IDENTITY

There is a spectrum of identities: from the mathematical, through cases
where specific criteria matter, to the complex or intuitive cases where we can
recognize identity but don't know what the criteria should be. In a series of essays
by senior figures in the sciences and humanities, this book examines what identity
means across a number of academic disciplines. Topics range from mathematics,
through the rules of recognition in biology and the law, to comprehending the
individual in the visual, performing and literary arts, and ultimately to notions
of the philosophy of existence. Using the theme of identity to make new
interdisciplinary connections, the contributors offer interested readers a glimpse
into their specialist subjects and suggest new ways for students and scholars
to think about identity in relation to their own work.

THE DARWIN COLLEGE LECTURES

These essays are developed from the 2007 Darwin College Lecture Series. Now in their twenty-fifth year, these popular Cambridge talks take a single theme each year. Internationally distinguished scholars, skilled as popularizers, address the theme from the point of view of eight different arts and sciences disciplines.

Subjects covered in the series include

23 DARWIN
    eds. William Brown and Andrew Fabian
    pb 9780521131957

22 SERENDIPITY
    eds. Mark de Rond and Iain Morley
    pb 9780521181815

21 IDENTITY
    eds. Giselle Walker and Elisabeth Leedham-Green
    pb 9780521897266

20 SURVIVAL
    ed. Emily Shuckburgh
    pb 9780521718206

19 CONFLICT
    eds. Martin Jones and Andrew Fabian
    hb 9780521839600

18 EVIDENCE
    eds. Andrew Bell, John Swenson-Wright and Karin Tybjerg
    pb 9780521710190

17 DNA: CHANGING SCIENCE AND SOCIETY
    ed. Torsten Krude
    hb 9780521823784

16 POWER
    eds. Alan Blackwell and David Mackay
    hb 9780521823717

15 SPACE
    eds. Francois Penz, Gregory Radick and Robert Howell
    hb 9780521823760

14 TIME
    ed. Katinka Ridderbos
    hb 9780521782937

13 THE BODY
eds. Sean Sweeney and Ian Hodder
hb 9780521782920

12 STRUCTURE
eds. Wendy Pullan and Harshad Bhadeshia
hb 9780521782586

11 SOUND
eds. Patricia Kruth and Henry Stobart
pb 9780521033831

10 MEMORY
eds. Patricia Fara and Karalyn Patterson
pb 9780521032186

9 EVOLUTION
ed. Andrew Fabian
pb 9780521032179

8 THE CHANGING WORLD
eds. Patricia Fara, Peter Gathercole and Ronald Laski
unavailable

7 COLOUR: ART AND SCIENCE
eds. Trevor Lamb and Janine Bourriau
unavailable

6 WHAT IS INTELLIGENCE?
ed. Jean Khalfa
pb 9780521566858

5 PREDICTING THE FUTURE
ed. Leo Howe and Alan Wain
pb 9780521619745

4 UNDERSTANDING CATASTROPHE
ed. Janine Bourriau
pb 9780521032193

3 WAYS OF COMMUNICATING
ed. D. H. Mellor
pb 9780521019040

2 THE FRAGILE ENVIRONMENT
ed. Laurie Friday and Ronald Laskey
pb 9780521422666

1 ORIGINS
ed. Andrew Fabian
pb 9780521018197

THE DARWIN COLLEGE LECTURES

IDENTITY

Edited by *Giselle Walker* and *Elisabeth Leedham-Green*

CAMBRIDGE
UNIVERSITY PRESS

CAMBRIDGE UNIVERSITY PRESS

Cambridge, New York, Melbourne, Madrid, Cape Town, Singapore,
São Paulo, Delhi, Dubai, Tokyo, Mexico City

Cambridge University Press
The Edinburgh Building, Cambridge CB2 8RU, UK

Published in the United States of America by Cambridge University Press, New York

www.cambridge.org
Information on this title: www.cambridge.org/9780521897266

First published 2010

Printed in the United Kingdom at the University Press, Cambridge

A catalogue record for this publication is available from the British Library

Library of Congress Cataloging-in-Publication Data

Identity / edited by Giselle Walker, Elisabeth Leedham-Green.
    p.   cm. – (Darwin College lectures)
  ISBN 978-0-521-89726-6 (Pbk.)
1. Identity (Philosophical concept)   I. Walker, Giselle.   II. Leedham-Green, E. S.   III. Title.
IV. Series.
  BD236.I38 2010
  111′.82–dc22

                                                                                2010025481

ISBN 978-0-521-89726-6 Paperback

Contents

List of figures   *page* viii
List of tables   ix
Acknowledgements   x

Introduction   1
GISELLE WALKER AND ELISABETH
LEEDHAM-GREEN

1   Identity of meaning   9
    ADRIAN POOLE

2   Identity and the law   26
    LIONEL BENTLY

3   Species-identity   59
    PETER R. CRANE

4   Mathematical identity   88
    MARCUS DU SAUTOY

5   Immunological identity   110
    PHILIPPA MARRACK

6   Visualizing identity   127
    LUDMILLA JORDANOVA

7   Musical identity   157
    CHRISTOPHER HOGWOOD

8   Identity and the mind   184
    RAYMOND TALLIS

    Notes on contributors   208
    Index   212

List of figures

3.1	Specimen of *Cannabis sativa*	*page* 62
3.2	Entry for *Cannabis* in Linnaeus' *Species Plantarum*	65
5.1	Location and specificity of innate immune receptors	112
5.2	Natural Killer cells kill targets that lack self class I	115
5.3	The clonal selection theory	118
5.4	Lymphocytes receptors for antigen are created from a few genes by a combinatorial process	120
5.5	Developing lymphocytes-bearing receptors that react with something in their environment die	123
6.1	John Hunter, line engraving by William Sharp, 1788	130
6.2	Oscar Wilde, photographed in 1891	136
6.3	William Cowper, stipple engraving by William Blake	139
6.4	William Cowper by Lemuel Francis Abbott	140
6.5	William Cowper by George Romney	142
6.6	Cover of Kenneth Franklin's book on Harvey	147
6.7	William Harvey, attributed to Daniel Mytens	149
6.8	William Harvey, line engraving, by unknown engraver	151
6.9	Frank Raymond Leavis, by Robert Sargent Austin	153
6.10	Frank Raymond Leavis, by Peter Greenham	154

List of tables

3.1 Comparison between the floras of the UK and Madagascar   *page* 71

3.2 Newly described species of plants from Madagascar   71

Acknowledgements

Many people, too many to list, have assisted in the organizing of the lecture series and the preparation of this book. We are grateful in particular to the following: Professor W. A. Brown, Dr Anthony Cox, Mrs Joyce Graham, Dr Felicity Henderson, Professor C. R. Leedham-Green, Espen Koht, Dr Ian McConnell, Lord Robert McCredie May, Mr Ryan Mark and, above all, Janet Gibson.

Introduction

GISELLE WALKER AND ELISABETH LEEDHAM-GREEN

'Identity' may seem a hard and fast concept: either this is your fingerprint, your DNA or it is someone else's; either this is the glove you mislaid yesterday or, at best, it is just one very like it. On waking in the morning you may have a brief 'who am I?' moment, but these appear to be familiar toenails and pyjamas. So, however reluctantly, you get up, perform the usual matutinal rituals and necessities and go to work. What awaits you there? An interview with the boss or a session with a distressed client? Probably you do not present the same *persona* to both. One is perhaps defensive, the other sympathetic. Quite probably neither is entirely sincere, so, in some sense, in either case you are shifting your identity, whatever that may be. If, in either case, you present yourself aggressively, the case may be different.

Simple identity reaches its physical extreme in immunology: the biology of recognizing self and non-self. As described in detail by Philippa Marrack in 'Immunological Identity', knowing oneself comes down to the molecular level – the presence of specific forms of molecules expressed on the surface of one's cells. Exceptions to such strict molecular rules occur only in cases where non-self is unrecognized or self is suppressed. However, while biological self appears uncontroversial (if imperfectly known), and there is one generally accepted grammar and syntax in mathematics (which gives everyone the same proof), it is often difficult to agree on the properties of elements on either side of non-mathematical equations. Most descriptions are not closed systems, so one has to look at *relevant* properties of identity, since *all* properties would be too numerous to let us get anywhere: as suggested by Marcus du Sautoy's predecessor in the Oxford mathematical world, Charles Lutwidge Dodgson:

> 'When *I* use a word,' Humpty Dumpty said in rather a scornful tone,
> 'it means just what I choose it to mean – neither more nor less.'
> 'The question is,' said Alice, 'whether you *can* make words mean
> different things.'
> 'The question is,' said Humpty Dumpty, 'which is to be master –
> that's all.'[1]

Humpty Dumpty is arguing for contextual identity, whereas Alice prefers a more essentialist view. Context is, of course, the key to Humpty Dumpty's appearance here: if all the king's horses and all the king's men put him back together again, is he the same egg? It depends on whether your important axis is 'unbroken topology' or 'time'.

As Marcus du Sautoy shows, many central mathematical results, old and new, trivial and profound, are expressed as identities or equations. These identities are often proved by counting the same set in two different ways, or by looking at the same object in two different ways: identifying one object with another. Here are two examples, one trivial and one not so trivial. Most people, when asked to explain why $a(b + c) = ab + ac$, have nothing to say. But suppose that a, b and c are positive whole numbers. Take a rows, each containing $b + c$ counters, and split this up into two sets of counters, one with a rows of b counters, and one with a rows of c counters. Now counting the same set of counters in two ways gives a small child a taste of how identities can be proved. On a less trivial level, Newton proved the identity

$$\pi = 6 \left(\frac{1}{2} + \frac{1}{2} \times \frac{1}{3} \times \frac{1}{2^3} + \frac{1 \times 3}{2 \times 4} \times \frac{1}{5} \times \frac{1}{2^5} + \frac{1 \times 3 \times 5}{2 \times 4 \times 6} \times \frac{1}{7} \times \frac{1}{2^7} + \cdots \right).$$

---

[1] Lewis Carroll, *Through the looking glass and what Alice found there* (London: Macmillan, 1871), 114.

This formula (in fact a variant on this formula) enabled Newton to compute π to 16 decimal places (though this was not the record). Now π is the ratio of the circumference of a circle to its diameter, and ancient calculations of π inefficiently estimated this directly. But Newton identifies π with the area of a circle, identifies the area with an integral, identifies the integral with a power series, using his famous generalization of the binomial theorem, and out pops the result.

Many, perhaps most, of the great mathematicians have produced famous identities: Newton, Euler, Gauss, Stokes, Hilbert, Ramanujan, du Sautoy's particular hero Riemann and, of course, the great mathematicians of today. The search for new identities will always remain at the core of mathematics.

Adrian Poole's chapter, 'Identity of meaning', highlights the importance of context, exploring the difference between words and what they convey. Different readings of plays like *Henry V* demonstrate that words on a page are only the beginning of communication: resonances differ according to the audience. The inevitability of such pluralism of interpretation should be recognized: as Poole points out, for better or for worse we are identified by others, each of whom sees what they want to see. This accords with Milan Kundera's view of identity: that *I* cannot know anything about *you* that is separate from myself and my standpoint. In Kundera's novel *Identity* two characters fail to communicate their thoughts to one another and, through a series of missed contacts, physical and mental, demonstrate that, no matter how much they stare into each other's eyes, neither will ever know what lies behind the other's eyelids during a blink.[2]

Ludmilla Jordanova's 'Visualizing identity' approaches the question from the angle of portraiture. Since identity, in the sense of personality, is here in the eye of the beholder, portraits frequently give clues to perceived features of identity that would not be picked up by a simple passport photograph. These may be conveyed by stance and expression in such a way that the style of execution gives an impression of the character of the sitter, while devices in the background frequently also represent concrete things emblematic of their profession, status or

[2] Milan Kundera, *L'Identité* (Paris: Gallimard, 1997).

preoccupations. The importance of the observer in establishing identity is just a special case of realizing that the criteria used to establish identity have to be the same, between presenter and observer.

Metaphysical questions exploring the essential nature of Theseus' ship after rebuilding, Locke's socks after darning, my grandfather's axe after replacement of handle and head, whether I can step in the same river twice and indeed whether Humpty Dumpty is the same egg ever again are only solved with reference to some criterion that matters in a given case. Leibniz might be invoked here – that nothing can ever have the 'same properties and relations' as anything else, and thus nothing is identical to anything else.[3] But this ignores the frame of reference in which most people care about rebuilt ships, darned socks, reconstituted axes, rivers and opinionated eggs sitting on walls.

In the absence of a clearly definable, long-term view, what matters above all else is that the hierarchy of characteristics which make up an identity – and their importance and mutability – be key to exploring current common usages of identity. While John Locke's metaphysical socks are still in his possession, it's the possession through time that counts, rather than the materials that constitute them. If possession is insufficient to the enquiry at hand, they cease to be the same socks once they've been darned, and stop being metaphysically interesting.

Lionel Bently's chapter, 'Identity and the law', explores the weighing of contingent characteristics in the context of property: where voice, name, appearance and so on are treated as representative of identity and thus used to imply endorsement by the owner of the identity. Bently points out that property in identity is problematic, because identity extends into so many areas – in complex human life it's unlikely that one specific characteristic can be taken as sufficient to distinguish someone – and identity so characterized can thus provide no solid foundation for property law. Nevertheless, the idea that something might be able to encapsulate identity – like a fingerprint on a human or in a computer – is extremely popular in these days of informational overload.

---

[3] Gottfried Leibniz, 'Discourse on metaphysics', in *Philosophical papers and letters*, ed. and trans. Leroy E. Loemker, 2nd edn (Dordrecht: D. Reidel, 1969).

Peter Crane's chapter, 'Species-identity', explores the degree to which Linnean binomials serve as fingerprints in current biological research. Only to a first approximation do names refer to comparable entities. In the absence of an ability to detect species and speciation (which probably has something to do with reproduction, immunology, anatomy... though we can't tell how much or what, a priori) all we have is bottom-up collections of individuals, or top-down observations of populations through time. Biologists endeavour to understand what these organisms share, or what distinguishes a population – seeking unique diagnostic criteria in the long list of features, criteria to which the species epithet is attached. Species descriptions are at best Platonic shadows with names, set down in the literature until some indeterminate intermediate makes us amend the criteria pertaining to the name. Complex systems of rules for attaching names to biology are actually silent on the biology – the zoological and botanical codes of nomenclature are only about names (ICZN, 4th edn, 1999; ICBN St Louis Code, 2000). But – although this may shock non-biologists – the fact a species epithet doesn't convey 'essence' doesn't mean that identities attached to names are unimportant or arbitrary. The name is there so that we know that the botanist, farmer, gardener, herbalist, poisoning victim, toxicologist, judge and jury are all talking about the same thing. The name is being used as an heuristic for the complex ecophysiological identity of a plant – so the distinguishing criteria attached to that name have to be adequate in all the different contexts where the name matters. Thus looking for something repeatable, and to do with a process apparently independent of our observation (such as evolution), is usually a good guiding principle for taxonomy, as for any form of finding shortcuts for identity. Biology gets it right more easily in other areas – Philippa Marrack, in her chapter, 'Immunological identity', discusses how recognition of non-self is often a good indicator that 'this is not me': for example an animal's innate immune system reacting to (uniquely) bacterial lipopolysaccharide, which suggests that this non-self will be very different from anything like the animal.

Distilling information about identities down to key characteristics like fingerprints has the advantage of ease and speed of communication. But the possibility of over-generalization always lurks, with doomsayers predicting disenfranchised Orwellian hordes at the mercy of a government wanting to impose identity cards on all the creative individuals that make up British society. Ludmilla Jordanova points out the failure of biometric information, or passport photos, to capture who we really are – the difference between fingerprint and portrait. We prefer portraits. But with so many of us here on the planet, administration prefers fingerprints, as a fast way of determining that most of us are harmless. Of course over-generalization stemming from fingerprints is precisely what many people are afraid of: the possibility that someone else could steal a place under the mantle of harmlessness, by stealing the details of someone else's day-to-day life. Identity theft brings home to us the point of bothering with trying to understand identities: self-determination. Although bank account fraud is where most of us chiefly think about identity theft, it's actually the bigger things that matter: one can usually recover the money stolen from bank cards – but what about getting arrested for a crime you haven't committed? We hang on to our identity because we want to control what we do with it – and we can't know what someone else will do with it – whether that someone be a criminal or a government facilitating with identity cards an unexpected attack of myopia. Adrian Poole points out that 'Identity is a powerful magnetizer and divider of "us" against "them", especially when annexed to class, gender, ethnicity or nation' – so hanging on to the high dimensionality of one's identity – and appreciating that of others – would seem to be key to promoting harmony. Politicians go a long way to try to convince the public that they, the rulers, share an identity with the ruled: if this is convincing it can lead the public to feel happy with having politicians extrapolate on their behalf. Frequently the extrapolation is from somewhere conveniently one-dimensional, and serves to silence groups who would perhaps prefer a different identity. A nice example is the magazine of the British National Party – too appropriately called *Identity*.

So the answer clearly matters when Adrian Poole asks, 'How do I know who I am? How do *you* know who I am?' Raymond Tallis may just provide the answer we need, in 'Identity and the mind'. The concept of identity that he advances here – the Existential Intuition – is the first-person mental and physical sense of being, within the context of the world: it is, in a way, taking responsibility for one's own biochemistry.

It is strictly in the first person: how *I* know who *you* are depends entirely on how I relate to you. Obviously, this identity-relation is only made explicit by wondering about identity – if you can't wonder about yourself, then your identity is imposed from without by something that *can* wonder about you. This brings us back to self-determination being a useful application of identity. The Existential Intuition implies that people can only know about themselves – making careful communication of the details of identity all the more important.

Some things, however, still defy all our attempts to pick out which details matter. Identity is complex – can we get at it when we don't know the relevant criteria, when all we have is the '=' but not the algebraic grammar to know how to deal with X and Y? Ludmilla Jordanova elaborates on the theme of visual recognition of people being based on a complex constellation of features; Christopher Hogwood's chapter, 'Musical identity', explores how we recognize the difference between Mozart and Haydn, and 'what *are* Brahms?'. Most of us can recognize faces, and most of us (with sufficient training) can recognize different pieces of music by the same composer, but we're not very articulate when we try to tell someone else about that recognition process. Despite knowing the salient features, say, of Mozart's style, and being able to trace these as influences from particular schools of composition, even the most informed musicologists have been known to misattribute work by Mozart's contemporaries. Is musical identity just too hard to recognize? Likewise, is visual identity still too difficult, in these days when a 'photo-fit' reconstruction of a face is almost pointlessly unnatural, but a witness can still recognize the face they've failed to reconstruct? Both visual and musical recognition are active areas of enquiry in machine learning, where one trains a computer to 'read' data and sort it into piles, in the hope that the computer will eventually decide what the rules are that keep the piles distinct. It's also possible to recognize individual recordings of music based on physical parameters like zero crossing rate (wavelength measurement when you have more than one note present), the distribution of frequencies across the spectrum. These techniques seem to be capturing important aspects of identity in modern popular music in the digital era, where the currency is specific recordings.

Western classical art music remains somewhat elusive, neither recognized by acoustic fingerprinting applications like Shazam, nor successfully synthesized by programmers of musical rules such as David Cope's *Experiments in Musical Intelligence.*[4] The latter area of enquiry, discovering the rules of style, harmony and counterpoint as known to a specific composer, and how to encode them in a way that a computer will find useful, is also an active area of enquiry. If successful, it could tell us all sorts of things beyond the compositional identity of a specific score: music is often a specifically personal reaction to perceptions of life and times in a particular society. These extremely complex types of identity might act as heuristics for much more than just one face or one song, if only we could work out the important criteria of recognition and how they relate to the wider world. But for the moment, 'music takes over where words leave off' – some areas of identity have to be understood in ways other than the plain English of this book.

[4] http://arts.ucsc.edu/faculty/cope/experiments.htm.

1 Identity of meaning

ADRIAN POOLE

Some titles are instantly intelligible. This is not one of them. So let me begin with some examples of what 'identity of meaning' might mean. Slightly less than 300 years before the birth of Christ, seventy-two translators travelled from Jerusalem to Alexandria. They were charged with rendering the Hebrew Scriptures into ancient Greek, and the result was known as the Septuagint. Seventy-two seems a sensible number for such a vast undertaking. It would be crazy to expect one man to do it all by himself. Yet the story that developed was indeed absurd, or miraculous. The legend was that the seventy-two all worked on all the Scriptures, but independently of each other. Incredibly, each arrived at exactly the same text. Unsurprisingly, the result carried enormous authority. When Jerome embarked on his historic translation of the same Scriptures into Latin he decided to go back to the original Hebrew and Aramaic texts. His colleague Augustine told him not to be silly. Who did Jerome think he was to challenge the divinely inspired translators of the Septuagint?

The Septuagint represents a great dream of redeeming the chaos of Babel and the confusion of tongues, akin to the legend of Pentecost. Yet a shift of perspective could easily turn this dream into nightmare, the bleak vision of George Orwell's *1984* in which a supreme political authority imposes a single common language from on high: Newspeak. Umberto Eco mildly notes that 'the dream of a perfect language has always been invoked as a solution to religious or political strife.'[1]

---

[1] U. Eco, *The search for the perfect language*, trans. James Fentress (Oxford: Blackwell, 1995), 19.

Identity, edited by Giselle Walker and Elisabeth Leedham-Green. Published by Cambridge University Press. © Darwin College 2010.

My second exhibit is a renowned short story by the Argentinian writer Jorge Luis Borges, entitled 'Pierre Menard, author of the *Quixote*'. This tale purports to memorialize a French man of letters whose greatest work is unfinished and unpublished. The narrator – let us call him Borges – tells us that Menard set out not to copy the work of Cervantes, nor to write another *Don Quixote*, but to create a new original, *ab initio*. Menard thinks of immersing himself in the past, of forgetting the history of Europe between 1602 and 1918, of identifying totally with Cervantes and his world. But this, he thinks, would be too easy: 'To be, in some way, Cervantes and reach the *Quixote* seemed less arduous to him – and, consequently, less interesting – than to go on being Pierre Menard and reach the *Quixote* through the experiences of Pierre Menard.'[2] And so, after innumerable drafts and immeasurable pains, Menard produces his fragments of a new *Don Quixote*, original, authentic, his own. It is, word for word, identical with Cervantes'. And yet, so the narrator asserts, this *Don Quixote* is quite different. Written in the twentieth century, the same words do not mean the same as they did in the early 1600s. When the seventeenth-century writer speaks of 'truth, whose mother is history, rival of time, depository of deeds, witness of the past, exemplar and adviser to the present, and the future's counsellor', it is 'a mere rhetorical praise of history'. When the twentieth-century writer speaks of 'truth, whose mother is history, rival of time, depository of deeds, witness of the past, exemplar and adviser to the present, and the future's counsellor', the idea is 'astounding'.[3] Identity of words, but not identity of meaning.

Thirdly, an anecdote from my old teacher and then colleague Theodore Redpath. In his memoir of Wittgenstein Redpath recalls buying some gramophone records. The ferocious philosopher called round and asked Redpath whether the records were 'any good'. Redpath replied, in the fashion of those days: 'It depends what you mean by "good".' Wittgenstein's response was 'rapid and decisive: "*I* mean what *you* mean." This shook me up,' confesses Redpath, 'and seemed to me tremendously illuminating. It still does.'[4] On a less theological level

---

[2]   J. L. Borges, 'Pierre Menard, author of the Quixote', in *Labyrinths*, ed. Donald A. Yates and James E. Irby (Harmondsworth: Penguin, 2000), 66.
[3]   Ibid., 69.
[4]   T. Redpath, *Ludwig Wittgenstein: a student's memoir* (London: Duckworth, 1990), 68.

than the mythic origins of the Septuagint, this suggests another brave bright dream. It's true that Redpath and Wittgenstein might then have listened to these records and come to blows over whether they were indeed 'any good'. But that would not invalidate the principle of good faith peremptorily summoned by Wittgenstein, the necessary if not sufficient condition for any collaborative enterprise. 'I mean what you mean' is a brilliantly economical way of proclaiming belief in the possibility of consensus and community — even, dare one say it, of love.

Lastly and less philosophically, a friend reports this from a menu in an Athens restaurant: 'Roquefort is Danish Blue.'

'I mean what you mean.' Imagine how difficult life would be without some such conviction in the identity of meaning carried by the words Friday, 2nd February, 2007, 5.30 p.m., Lady Mitchell Hall, Darwin Lecture. The Master of Darwin is a patient man but even he might have been irritated if I had responded to his invitation with: 'It depends what you mean by Friday,' and so on. (Philosophers would tell us that Frege's distinction between 'sense' and 'reference' would solve this difficulty.) Of course, things do get trickier with the words 'Darwin Lecture'. But 'I mean what you mean' is a good motto for people who want to stick together, in a church, in an army, in a political party, in love. It is at least the official party line followed by Tony Blair and Gordon Brown, as it is, more enthusiastically, by Shakespeare's Romeo and Juliet or Wagner's Tristan and Isolde.

It's at best a good dream and at least a necessary fiction, such 'identity of meaning'. For we all know that in reality 'I mean what you mean' is under constant siege from 'Oh no you don't.' Every day, even when you and I 'speak the same language'. There's a delightful passage in a novel by José Saramago, the Nobel-prize-winning Portuguese writer. It's entitled (in English) *The double* and, along with Dostoevsky's tale of the same name (and others), it bears an obvious relevance to the theme of this whole series of lectures. The passage I am about to quote is part of a telephone conversation between the main character and his girl-friend just after they have been to bed together for the first time. This dialogue, the narrator tells us, would have been 'found in the index of any Manual of Human Relations under Mutual Incomprehension'. (Note the lack of typographical assistance the reader receives in distinguishing between the two speakers – no inverted commas but only an initial upper case.)

> I was beginning to think you weren't going to phone me, said Maria da Paz, As you see, you were wrong, here I am, Your silence would have meant that today didn't mean the same thing to you as it did to me, Whatever it meant, it was the same for us both, But perhaps not in the same way or for the same reasons, We don't have the instruments to measure such differences, if there were any, You still care about me, Yes, I still care about you, You don't sound very enthusiastic, all you did was repeat what I said, Tell me why those words shouldn't serve me as well as they served you, Because in being repeated they lose some of the conviction they would have carried if they had been spoken first, Of course, a round of applause for the ingenuity and subtlety of the analyst, You'd know that too if you read more fiction.[5]

Later in this same tortured conversation he sadly concludes that 'All the dictionaries put together don't contain half the terms we would need in order for us to understand each other.'[6]

Even the best of lovers can't always be sure that 'I mean what you mean'; not this side of paradise. Imagine how tedious it would be if they did. But imagine too how drastically the chances of such ethereal agreement are reduced when you and I do not 'speak the same language'. Especially when it comes to words more heavily fraught than those which mark our basic needs for food, shelter and clothing. It's not hard to imagine one American citizen saying to another: 'What *you* mean by glory, virtue, wisdom, justice, duty, sacrifice, democracy, freedom, human rights, peace process and the rule of law, is not what *I* mean.' It is even less difficult to imagine such an exchange between an American and a citizen of the developing world. If you add to differences of language and culture those made by time and history, the chances of brute mutual rebuff increase. Nor should we delude ourselves: Homer, Cervantes, Shakespeare, Voltaire would all have demurred at our eagerness to claim that we mean what they meant.

The roots of the word 'identity' come from (late) Latin *identitas*. 'Identity' represents the idea of 'sameness' (from *idem*), parallel with

[5] J. Saramago, *The double*, trans. Margaret Jull Costa (New York: Harcourt Inc., 2004), 119–20.
[6] Ibid., 122.

the ideas of 'likeness' (*similitas*) and of unity (*unitas*). Identity, likeness, unity: this is a powerful trinity, and its three terms easily blend into each other. In 1855 Herbert Spencer observed that: 'Resemblance when it exists in the highest degree of all . . . is often called identity.'[7] We might think of identical twins, such as the masters and servants in Shakespeare's *The comedy of errors*. Or we might think of the perverse logic that allows Hamlet to address his loathed stepfather Claudius as his – mother: 'Father and mother is man and wife; man and wife is one flesh; and so, my mother.' From Plato's *Symposium* onwards, myths about erotic love have figured a state in which two lovers become (or return to) 'one and the same'. In a benign perspective the idea of identity indicates forms of passionate attachment, whether of two persons or many, united by shared beliefs, interests or values. 'Identity' is a powerful magnetizer and divider of 'us' against 'them', especially when annexed to class, gender, ethnicity or nation.

To say that this has a dark side would be an understatement. The danger of identifying ourselves or others as members of a single group is precisely the target of Amartya Sen's recent book *Identity and violence*.[8] To look ahead to our other key word 'meaning': those who applaud Sen's eloquent assault on the illusion of singular identity might also wish to deplore the illusion of singular meaning. The *Oxford English Dictionary* is not immediately helpful to Sen's argument. For its first main definition of identity it offers us this: 'absolute or essential sameness; oneness' (1a). But its second definition introduces the crucial conditions of time and space: 'The sameness of a person or thing *at all times or in all circumstances* (emphasis added); the condition or fact that a person or thing is itself and not something else; individuality, personality' (2a). Where the first definition is angelically relaxed about the possibility of identity being shared by different or separate entities, the second is bristling with defiance and defensiveness. 'The sameness of a person . . . at all times or in all circumstances': this might be an ideal of stoic endurance and reliability. It's certainly an important legal and political fiction, as the need for proof of identity, the danger of identity theft and the politicians'

---

[7] Cited by *The Oxford English Dictionary*, 2nd edn online, under 'Identity', 1a.
[8] A. Sen, *Identity and violence: the illusion of destiny* (London: Allen Lane, 2006).

dream of identity cards all suggest. But 'sameness at all times or circumstances'? This sounds like a recipe for terminal boredom. For a person to be the same at all times or in all circumstances might be an heroic feat of endurance but it could also be a crazy, mulish refusal to adapt. Or it could be both at once – as exemplified by Sophocles' tragic heroes and Joseph Conrad's imperturbable sea-captains. Or it could be worse than this. Amartya Sen argues that to be one and the same, or to suppose *others* to be one and the same, at all times or in all circumstances – this could well prove an incitement to violence.

Sen urges us to recognize our several identities, and those of others. There is a comical aspect here in the several identities to which the same name can lay claim. How do I know who I am? How do *you* know who I am? We can't rely on mere words. The Web will tell you that there are Adrian Pooles who work for the Open University, who take photographs for the Powerboat World Championship Yearbooks, who support Peterborough United Football Club. Adrian Poole is a New Business Manager with Norwich Union, an assistant solicitor with Porter and Dodson (they help people apply for new liquor licences), an Executive Vice-President for a company called FearSelling (their motto is 'Proven Systems + Emotional Triggers = More Sales'). In the late 1990s Adrian Poole was a leading member of the Emory University Women's Tennis Team (sic), and in 2004 she enjoyed a Resident Fellowship at the University's Department of Gynecology and Obstetrics. In June 2006 she was Recycler of the Month – somewhere in Texas, I think.

So much for comic relief. There are times and places in which your name can be a matter of life and death. In Shakespeare the Roman mob lynch a man who shares the same name as one of Julius Caesar's murderers: 'I am Cinna the poet! I am Cinna the poet! . . . I am not Cinna the conspirator.' 'It is no matter; his name's Cinna! Pluck but his name out of his heart, and turn him going.' For many years after the massacre of the Macdonalds there were parts of Scotland where it could have been fatal to let on that your name was Campbell. (It is still not wise.) Over the past year or so many Iraqi citizens have changed their names. If a Shiite death-squad at an illegal checkpoint sees a Sunni name on your identity card (or vice versa) they will not bother to stop and ask questions. No wonder that young men named Saddam try to get it changed to something safer such as Sajad or Jabar. Here is an extreme and lethal consequence of the singularizing of identity against which Amartya Sen protests.

If beauty is at least partly in the eye of the beholder, so too is identity. For better or worse, for richer or poorer, we are identified by others. What of our other key word, 'meaning', and the verb that goes about its business, 'to mean'? In everyday speech the words 'mean' and 'meaning' are strongly bound up with intention and purpose. Think of such daily sayings as: 'She means business', 'I meant no harm', 'He meant to catch the 7.15', 'What's the meaning of this?', 'Do you mean to say they're *still* married?', 'The bullet was meant for the President', 'These things were meant to be'. There are two main senses of the verb still current (there are several that are obsolete). The first is 'to intend' (*OED*, 1), and the second, 'to signify; to convey or carry a meaning, significance, consequence' (*OED*, 2). There seems to be a clear distinction between these two, between intention and reference. As between the statement: 'I mean to be Prime Minister' and 'By the person best qualified to be Prime Minister I mean myself'. Or 'I mean to drink in moderation tonight' and 'By drinking in moderation I mean less than the two bottles I normally drink'. In the first case we can substitute the word 'intend' and in the second some such verbal form as 'I am referring to' or 'I am defining this as'. All statements of this second kind can be roughly categorized thus, as 'By this I mean that'. Here 'meaning' is something that 'carries' between 'this' and 'that', where there is a happy doubleness to a verb that can be either transitive (as a cart carries turnips) or intransitive (as my voice carries to the back of this hall). Meaning carries through space and time, or hopes to. So too does identity strive to stay the same. This metaphor of 'carrying' associates both meaning and identity with words we have inherited from Greek and Latin. The words 'metaphor' and 'translation' both mean to carry across. Across what? Across some distance between 'this' and 'that', or 'here' and 'there', or 'now' and 'then', this speaker and that auditor, this writer and those readers, a rift more or less wide, from crack to abyss, in which meaning may fail. Essential to this drama is the desire for identity of meaning, that what the speaker or writer intends to signify is the same as what the auditor or reader will grasp.

'Meaning' is a matter of intention *and* consequence. We are familiar with such statements as 'This means another eight hours on the motorway', 'This means a rise in world oil prices', or 'This means war'. But this sense of 'to mean' as 'to require, entail, necessitate; to produce as an effect or result' (*OED*, 8) appears to be less than 200 years old. The first usage recorded by the *OED* is from 1841 (though of course the *OED* is scarcely infallible). By 5 February 1894 it was firmly established. You could read in *The Times*: 'That would mean taking up all the streets in South London.' There's a further new sense of 'meaning' (*OED*, 9) that focuses on the consequences to a particular person. 'Dearest, it means so much to me': you will not find this sentence in Jane Austen but in Louisa May Alcott's *Little Women* (1869). It seems that only since the 1860s have we become used to hearing 'She meant the world to him' or saying 'That means nothing to me'. This emphasis on consequence extends already well-established senses of meaning. But it also enhances the possibility that meaning might be a subjective affair, as when we speak of what an old photograph or family heirloom might 'mean' to a particular person. Events and the material objects that help to compose them can mean such different things to different people as to undermine the possibility of identity of meaning, and test to the limit Wittgenstein's good faith that 'I mean what you mean'.

To summarize: within the whole range of the meanings of meaning both current and obsolete, the sense of intention or purpose or will to signify, communicate or make something happen is inalienable. So too is the sense of effect and impact and consequence, of meaning as something that passes between speaker and listener, between artist and audience, between lovers and between warriors. It is something that goes through a process in time, space and history. Against this there is the desire for meaning that lies outside vicissitude and even intentions, at least human intentions, a desire especially invested in great religious symbols that command widespread belief, such as the Cross and the Crescent. Yet even the most sacred objects of contemplation require stories to be told about them if their meanings are to be grasped. Meaning means interpretation in the sense that it requires and entails it. 'Know what I mean?' Think of the way we appeal to such harmless, pathetic everyday fillers. Almost devoid of content, they mark the desire for connection, sometimes minimally, as who should say, 'you know, like, uh, hey, man, I mean, cool, huh?' (from a 1992 publication cited by the *OED*, under 6e).

Make love not war, as we used to say in the 1960s. Both love and war put great pressure on the idea of 'identity of meaning'. Love binds people and their meanings together, but war binds them together against each other under a banner that declares: '*We* do not mean what *they* mean'. I turn now to two fictional scenes that debate the relation between war and love, one from Homeric epic, the other from Shakespearean drama. One takes place in the thick of war while the other seeks to conclude it, but both question the meaning of war, what war is for, in defence or pursuit of what good or goods.

The first is from Book 6 of Homer's *Iliad*. It is a famous scene in which Andromache pleads with her husband, Hector, the Trojan's warrior-hero, not to go out to battle (369–502). Achilles has killed Andromache's father and seven brothers; her mother too has died. She says to Hector, unforgettably, that for her he is now father and mother and brother and husband. Nowadays we might say he means everything to her – and to their little boy, Astyanax. Have pity on us, she pleads. Don't leave your son an orphan and your wife a widow. But Hector has been brought up to win 'great glory' for his father and himself. He thinks of the shame he would feel if he were to do as she says and 'play the coward'. Like Andromache, Hector foresees the day when Troy will fall, his father and all the people. Yet this vision of disaster is not what moves him most, he says, so much as the thought of Andromache's future, of what it will mean for her to be humiliated and enslaved. He stretches his arms out to their little boy, but the child is scared by the bronze helmet with its nodding plume. His parents laugh. His father takes off the helmet, catches the boy in his arms and prays to the gods that the child may grow up to be 'just like me' or even better, so that one day he will come back from battle with the blood-stained spoils of the enemy he has killed, and his mother's heart will rejoice. He passes the boy to his wife, who is smiling and weeping. Though he will not do as she asks, Hector feels pity for her and touches her gently. She should not grieve for him too much, for no one can escape their fate – what is meant to be, we might say. She must go back to her women's work, while he goes to his, the men's work that is war. She goes home to weep with her servants, as for a man they don't expect to see alive again, a man already dead. They correctly envisage the corpse that will be returned to Troy in Book 24.

There is a whole group of words in this passage that seek to define who they are, this man and this woman and boy. These are formulaic words, easily repeated. Andromache is *leukôlenos* (371, 377, 'white-armed'), and *amumôn* (374, a fairly empty term of praise). Such words go with the epithets applied to other Trojan women, such as *eupeploi* (372, 378, 'fair-robed'), and *euplokamoi* (380, 385, 'fair-tressed'). Hector too attracts such impersonal words as *koruthaiolos* (369, 'of the flashing helmet'), *phaidimos* (466, 472, 'glorious'), and later, *androphonoios* (498, 'man-slaying'). They are reassuring words, or they aim to be. They are familiar, predictable, stabilizing. They possess an identity of meaning for all concerned, both poet and characters and audience. They promote the vision − or mirage, one might say − of a regulated world in which men and women conform perfectly to type.

But then this man and this woman begin to speak for themselves, and we encounter a language more loaded with personal meaning. There is the terrible shame Hector feels at the thought of being a coward (442–3); there is the 'heart' (*thumos*, 444) in him that urges him otherwise. He has always aimed to excel (to be *esthlos*, 444) and to win the 'great glory' (*mega kleos*, 446) for which he risks his life. These words are a part of what makes Hector who he is and help him know who he is. He can understand what Andromache means, in the sense that he imagines what her life will be like without him. But there's an impossible rift between what it means for Hector to continue being who he is and what it would mean for him to show pity for Andromache by not risking his life in battle. And then there is the wonderful touch of the little boy's terror. The child is right. The helmet belongs to the realm of mortal risk to which his father is going and from which he will never return. It is the realm to which the boy too will be consigned when (or if) he grows up, and to which his father now proudly dedicates him. His parents laugh at his failure to realize that this is not the real thing, at his premature terror. (But he is as wise as they.) His father is committed to a belief that 'great glory' will continue to have meaning, and that this meaning will be one and the same, handed on and sustained from father to son. Whether Andromache's heart would really rejoice at the sight of her son coming home with blood-stained spoils is another matter. Hector does not pause to wonder.

What does the scene mean to readers now, in ancient Greek or English or any other language? Unless inspired by divinity, like the translators of the Septuagint, the passage of meaning from one language to another is fraught with resistance and coloured by more or less flagrant variations. There could be no absolute identity of meaning, even if we were to emulate Pierre Menard and rewrite the *Iliad* into the identical words accumulated by 'Homer'. What is more, war cannot mean the same for us as it did for Homer. The meanings of war are affected by changing ideas about its justice, justifiability, aims and limits, ideas at once theological and political; they are also radically affected by the means of waging it, the weapons of destruction. There can be no identity between the meanings of war for Homer, Shakespeare (*Troilus and Cressida*), Tolstoy (*War and peace*), Stephen Crane (*The red badge of courage*), Kurt Vonnegut (*Slaughterhouse five*) and Oliver Stone (*Platoon*, the movie). And yet to suppose that we cannot recognize resemblance between these meanings would be absurd.

We have often been told, not least by those who went through it, that the Great War or World War I changed the meaning of words such as courage, cowardice, heroism, glory. Samuel Hynes writes: '[T]he Big Words of war, if they could be used at all, would have to be redefined.'[9] But this is true of all great wars, including the one that Homer describes. The *Iliad* certainly questions and tests, if it does not redefine, 'the Big Words of war'. However remote we may be from the world Homer portrays, we believe that *some* meaning carries to us from it, especially through the words with which Andromache and Hector utter their deepest needs and fears and desires and beliefs: her expression of total dependence on him; his adherence to the values in which he has been trained. War means different things to the two of them; so too does their little boy. They are bound, in their different positions, by the code of war and martial glory from which they both, indeed all three of them, cannot break free. (There is in fact a fourth figure, the nurse who

---

[9] S. Hynes, *The soldiers' tale: bearing witness to modern war* (Harmondsworth: Penguin, 1998), 57.

holds the wee boy. Almost invisible in Homer, she gains new substance in a recent retelling by Alessandro Baricco when she becomes the narrator of this scene.)[10] This too is one of the meanings of this scene that some thousands of years later we can 'identify', when we recognize the force of such value-systems and the difficulty of changing or escaping from them.

My second main exhibit is from *Henry V.* Shakespeare's martial heroes form a large and complex group. Some fight (and die) bravely for their country against the enemy, like the legendary Lord Talbot in *Henry VI, Part I*; others are more problematically and even treacherously embroiled in civil wars, English, Scottish and Roman, including Hotspur, Brutus, Macbeth, Mark Antony and Caius Martius Coriolanus. King Henry V seems a blessed exception, if – but it is a big if – the claims on which he bases his claim to the French crown are just. Shakespeare's contemporary Samuel Daniel had described Henry's invasion and conquest of France as a theme 'Whence new immortal Iliads might proceed', and there is evidence that just before or during the first writing of *Henry V* in 1599 Shakespeare had read the recently published translation of *Seaven bookes* of the *Iliad* by George Chapman. But Henry, so Shakespeare's Chorus would have us believe, is 'the mirror of all Christian kings'. Amongst other things Shakespeare's Henry V prays to a singular and different god from those in whom Hector and Achilles believe.

Universal Shakespeare? Not *Henry V.* 'No other Shakespeare play has been so ignored outside the English-speaking world', writes Emma Smith.[11] It may seem unsporting of the French but they have found it harder to admire *Henry V* than *Hamlet, Le Roi Lear*, and so on. Apart from anything else, translating the play into French is a nightmare. How do you translate the French spoken by Shakespeare's characters when all the English are already speaking French? (Jean-Michel Déprats has some answers to this.)[12] It is hardly surprising that Shakespeare's

[10] A. Baricco, 'The nurse', in *An Iliad*, trans. Ann Goldstein (New York: Alfred A. Knopf, 2006), 41–6.
[11] E. Smith (ed.), *King Henry V, Shakespeare in production* (Cambridge University Press, 2002), 1.
[12] J.-M. Déprats, 'A French history of Henry V', in *Shakespeare's history plays: performance, translation and adaptation in Britain and abroad*, ed. Ton Hoenselaars (Cambridge University Press, 2004), 75–91.

play had to wait 400 years for its first professional production in French, at Avignon in 1999. Meanwhile, recent English productions have been known to make Henry's army such despicable hooligans that one theatre critic was moved to say that it was the first version he'd seen where you wanted the French to win.

The play *Henry V* can be interpreted as patriotic propaganda and it can be interpreted as a scathing indictment of realpolitik. You can see the play as a rabbit; you can see it as a duck; you can try to see it as both at once. But before we even begin worrying about the meaning of the play, we must be clear what we mean by 'the play'. For the identity of this play is uncertain. Are we talking about a written printed text that we read, or about a performance that we witness? If the former, which printed text exactly? There are two early witnesses in the so-called 'bad' Quarto (1600) and the Folio (1623): the former is much shorter than the latter, and it lacks all sorts of things we have grown to expect from the play, including the Chorus. Very well, let's ignore the Quarto and just perform the Folio text. But Gary Taylor tells us that the Folio contains forty-two readings 'unanimously rejected by modern editors'.[13] And in any case performances rarely if ever follow the printed text to the letter, even if such an ideal were possible. This is true of all Shakespeare's plays. For many years on the English stage Edgar and Cordelia got happily married at the end of *King Lear*, and the Fool was nowhere to be seen (the two most arresting 'adaptations' of Shakespeare in Nahum Tate's 1681 version); Richard III has a famous line: 'Off with his head. So much for Buckingham' – but Shakespeare didn't write it (Colley Cibber did, in 1700); you can attend many performances of *Hamlet* without ever meeting Fortinbras; nowadays productions of *The Merchant of Venice* frequently sanitize Portia by cutting her embarrassing remark, as she sees off her unwanted suitor, the Prince of Morocco: 'Let all of his complexion choose me so.' As for *Henry V*, Olivier's famous film of 1944 diminishes many of the play's problematic aspects, especially as they affect the King's leadership qualities, the political justification for invading France, the threat of the conspirators, the challenge to his authority from

---

[13] W. Shakespeare, *Henry V*, ed. Gary Taylor (Oxford: Clarendon Press, 1982), 17.

Michael Williams in the great night-scene before Agincourt. So too does Kenneth Branagh's film of 1989, for all its apparently greater realism.

I want to consider the final scene (Act 5, scene 2). King Henry and his band of brothers have conquered their opponents at Agincourt. Now they meet the defeated French King and his counsellors, though not the conveniently absent Dauphin. A deal is struck by which Henry is named as his erstwhile enemy's son and heir, and this is sealed by the promise of marriage to the French princess, Katherine. Shakespeare could have chosen to make this a formality, but he likes to stage these awkward scenes of negotiation, so he gives us the long 'wooing scene', as it's quaintly called, in which Henry seeks Katherine's consent. She could choose to be a shrew, like her near name-sake Katherina Minola, but the political reality is that she has no choice. A fine recent critic of the play speaks of 'the Bismarckian brutalities' of this scene;[14] another declares that 'rape is sanctioned . . . civilly, ceremoniously'.[15]

For Henry this scene is a final challenge. There is the language problem, but you have to try. The languages and nationalities over which Henry aspires to reign have proliferated in this play: Welsh, Scots, Irish, English – and now French. There is the problem of genre: Henry needs to resolve the uncertainty about what kind of story this play has told. He has to find a comic ending, that is to say – a wife. He has never had anything to do with respectable women (Mistress Quickly and Doll Tearsheet don't qualify), and he needs to prove that he is loveable as well as admirable. He still has to settle an old score with his rival Hotspur, whom he killed at the end of *Henry IV, Part I*. For the reckless headlong Hotspur *was* loveable. He enjoyed a lively marriage with another woman called Kate, and the quarrel between husband and wife as Hotspur sets off for man's work enjoys a generic affinity with the Homeric scene between Hector and Andromache. This is what the martially triumphant Henry has now to emulate, an ability to 'deal with women', as it were. There are all sorts of ways of playing

[14] E. Smith (ed.), *King Henry V, Shakespeare in Production* (Cambridge University Press, 2002), 226.
[15] Joel Altman, cited in M. Neill, 'Broken English and broken Irish: nation, language and the optic of power in Shakespeare's Histories', in *Putting history to the question: power, politics, and society in English Renaissance drama* (New York: Columbia University Press, 2000), 361.

this scene: you can play Henry (as Olivier did) as a fluent romantic lover. You can make him charming, chilling, bumbling, bullying, just as you can make Katherine naive, shrewd, calculating, compliant, resistant.

Identity, similitude, unity. The union of two people or two nations can create a new identity. But what will this new identity 'mean', in every sense of this complex word? What will it signify, entail, portend? Within the play there are many who would like the carnage of war to end. The Duke of Burgundy has a fine long speech in praise of peace, 'Dear nurse of arts, plenties and joyful births'. The Queen of France has a beautifully eloquent prayer (though in performance it's often wrested away from her and given to the French king or to Henry himself). We should also think of audiences exhausted by war as Britain was in 1944, and as England was in 1599, audiences to whom the prospect of peace and a good new future would speak with less irony, if any, than at other moments in history (as for example during the Falklands war in the 1980s, or during the wars in Iraq and Afghanistan now). The meaning of this play is never constant, let alone identical, one and the same, but always multiple and various.

But there is a particular identity to those moments when characters look forward to a future that we know and they perforce don't. We can focus here on the children. We can make a connection between the little boy Astyanax in Homer and the son and heir to whom Shakespeare's Henry desires to bequeath the great glory that Hector hoped to hand on to his. Henry urges the French princess that she will need to be 'a good soldier-breeder'. This is not a line you'd think of trying on many young women in the West today. (Kenneth Branagh does not risk it.) Henry goes on: 'Shall not thou and I, between Saint Denis and Saint George, compound a boy, half French and half English, that shall go to Constantinople and take the Turk by the beard? Shall we not? What sayest thou, my fair flower de luce?' 'I do not know dat,' she replies. Indeed. But *we* know that the boy they compounded grew up to do no such thing, that their son was incapable of taking anyone by the beard, let alone 'the Turk'. We know the calamitous future that lies ahead for the feeble King Henry VI as it does for the doomed young Astyanax. We can try to forget or suppress this knowledge, as productions of the play often have when they cut some embarrassing lines from the Epilogue. The Chorus celebrates the triumph of 'This star of England' and his conquest of 'the world's best garden', but then goes on to remind us that under the infant son who succeeded him everything went wrong – Henry VI,

> Whose state so many had the managing
> That they lost France and made his England bleed,
> Which oft our stage hath shown. . . .

No wonder that many productions over the years (including Olivier's film) have chosen to censor this crushing reminder.

To conclude, a thought about endings. In the opening lines of the *Iliad* Homer asks the Muse to sing the wrath of Achilles that sent 'countless' Greeks to their death. (From the Greek word *murios* (countless) we get our word 'myriad'.) Most wars entail countless casualties, fatal and otherwise, actors and victims and witnesses beyond number. These stretch into the illimitable future, including those who will read and hear all the stories about it. Who could hope to impose identity of meaning on events that mean such different things to so many people? In his fine survey of 'soldiers' tales' from the twentieth century, Samuel Hynes notes the different ways that stories of World War I choose to conclude. Endings impose meaning on narratives, 'and not all meanings of that war were the same'. James Jones strikes a similar note at the end of his World War II novel, *The thin red line*, about the capture of Guadalcanal by American troops: 'One day one of their number would write a book about all this, but none of them would believe it, because none of them would remember it that way.'[16] No wonder politicians are anxious to control the way we remember the countless casualties of war. These must be marshalled into identity of meaning, by the funeral oration, by words engraved on stone, by the cult of the national flag, by the day of remembrance, by the trees being planted along 'Warriors' Walk' for the American servicemen who have died in 'Operation Iraqi Freedom'.

Identity of meaning is a dream, a fiction, a kind of heaven, a kind of hell. The heaven would be a matter of perfect love, where identity of meaning is its cause and its consequence, freely given and received,

[16] J. Jones, *The thin red line* (New York: Charles Scribner's Sons, 1962), 510.

beyond all vicissitude. The hell would be one in which identity of meaning is a matter of violent coercion, imposed from on high, depriving its victims of all choice and agency. In the circumstances we might welcome something less absolute than 'identity of meaning'. We might prefer the struggle to recognize each other's meanings through likeness, resemblance, conjecture, speculation and imagination. We could work for a state of affairs in which 'I mean what you mean' might just be truer more often than not.

FURTHER READING

S. Clark (ed.), *Shakespeare made fit: Restoration adaptations of Shakespeare* (London: J. M. Dent, 1997).

C. Fitter, 'A Tale of Two Branaghs: *Henry V*, ideology, and the Mekong Agincourt', in *Shakespeare left and right*, ed. I. Kamps (New York and London: Routledge, 1991), 259–76.

R. Fowler (ed.), *The Cambridge Companion to Homer* (Cambridge University Press, 2004).

Homer, *Iliad*, trans. A. T. Murray, rev. W. F. Wyatt, 2 vols, *Loeb Classical Library* (Cambridge, MA and London: Harvard University Press, 2001).

K. Miller, *Doubles: studies in literary history* (Oxford University Press, 1985).

N. Rabkin, 'Either/or: responding to *Henry V*', in *Shakespeare and the problem of meaning* (Chicago University Press, 1981), 33–62.

W. Shakespeare, *Julius Caesar*, ed. Martin Spevack, 2nd edn (Cambridge University Press, 2004).

W. Shakespeare, *King Henry V*, ed. Andrew Gurr, 2nd edn (Cambridge University Press, 2005).

D. Weissbort and A. Eysteinsson (eds.), *Translation – theory and practice* (Oxford University Press, 2006).

2 Identity and the law

LIONEL BENTLY

Although issues of 'identity' have frequently been the subject of legal regulation and legal decision-making in legal areas as disparate as child law, contract law and criminal sentencing, the concept of 'identity' has not hitherto occupied a central place in English law. In contrast, in the United States, in particular, the idea that a person has property in their identity, including their image, name or voice, is one which is gaining increasing acceptance. Under these laws (which operate primarily at state level and vary in detail from state to state) a person may be able to object if their name is used on a product, or as a domain name, or their face on posters, t-shirts, mugs, video games or memorabilia, or their voice in a television advertisement. Thus it has been held that a famous baseball player could prevent use of his image on baseball cards,[1] a famous athlete use of his nickname 'crazylegs' on shaving gel,[2] and a famous singer could prevent advertisers using vocal imitations in association with the sale of snack food.[3] Some

---

[1] *Haelen Laboratories. Inc.* v. *Topps Chewing Gum Inc.* 202 F. 2d 866 (2d. Cir. 1953).

[2] *Hirsch* v. *S. C. Johnson & Son, Inc.*, 90 Wis 2d 379, 280 N.W. 2d 129 (S. Ct Wisconsin, 1979) (appeal allowed from dismissing action by famous 1940s and 50s footballer and basketball player Elroy Hirsch, nicknamed 'Crazylegs', who objected to Johnson & Son's use of the name on shaving gel for women). See also *John Doe, a.k.a. Tony Twist* v. *TCI Cablevision*, 110 S.W. 3d 363 (Sup. Ct Miss., 2003) (notoriously violent ice hockey player Tony Twist could succeed in action objecting to use of name Tony Twist as that of evil mafia don in comic book, *Spawn*, even though there was no physical resemblance); *McFarland* v. *Miller et al.* 14 F. 3d 912, 914 (USCA 3d. Cir. 1994) (actor who played 'Spanky McFarland' could bring action against restaurant using the name).

[3] *Midler* v. *Ford Motor Co.*, 849 F. 2d 460 (9th Cir. 1988); *Waits* v. *Frito-Lay, Inc.*, 978 F. 2d 1093 (9th Cir. 1992) cert. denied 113 S. Ct 1047, 122 L. Ed. 2d 355 (1993). Cf. *Booth* v. *Colgate-Palmolive Co.* 362 F. Supp. 343, 347 (USDC, SDNY 1973) (right of publicity under New York law confined to name or likeness so did not cover sound-alike voice).

Identity, edited by Giselle Walker and Elisabeth Leedham-Green. Published by Cambridge University Press. © Darwin College 2010.

commentators are suggesting that the European Convention on Human Rights now requires the United Kingdom to take a similar position. In this essay I want to argue that the United Kingdom is not obliged, as yet, to adopt such a law, and would be well advised to think twice before doing so. Whereas other critics of identity-rights have questioned the underlying justification for creating such rights, I want to highlight some other potential problems with the idea of property in identity. I will suggest that 'identity' is a particularly problematic concept around which to build legal structures. The first reason is because it eludes definition, or, to the extent to which it can be defined, raises problems of subjectivity. The second is because, even as regards the core aspects of identity that have been subject of legal protection – name, image and voice – the nature of these attributes is contested and may, therefore, warrant different legal treatments. In particular, echoing Rosemary Coombe,[4] I want to highlight the possibility that property in identity may well conflict with the legitimate freedoms of others to develop their identities.

1   Comparative legal development of property in identity

1.1   The United States

The US protection of a person's identity has its origins in the development of a right of privacy. The story of the development of this right begins with 'that most influential law review article of all',[5] written by Samuel D. Warren and Louis Dembitz Brandeis in the 1890 *Harvard Law Review*.[6] In this article, the authors sought to discover whether the common law offered any remedy to protect the privacy of an individual: 'of the desirability – indeed the necessity – of some such protection, there can, it is believed, be no doubt'.[7] They argued there was such a remedy,

---

[4] Rosemary Coombe, 'Objects of property and subjects of politics: intellectual property laws and democratic dialogue' (1991) 69 *Texas l. r.*, 1853.

[5] H. Kalven, Jr, 'Privacy in Tort Law – were Warren and Brandeis wrong?', 31 *Law. and cont. probs.*, 326, 327; *Hirsch* v. *S. C. Johnson & Son, Inc.*, 90 Wis 2d 379, 280 N. W. 2d 129, 133 (S. Ct Wisconsin, 1979) (Heffernan J.)

[6] Samuel D. Warren and Louis Dembitz Brandeis, 'The right of privacy' (1890) 4 *Harv. l. r.*, 193–220. William L. Prosser, 'Privacy' (1960) 48 *Cal. l. r.*, 383. ('It has come to be regarded as the outstanding example of the influence of legal periodicals upon American law.')

[7] (1890) 4 *Harv. l.r.* 193, 196.

not based, as one might perhaps have expected, through an extension of the law of defamation's protection of 'reputation',[8] but rather through case-law, which had protected authors and artists against unauthorized publication of their works. Using the classic methodology of searching for an 'underlying principle' or 'golden thread' to explain existing cases, the authors 'discovered' that the common law sought to protect 'the right to one's personality'.[9] The relevant case-law related to the recognition of an author's right to decide on the publication of their unpublished manuscripts and artistic works.[10] For Warren and Brandeis these cases were not properly explained as cases of 'property' in the products of one's labour, but were better seen as 'instances and applications of a general right to privacy'.[11] The cases protected private 'thoughts, emotions, and sensations' and the authors argued 'these should receive the same protection, whether expressed in writing, in conduct, in conversation, in attitudes or in facial expression'.[12]

After some hesitation,[13] the Warren and Brandeis analysis was accepted in a case of the use of an individual's image, without consent, in an advertisement. In *Pavesich* v. *New England Life Insurance Co.*,[14] the plaintiff was an artist who discovered his photograph (which, it seems,

[8] Ibid. 193, 197–8.
[9] See James Q. Whitman, 'The two western cultures of privacy: dignity versus liberty' (2004) 113 *Yale l. j.* 1151, 1202 (arguing that the 'Warren and Brandeis tort' is best thought of not as 'a great American innovation' but as 'an unsuccessful continental transplant'. Whitman claims that the American conception of 'privacy' concerns freedom in the home, particularly from interference by the state, whereas 'continental' conceptions are grounded in notions of dignity and honour originally afforded only to an elite but in modern times generalized to the whole population. For Whitman, the Warren and Brandeis tort was grounded in this latter conception, specifically drawing on French and German law and scholarship.)
[10] *Prince Albert* v. *Strange* (1849) 2 De G. & S. 652; *Nicols* v. *Pitman* (1884) 26 Ch. D. 374; *Lee* v. *Simpson* (1847) 3 C.B. 871, 881; *Turner* v. *Robinson* (1859–60) 10 Ir. Ch. 121. The authors also relied on implied contract and trade secret cases: (1890) 4 *Harv. l. r.* 193, 210–14.
[11] Ibid., 193, 198.   [12] Ibid., 193, 206.
[13] For the immediate case-law, see (1960) 48 *Cal. l. r.* 383, 384–5. Most important amongst these was a decision of the New York Court of Appeal, *Roberson* v. *Rochester Folding Box Co.* 171 N.Y. 538, 64 N.E. 442 (1902), where a complaint by a young woman to the use of her image in an advertisement for flour, with the caption 'The Flour of the Family', was rejected. Significantly, this prompted the New York legislature to introduce statutory protection to prevent the use of the name, portrait or picture of any person for 'advertising purposes or for the purposes of trade' without consent.
[14] 50 SE 68 (1905) (Sup. Ct Georgia).

had been taken with consent) was being used by the defendant in an advertisement for its insurance services. The advertisement depicted the plaintiff alongside a sickly-looking man and suggested that the plaintiff's comparative good health was attributable to the fact that he had insurance with the defendant, whereas the sickly-looking man did not. The plaintiff's action was for trespass on the plaintiff's right of privacy, caused by breach of confidence and trust reposed in the photographer. At first instance the claim was rejected, but the Supreme Court of Georgia allowed an appeal. Cobb J., for the Court, acknowledged that the Court had to determine whether an individual had a right of privacy which the courts would protect against invasion. Despite the fact that neither previous case-law nor commentary mentioned such a right, the Court found that this did not mean there was not such a right. The Court based its reasoning in 'natural law' arguing that the right of privacy 'has its foundation in the instincts of nature. It is recognized intuitively, consciousness being the witness that can be called to establish its existence.'[15] Just as a person had liberty to decide whether to expose their bodies to the public gaze (or to stay in seclusion), so they should have the power to decide whether their image was placed before the public eye.[16] For Cobb J., this right of privacy could be waived, but such waiver could be 'for one person, and still asserted for another; it may be waived in behalf of one class, and retained as against another class; and it may be waived to one individual, and retained as against all other persons'.[17] Moreover, the right would, where appropriate, give way to competing interests in free speech.[18]

In the case in hand there was little difficulty in reconciling the two, often competing, interests of privacy and free speech. The 'form and features of the plaintiff are his own' and the defendants had 'no more authority to display them in public for the purpose of advertising the business in which they were engaged than they would have had to

---

[15] 50 SE 68, 69. See also at 71 ('the right of privacy . . . is a right derived from natural law, recognized by the principles of municipal law, and guaranteed to persons in this state both by the Constitution of the United States and of the state of Georgia, in those provisions which declare that no person shall be deprived of liberty except by due process of law').

[16] 50 SE 68, 70.   [17] 50 SE 68, 72.

[18] 50 SE 68, 73–4 ('The right of privacy is unquestionably limited by the right to speak and print').

compel the plaintiff to place himself upon exhibition for this purpose'.[19] Such use in advertising involved 'not the slightest semblance of an expression of an idea, a thought or an opinion'.[20] The right of privacy, described in this way as an extension of liberty of movement and self-determination, was thus violated.

Pavesich recognized that privacy interests could be affected by unwanted exposure of one's image in association with advertising. However, *Pavesich* concerned an image of an unknown person, where the wrong was perceived in non-pecuniary terms: the publication was 'peculiarly offensive to him' and 'tends to bring plaintiff into ridicule before the world'.[21] Although the Court spoke in terms of 'liberty' and thus might have foreshadowed a general right to control all uses of one's image, subsequent courts declined to protect well-known personalities where claims of injury to solitude or feelings were implausible. In *O'Brien* v. *Pabst Sales Co.*,[22] for example, the plaintiff, football-player Davey O'Brien, who had allowed Texas Christian University to take photographs for publicity purposes, was held not to be entitled to prevent the use of his photograph in football strip on a calendar, the *Pabst Blue Ribbon Football Calendar*, 1939. The Court of Appeals for the Fifth Circuit held that a person who had courted celebrity could not complain of intrusion into their privacy when they received the very publicity the Court said they had 'been constantly seeking and receiving'.

In *Haelen Laboratories Inc.* v. *Topps Chewing Gum Inc.*,[23] the US Court of Appeals for the Second Circuit extended the logic of *Pavesich* into a right to control not privacy but 'publicity'. In *Haelen*, the facts of which 'were not too clearly found',[24] the plaintiff claimed the exclusive right to use

---

[19] 50 SE 68, 79.   [20] 50 SE 68, 80.
[21] 50 SE 68, 68. Jonathan Kahn, 'Controlling identity: Plessy, privacy and racial defamation' (2005) 54 *De Paul l. r.*, 755, 767 (emphasizing that *Pavesich* involved 'a dignitary harm – and infringement of a personal interest – not a property right').
[22] 24 F. 2d 167 (5th Cir. 1941), cert. denied 315 U.S. 823, 62 S. Ct. 917, 86 L. Ed. 1220 (1942). *Pallas* v. *Crowley-Milner & Co.*, 334 Mich 282, 54 N.W. 2d 595 (1952). See Melville B. Nimmer, 'The right of publicity' (1954) 19 *Law and cont. probs.*, 203, 204–9 (explaining limitations of 'privacy'-based conception of right over name and likeness).
[23] (1953) 202 F. 2d 866. For background to the case, see J. Gordon Hylton, 'Baseball cards and the birth of the right of publicity: The curious case of Haelan Laboratories v Topps Chewing Gum' (2001) 12 *Marquette sports law review*, 273.
[24] (1953) 202 F. 2d 866, 867.

photographs of famous baseball players in connection with the sale of its
chewing gum, basing its claim on contracts entered into with the players.
The defendant, a rival chewing-gum manufacturer, used the same players'
images on its cards. The plaintiff objected on the basis of both inducing
breach of contract (a recognized tort) and the exclusive rights in the
images. The defendant argued that the baseball players had only non-
assignable rights of privacy, which they could waive vis-à-vis the plaintiff
(or the defendant) so that its use of the images was non-infringing, but
they could not assign the right to the plaintiff. Judge Jerome Frank, held
that 'in addition to and independent of the rights of privacy (which in New
York derives from statute), a man has a right in the publicity value of his
own photograph i.e., the right to grant the exclusive privilege of publishing his picture' which was assignable.[25] These rights of 'publicity' were
particularly relevant to the 'many prominent persons' who objected to use
of their images not because of 'bruised feelings' from exposure of their
likenesses but because they 'no longer received money for authorizing
advertisements, popularizing their countenances'.

Haelen inaugurated a second wave of cases (and statutes) in which
famous plaintiffs were permitted to claim for misuse of their names or
likenesses, particularly by their use, without authorization, in advertising.[26] While *Pavesich* had recognized that such actions might involve
invasions of the privacy of relatively unknown individuals, *Haelen* held
that public figures had similar rights. But while the two actions bore a
superficial similarity, the exact relationship between them was to become
a matter for debate. Dean William L. Prosser,[27] sought to incorporate
the publicity right within the rubric of privacy.[28] Prosser asserted that

[25] (1953) 202 F. 2d 866, 868. Distinguishing *Pekas Co. Inc.* v. *Leslie*, (1915) 52 N.Y.L.J.
1864 on the basis that the judge's attention was directed purely at the New York
statute protecting privacy.
[26] According to the National Conference of State Legislatures, there are nineteen
states with statutory publicity laws and eleven which recognize a right at common
law only. In California, actions arise under Civil Code section 3344 and the common
law. Section 3344 (a) provides that 'any person who knowingly uses another's name,
voice, signature, photograph or likeness, in any manner . . . for purposes of
advertising or selling, . . . without such person's prior consent . . . shall be liable
for any damages sustained by the person or persons injured as a result thereof'. In
New York, the action is based on sections 50 and 51 of the Civil Rights Law.
[27] Dean of University of California School of Law, Berkeley.
[28] (1960) 48 *Cal. l. r.*, 383, 388.

'privacy' comprised not a single cause of action, but instead 'a complex of four' distinguishable strands. These 'four distinct kinds of invasion of four different interests' were intrusions upon another's seclusion or solitude, public disclosure of embarrassing private facts, placing another in a false light and appropriation for the defendant's advantage of the plaintiff's name or likeness. Prosser argued that, as regards the fourth tort, '[t]he interest protected is not so much a mental as a proprietary one, in the exclusive use of the plaintiff's name and likeness as an aspect of his identity'. In contrast Edward Bloustein[29] claimed that the publicity right lay outside the concept of privacy. Privacy, he said, protects 'the individual's independence, dignity and integrity; it defines man's essence as a unique and self-determining being' and argued that Prosser's division into parts neglected this significant unifying characteristic. Bloustein denied that protection of one's name or image can be reduced to a proprietary interest, emphasizing that cases such as *Pavesich* concern preservation of 'individual dignity'. For Bloustein, the '[u]se of a photograph for trade purposes turns a man into a commodity and makes him serve the economic needs and interests of others'. He denied that there is a 'right of publicity' and preferred to see commercial dealings as situations where a person abandons his or her privacy right.

Although Prosser's categorization of 'four torts of privacy' has received widespread judicial acceptance,[30] the question of the relation between protection of 'identity' through rights of privacy and publicity has continued to engage scholars and law-makers.[31] Perhaps the most important development has been the 'Restatements' produced by the American Law Institute. Here the rules on commercial appropriation of identity are summarized in two restatements, under rubrics of both 'privacy' and 'unfair competition.'[32] The Restatement (Second) of Torts

[29] Edward J. Bloustein, 'Privacy as an aspect of human dignity: An answer to Dean Prosser' (1964) 39 *N. Y. U. l. r.*, 962, 971.

[30] *White v. Samsung Electronics America Inc.*, 971 F. 2d 1395 (9th Cir. 1992), cert. denied 113 S. Ct 2443, 124 L. Ed. 2d 660 (1993) ('one of the earliest and most enduring articulations of the common law right of publicity cause of action'). J. Thomas McCarthy, 'Public personas and private property: the commercialization of human identity' (1989) 79 *Trademark reporter* 681, 685–6.

[31] Jonathan Kahn, 'Privacy as a legal principle of identity maintenance', 33 *Seton Hall l. r.* 37; 54 *De Paul l. r.*, 755.

[32] The Restatement (Second) of Torts (1977), section 652 and the Restatement (Third) of Unfair Competition (1995), section 46.

includes a rule imposing liability for an invasion of privacy against 'one who appropriates to his own use or benefit the name or likeness of another'.[33] The Restatement (Third) of Unfair Competition states that '[o]ne who appropriates the commercial value of a person's identity by using without consent the person's name, likeness, or other indicia of identity for the purposes of trade is subject to liability for the relief appropriate under the rules stated in sections 48 and 49'.[34]

The Restatement explains that this parallels the provisions of the Restatement of Torts on privacy, which relate to the protection of personal interests that are affected by the appropriation of another person's identity. Thus 'similar substantive rules govern the determination of liability' in privacy and unfair competition, the difference relating primarily to the nature of the harm suffered.[35]

The identity right is, of course, limited by various doctrines: incidental uses are not covered,[36] nor are non-commercial uses, and artistic uses may benefit from exemption under the First Amendment.

1.2   The UK protection of identity

As I mentioned at the outset, English law does not have a corresponding action for 'commercialization of identity'. The English common law declined (until recently) to recognize a right of privacy and has not come close to accepting the idea of a right of publicity. Baroness Hale explained in 2004 that '[u]nlike in France and Quebec, in this country we do not recognize a right to one's own image',[37] and, as recently as May 2007, other members of the House of Lords reiterated the point.

---

[33] Restatement (Second) of Torts (1977), section 652. The commentary, written by Prosser, states that 'the interest protected by the rule stated in this Section is the *interest of the individual in the exclusive use of his own identity*, in so far as it is represented by his name or likeness, and in so far as the use may be of benefit to him or others' (emphasis added).

[34] Section 46 of the Restatement (Third) of Unfair Competition (1995).

[35] Restatement (Third) of Unfair Competition (1995), Comment (b). The commentary to the Restatement also notes that 'like the right of privacy, the right of publicity protects an individual's interest in personal dignity and autonomy'.

[36] *Preston v. Bregman Productions* 765 F. Supp. 116 (USDC, SDNY 1991) (inclusion of plaintiff, a prostitute, in opening titles for film, *Sea of Love*, for nine seconds, with face showing for four and a half seconds, was incidental use so not a violation of New York privacy statute).

[37] *Campbell v. Mirror Group Newspapers* [2004] A.C. 457, 501, para. 154.

While recognizing that 'the position is different in other jurisdictions', in *Douglas* v. *Hello*, Lord Walker stated that 'under English law it is not possible for a celebrity to claim a monopoly in his or her image, as if it were a trademark or a brand'.[38] Lord Hoffmann agreed that, while he and Lord Walker might differ as to the result of the case before them (which involved interpretation of the law of confidentiality), there was no question of creating 'an "image right" or any other unorthodox form of intellectual property'.[39]

Of course, to deny the existence of an image right (let alone an 'identity right') is not to say that an aggrieved party cannot, in certain circumstances, gain judicial assistance in preventing certain uses of his or her image or identity. In the UK the claimants have sought to use any of a number of different legal bases for their claims (depending, in part, on the regulatory context, and the type of damage that the appropriation has brought about). Although claimants have used defamation,[40] contract,[41] copyright,[42] and other regulatory mechanisms (such as complaining to Ofcom or the Advertising Standards Authority),[43] until recently the most promising option seemed to be the action to prevent passing-off.

---

[38] *Douglas* v. *Hello!* [2008] 1 A.C. 1 para. 293. Lord Walker observed, 'Their claims come close to a "character right" protecting a celebrity's name or image such as has consistently been rejected in English law'(para. 285). See also *Elvis Presley Trade Mark* [1999] R.P.C. 567, 580–2, 597–8; Brooke L.J. [2001] Q.B. 967 paras 74 and 75.

[39] *Douglas* v. *Hello!* [2008] 1 A.C. 1.

[40] *Tolley* v. *J. S. Fry & Sons* [1931] A.C. 333 (amateur golfer's action for defamation succeeded when caricature included in plaintiff's advert showed him having a bar of Fry's chocolate in his trouser pocket).

[41] *Pollard* v. *Photographic* Co. (1888) 40 Ch. D. 345.

[42] *Merchandising Corporation* v. *Harpbond* [1983] F.S.R. 32 (pop star Adam Ant unable to protect new image as a painting).

[43] *The Number UK (Ltd), regarding complaint by David Bedford* (27 January 2004) (unsuccessful appeal of finding that advertisement for phone company which featured two runners caricatured the athlete David Bedford, contrary to ITC Advertising Standard Code, rule 6.5, available at www.ofcom.org.uk/tv/obb/adv_compl/content_board/). Note also the decision of WIPO Arbitrator David Perkins in *Winterson* v. *Hogarth* [2000] E.T.M.R. 783 (holding that English law recognized 'jeanette winterson' was a trade mark for the purposes of the Uniform Domain Name Dispute Resolution Policy, that Hogarth's registration of, *inter alia*, jeanettewinterson.com, had been in bad faith, and requiring a transfer of the domain name to Winterson).

1.2.1 PASSING-OFF

The central precept of the English law of passing-off is that 'no man has a right to sell his own goods as the goods of another'.[44] Under conventional rules, a claimant, to succeed, would have to show that he was a trader and had a trading reputation (so called 'goodwill') and that another's use of his name or image amounted to a misrepresentation that would damage the claimant's goodwill. While the mere use of the name or image of a private or public figure will not always amount to passing-off, it might well do so in cases where the person in question sold goods or provided services that had become associated with the particular name or image in such a way that the latter would be understood as indicating the origin of the goods or services. The actor Paul Newman, or celebrity Loyd Grossman, might for example take up the manufacture of various foods, and, having done so, would be able to stop other traders 'passing their goods off' as 'Newman's Own' pasta sauce or 'Loyd Grossman Madras Curry Sauce'.

However, claimants seeking to protect their names and images have frequently failed to establish relevant elements of the action for passing-off. As early as 1848,[45] the Physician in Ordinary to the Queen, Sir James Clark, was denied an injunction against a defendant who was selling 'Sir J. Clarke's Consumption Pills' because Clark was not himself 'in the habit of manufacturing and selling pills' so there was no damage 'to property by the fraudulent misuse of the name of another, by which his profits are diminished'. Virtually 100 years later Derek McCulloch, the presenter of the BBC's very popular radio broadcast programme *Children's Hour*, was denied an injunction preventing the defendants from selling 'Uncle Mac's Puffed Wheat'. Passing-off required that the defendant's misrepresentation damaged the goodwill of the plaintiff's business and, given that McCulloch was 'not engaged in any degree in producing or marketing puffed wheat', the court was unable to see how his business could be damaged.[46] In *Lyngstrad* v. *Annabas Products*,[47] the pop group ABBA complained that the defendant was selling paraphernalia that bore the name and image of the group. Refusing to grant relief, Oliver J. said

[44] *Perry* v. *Truefit* (1843) 7 Beav. 84, 88.
[45] (1851) 11 Beav. 112; 8 *Law magazine*, 236.
[46] *McCulloch* v. *May* (1948) 65 R.P.C. 58.   [47] [1977] F.S.R. 62.

that he did not think anyone could reasonably imagine that the pop stars had given their approval for the paraphernalia. He also added that the defendants were not doing 'anything more than catering for a popular demand among teenagers for effigies of their idols'.[48]

Despite these precedents, in 2002 a celebrity finally succeeded with the decision of Laddie J. in *Irvine* v. *Talksport*.[49] In this case the famous Formula One racing driver brought an action against Talksport for using his image on a promotional brochure (used to attract advertising for the radio station). The brochure comprised a picture of Irvine, which had been modified so that he was listening to a radio bearing the Talksport logo. Irvine brought an action for passing-off, and Laddie J. found in his favour. Laddie J. reviewed the cases on personalities and passing-off and held that they indicated that a person might be able to utilize the action to prevent a misrepresentation by a trader that its products or services had been endorsed by the personality. (In so doing the judge made it clear that endorsement was a narrower notion than merchandising.) On the facts in front of him, Laddie J. found that Talksport's brochure had given the impression that Irvine endorsed the radio station. In particular, Laddie J. was impressed by evidence from an associate of Irvine to the effect that he sought a free radio from the racing driver, an act which indicated that he believed Irvine had done a deal with the radio station. The Court of Appeal affirmed Laddie J.'s decision, emphasizing, in particular, that the actual image of Irvine listening to the radio gave an impression of endorsement.

1.2.2 PRIVACY

While passing-off has long seemed the most promising avenue for those seeking to prevent the commercial use of their name or image – not least because there was no common law of privacy – exciting new possibilities were presented for the development of the law of privacy in October 2000 when the Human Rights Act 1998 came into force. As is well known, the Act gave legal force within the United Kingdom to the European Convention on Human Rights, as well as jurisprudence to the European Court of Human Rights ('the Strasbourg Court'). Importantly, Article 8 of that Convention states that 'everyone has the right to

---

[48] Ibid.   [49] [2002] F.S.R. 943.

respect for his private and family life, his home and his correspondence'. Because of the wording relating to 'respect', Article 8 does not merely compel the state to abstain from interfering with private and family life but also requires the state positively to act to protect privacy, even in the sphere of the relations of individuals between themselves. In so doing, the state has 'a certain margin of appreciation'.

The impact of Article 8 on English law has not been straightforward, primarily because English law continues to deny the existence of a tort of invasion of privacy. Instead, the judiciary has acknowledged that it should develop existing causes of action to provide protection sufficient to comply with Article 8. The most important decision so far is that of the House of Lords in *Campbell* v. *MGN Ltd.*[50] As was widely reported in the media, this case concerned the famously irascible model, Naomi Campbell. The *Daily Mirror* had published articles relating to the fact that she was receiving treatment for drug addiction ('Naomi: I am a drug addict'), and these were illustrated with photographs of Campbell leaving meetings of Narcotics Anonymous ('Therapy: Naomi outside meeting').[51] Campbell sued, claiming invasion of her privacy. The House of Lords held in her favour by three votes to two, though the disagreement was more about application of the principles than over what they were. The House indicated that Article 8 was to be given effect through adaptation of the rules on breach of confidence.[52] The key question was whether the photographs related to matters with respect to which Campbell had a reasonable expectation of privacy.[53] Given that Campbell's medical treatment was a private matter, and that the newspaper was aware of this, the majority held that the *Mirror* had breached an obligation of confidence.[54]

---

[50] [2004] A.C. 457; [2004] 2 All E.R. 995; [2004] 2 W.L.R. 1232 (House of Lords).
[51] Published on 1 February 2001.
[52] [2004] A.C. 457, 465 per Lord Nicholls, para. 17 ('the values enshrined in Article 8 and 10 are now part of the cause of action for breach of confidence'). See also Lord Hoffmann, at para. 51, referring to a 'shift in the centre of gravity' of the cause of action for breach of confidence.
[53] [2004] A.C. 457, 466, para. 21 per Lord Nicholls.
[54] Lord Nicholls said that Campbell had put the issue of whether she was addicted to drugs into the public domain, and that the photographs disclosed nothing further than that she was attending Narcotics Anonymous and so did not relate to material over which she had a reasonable expectation of privacy. Lord Hoffmann held that the *Mirror*'s freedom of expression justified the publication of the photographs.

The *Campbell* case certainly indicates potential for the law of privacy
to give a person control of their image, but that potential is limited to
images over which a person has a reasonable expectation of privacy.
The effect is thus limited to photographs that disclose private matters,
or implicate the dignity of the individual. In *Campbell* itself, Lord
Nicholls argued that (once it was accepted that the fact she was receiving
treatment was in the public domain) the photographs contained no
private information: she was shown in the street exchanging greetings
with others and 'there was nothing undignified or distrait about her
appearance'.[55] Lord Hoffmann too said that, even where a photograph is
taken of someone in a public place, its publication could be restrained if
it revealed him or her 'to be in a situation of humiliation or severe
embarrassment' but that here there was 'nothing embarrassing' as
Ms Campbell was 'neatly dressed and smiling'.[56] Baroness Hale too
agreed that, had the picture been presented merely as one of Ms Campbell
going about her daily business in a public street, there could have been
no complaint (though she, and the majority, took the view that in the
context of the disclosures about her medical treatment, there was a
reasonable expectation of privacy).[57] The clear view that a public figure
has no expectation of privacy when going about their business in public
was applied in *Elton John* v. *Associated Newspapers*.[58] Here, Elton John
sought to prevent the *Daily Mail* from publishing a photograph of him
standing in the street outside his home wearing a baseball cap and
tracksuit. Denying interim relief, Eady J. explained that nothing in the
photograph pertained to Mr John's health, or social, personal or sexual
relationships, and thus there was nothing relating to which John could
be said to have a reasonable expectation of privacy. While the Judge
expected that the article would likely be dismissive or personally offensive, he said that as yet there is not 'any doctrine operative in English
law whereby it is necessary to demonstrate that, to publish a photograph, one has to show that the subject of the photograph gave consent'.

---

[55] [2004] A.C. 457, para. 31.   [56] Ibid. 457, paras. 75–6.
[57] Ibid. 457, para. 154.   [58] [2006] E.M.L.R. 772.

1.2.3 CONFIDENTIALITY

The recent decision of the House of Lords in *Douglas* indicates that, even without circumstances that give rise to a reasonable expectation of privacy, the law of breach of confidence can itself provide some protection against use of one's image. The case arose out of events following the wedding of Catherine and Michael Douglas in New York in 2000. Ten days before the wedding, the bride and groom entered into an arrangement with *OK!* Magazine concerning photographs of the wedding, for which Douglas and Zeta-Jones each received £500,000. The Douglases were to arrange security for the wedding (so that no publishers other than *OK!* could obtain images), to commission the photography and then select photographs for publication by *OK!* (by 22 November). The agreement purported to transfer 'the exclusive right to publish . . . the photographs . . . from the date of the wedding and for nine months thereafter' and the Douglases undertook not to publish or authorize publication of any photographs during that period. There were some 350 guests at the wedding, all of whom had been informed that there was to be no photography.

OK!'s chief rival, *Hello!* obtained (for £125,000) six photos of the wedding taken by a paparazzo, Mr Rupert Thorpe, and sought to publish them. *Hello!* was initially enjoined by Court order, but the Court of Appeal reversed this on 23 November 2000, and *Hello!* published the photographs that day. The, by now, not so 'happy couple' – and *OK!* – responded to these developments by rushing a selection of the photographs into publication, so that *OK!* in fact was able to release its authorized coverage on 23 November too. The Douglases and *OK!* sued for damages, claiming breach of confidence, invasion of privacy and deliberate interference with business relations. At first instance, before Lindsay J., they succeeded. The Douglases were awarded £3,750 damages each for mental distress; and £7,000 for inconvenience they suffered as a result of the wrongful publication. *OK!*, in contrast, were awarded what would be called in tabloid language a 'whopping' £1,026,706 for loss of profit. The defendants appealed. The Court of Appeal allowed the appeal in part – indeed, the most financially significant part – as regards *OK!*'s claim. Lord Phillips MR, giving judgement for the Court, accepted that the photographs 'plainly portrayed aspects of the Douglases' private life and fell within the protection of the law of confidentiality, as extended to cover private or personal information'.[59] Moreover, the fact that the Douglases had entered a contract with *OK!* allowing the latter to exploit some of the information did not mean all details of the wedding were in the public domain.

However, the Court observed that *OK!*'s claim was wholly based on interests purportedly derived from the Douglases. Scrutiny of the agreement between the Douglases and *OK!* revealed that it did not purport to give any rights in the residual details of the wedding (but only related to the authorized photographs).[60] The agreement gave *OK!* the right to use the pictures of the wedding that the Douglases had selected, but the residual rights over all the other photographs (including unauthorized ones) remained with the couple. Crucially, the unauthorized photos 'invaded the area of privacy which the Douglases had chosen to retain. It was the Douglases, not *OK!*, who had the right to protect this area of privacy or confidentiality.'[61]

On appeal the House of Lords reversed the ruling in respect of *OK!*. Lord Hoffmann, with whom Lord Brown and Baroness Hale agreed, took the view that photographic images of the wedding were regarded by the Douglases and *OK!* as confidential, and observed that *OK!* had required the Douglases to use their best efforts to ensure that no one else would take any photographs. *Hello!* knew that there was an exclusive arrangement between the Douglases and *OK!* and the sort of provisions it would contain. Consequently, *Hello!* came under an obligation of confidence to *OK!* itself.[62] Lord Hoffmann described the key matter as the fact that '*OK!* had paid £1m for the benefit of the obligation of confidence imposed upon all those present at the wedding in respect of *any* photographs of the wedding.'[63] Lords Walker and Nicholls had difficulty with this analysis. Lord Nicholls held that *Hello!*'s actions did not reveal any information not already made public when *OK!* published its authorized photographs.[64] Lord Walker emphasized that

---

[59] [2006] Q.B. 125, 159, para. 94.   [60] Ibid. 125, 168, para. 132.
[61] Ibid. 125, 169, para. 136.   [62] [2008] 1 A.C. 1, para. 129.
[63] Ibid., para. 117.   [64] Ibid., paras. 257–9.

OK!'s right depended on establishing confidentiality, and he could not see any basis for treating *Hello!*'s photographs of the event as confidential.

1.2.4   SUMMATION

Although English law offers protection to persons for unauthorized use of their names and likenesses, it seems that at present this is only so where the effect of publication is to imply endorsement of a product, or where the photograph discloses matters in relation to which there exists a reasonable expectation of privacy, or which are subject to obligations of confidence. What we should draw from this, however, is that, while in specific contexts English law (or self-regulation) may provide remedies to those who find that their identities have been used for commercial purposes, English law has never done so on the basis that 'identity' is an attribute that deserves protection for its own sake. This leaves a number of circumstances where protection would probably be available in the United States but not in England. For example, a depiction of a look-alike, such as Jackie Onassis at a party on a Dior advertisement,[65] would not incur liability under the law of passing-off in the absence of a belief on behalf of consumers that Onassis endorsed the product. Equally, no action could be brought based on privacy or confidentiality had the picture been one of Onassis from a photo library of publicly available images, or indeed of her standing in an unembarrassing manner in a public place.

1.3   Potential implications of case-law of the European Court of Human Rights

If English law currently contains large gaps compared to that in the US, there are some who argue that the logic of the European Court of Human Rights' decision in *von Hannover* v. *Germany* effectively demands that English law fill those gaps.[66] In this case, Princess Caroline of Monaco had sought to restrain the publication of various pictures of her in a

---

[65] *Onassis v. Christian Dior New York, Inc.*, 472 N.Y.S. 2d 254, 260 (S. Ct N.Y., 1984.
[66] Appn 59320/00, (2005) 40 E.H.R.R. 1. For reviews of *von Hannover*, see M. A. Sanderson, 'Is *von Hannover* v. *Germany* a step backward for the substantive analysis of free speech and privacy interests' (2004) 6 E.H.R.L.R. 631; N. A. Moreham, 'Privacy in public places' (2006) 65 (3) C.L.J. 606.

number of German newspapers and magazines. The pictures included some in a courtyard restaurant, some on a beach, some horse-riding, some on a ski-ing holiday, some leaving her Parisian home, and some shopping. She had relied initially on the German Civil Code's provision protecting personality, as well as specific provisions in German copyright law enabling a person to protect their image.[67] The Hamburg Court had held that, as a figure of contemporary society *par excellence*, Caroline had to tolerate this kind of publication, and this view was affirmed on appeal. The Federal Court of Justice allowed a further appeal in relation only to the pictures in the restaurant courtyard, since it was clear to third parties that she and her companion wanted to be alone. On further appeal, the Federal Constitutional Court also took the view that pictures of her with her children infringed her basic right to protection of her personality. Unhappy with the outcome under German law, Caroline took the German Government to the European Court of Human Rights, where it was held that the German law had not balanced appropriately the right to freedom of expression contained in Article 10 of the Convention with the right to respect for one's private life (in Article 8).

The Court began by considering the concept of private life in Article 8. It defined the concept broadly, as encompassing 'a person's physical and psychological integrity'. It 'extends to aspects relating to personal identity, such as a person's name, or a person's picture'. The Court explained: 'the guarantee afforded by Article 8 of the Convention is primarily intended to ensure the development, without outside interference, of the personality of each individual in his relations with other human beings. There is therefore a zone of interaction of person, with others, even in the public context, which may fall within the scope of "private life"'.[68] The Court said that there 'is no doubt that the publication . . . of photographs of the applicant in her daily life either on her own or with other people falls within the scope of her private life'.[69] Effectively,

---

[67] German Basic Law, Art. 2 ('Everyone shall have the right to the free development of their personality provided that they do not interfere with the rights of others or violate the constitutional order or moral law'); Copyright (Arts Domain) Act, section 22 (images can only be disseminated with the express approval of the persons concerned).

[68] (2005) 40 E.H.R.R. 1, para. 50.   [69] Ibid., para. 53.

Article 8 was engaged. The Court then went on to examine the inter-relationship between Articles 8 and 10, the latter guaranteeing freedom of expression. The Court noted that, although freedom of expression

> extends to the publication of photographs, this is an area in which the protection of the rights and reputation of others takes on particular importance. The present case does not concern the dissemination of "ideas", but of images containing very personal or even intimate "information" about an individual. Furthermore, photographs appearing in the tabloid press are often taken in a climate of continual harassment that induces in the persons concerned a very strong sense of intrusion into their private life or even of persecution.[70]

The Court also observed that the pictures in the case 'show her in scenes from her daily life' and that the 'accompanying commentaries relate exclusively to the details of the applicant's private life'. The 'sole purpose was to satisfy the curiosity of a particular readership regarding the details of the applicant's private life'.[71] As she was not exercising any official functions, and the photographs related exclusively to details of her private life, there was no contribution 'to a debate of general interest' such as to require their publication under Article 10.[72]

Beverley-Smith, Ohly and Lucas-Schloetter, in their book *Privacy, property and personality: Civil law perspectives on commercial appropriation*, have argued that *Von Hannover* does seem to require recognition of a right to identity:

> In typical appropriation cases the case for the protection of privacy is even stronger. The use of a celebrity's picture or name in advertising or merchandising does not provide the public with socially useful information or contribute in any way to a debate of public interest. Following the ECHR's reasoning, article 8 of the Convention arguably imposes an obligation on the member states to protect individuals against any misappropriation of their personal indicia in advertising or merchandising. A free speech defence will only be available in exceptional cases.[73]

---

[70] Ibid., para. 59.   [71] Ibid., para. 65.   [72] Ibid., para. 76.
[73] H. Beverley-Smith, A. Ohly and A. Lucas-Schloetter, in their *Privacy, property and personality: Civil law perspectives on commercial appropriation* (Cambridge University Press, 2005), 222–3.

The authors argue that the jurisprudence 'will inevitably force English law to confront the issue of how best to develop a remedy for appropriation of personality'.[74]

There are four aspects on *von Hannover* that seem, possibly, to point towards recognition of identity-rights (or at the very least 'image rights'). The first is the occasional use of the language of image rights. For example, the Court refers to the 'positive obligation under the Convention to protect private life and the right to control the use of one's image'. (And, as we noted, the Court also said that 'the concept of private life extends to aspects relating to personal identity, such as a person's name, or a person's picture'.) These comments could be taken to imply absolute rights of control over one's image (and identity) subject to contravening Article 10 interests.[75]

The second is the implication, from the decision itself, that all photographs of an individual engage the Article 8 right, even mundane ones of a person shopping or horse-riding. In this respect the case went well beyond its previous holding in *Peck* (where the protected images were of *Peck* carrying a knife after attempting to commit suicide in public),[76] and the House of Lords' decision in *Campbell* (where, subject to a difference of opinion, the pictures were of the model outside the venue of a Narcotics Anonymous meeting which could be identified). If protection must also be provided over the mundane, one might ask, are not all photographic images protected? Indeed, subsequent case-law of the Court indicates that 'private life' was engaged in relation to publication by the press of a photograph of a person taken for the purposes of an official file.[77]

The third is the heavy emphasis on the privacy interests in the balancing exercise between Articles 8 and 10 (freedom of expression). It is this latter aspect, particularly, that seems to inform Beverley-Smith, Ohly and Schloetter's views. These commentators seem to treat *von Hannover* as suggesting that all uses of photographs impact on private

---

[74] Ibid., 225.
[75] A dissenting minority comprising Judges Spielmann and Jebens interprets *von Hannover* as having established 'the right to one's image' under Article 8. See *Vereinigung Bildener Künstler* v. *Austria*, Appn 68354/01 (25 January 2007), para. 14.
[76] *Peck* v. *United Kingdom*, Appn 44647/98 (2003) 36 E.H.R.R. (41) 719.
[77] *Sciacca* v. *Italy*, Appn 50774/99 (11 January 2005).

life, and thus require justification under Article 10.[78] Because there is little such justification for merchandising or advertising uses, they argue that consent is needed for any use of any picture.

The fourth reason why *von Hannover* might be taken as indicating a requirement to recognize a right to identity lies in the justification offered for the protection of private life. Following earlier case-law, the Court twice refers to 'ensuring the development, without outside inter-ference of the personality of each individual in his relations with other human beings' (para. 50) and 'the fundamental importance of protecting private life from the point of view of the development of every human being's personality'.[79] Given the emphasis on self-determination, it might be argued, *von Hannover* does require that a person identified consent to any and every new use of the indicia of their identity (in particular, image, but also name or voice).

There are, I would suggest, two reasons to be sceptical about this understanding of *von Hannover*. Firstly, we should note that the language of the case, in particular the references to image rights, reflects the German legal provisions under consideration (Article 22 of the Copy-right Act), which protects a person's image whether it relates to private life or not. German law, is of course, entitled to give individuals greater protection than that required under Article 8. The Court objected to the derogation from the German law on image rights (in Article 23), which applied to figures of contemporary society, and according to the Court seemed to deprive these persons of their rights under Article 8. Seen in this light, the Court's comments on 'image rights' should be seen as part of the context of the decision, not statements as to the content of Article 8.

Secondly, while the *von Hannover* case does clearly cast doubt on the assumptions of English law present in *Campbell* and *Elton John* that 'ordinary photos taken of a famous person in a public place' are within

---

[78] *White v. Sweden*, Appn 42425/02 (19 September 2006) may support this view, for in this case the European Court of Human Rights assumed, without examining the circumstances in which the photographs were initially created or disclosed, that the publication of pictures of White in several Swedish papers engaged Article 8, with the critical issue being whether this was justified under Article 10.

[79] Citing *Stjerna v. Finland*, Appn 18131/91 (1997) 24 E.H.R.R. 195 Commission, para. 56 (Article 8 ensures a sphere within which everyone can freely pursue the development and fulfilment of their personality.)

the remit of Article 8,[80] it does not follow from the decision that all photographs, *however made and whatever their content*, contain private information. After all, there is authority that an act must engage 'private life' in a non-trivial way before Article 8 is engaged.[81] There must be some 'legitimate expectation' of protection and respect for the person's private life. In the *von Hannover* case, the images may have been essentially uninteresting in that Caroline was not doing anything controversial (carrying a knife, attending a meeting of NA), but as far as the Court was concerned it was exactly these sorts of quotidian, routine actions that were private. They concerned her daily life. Moreover the images were created without Caroline's consent, and distributed well beyond any audience to which she could have been taken to consent. As the Court said 'the context in which these photos were taken – without the applicant's knowledge and consent – and the harassment endured by many public figures in their daily lives cannot be fully disregarded'.[82] Importantly, then, images such as those of Eddie Irvine in *Irvine* v. *Talksport* or the baseball players in *Haelen* seem to fall well outside the scope of the *von Hannover* holding. For *von Hannover* to encompass such acts we would have to accept that photographs taken *with the consent* of the person depicted and distributed in public with their consent nevertheless involved aspects of the person's private life so that explicit consent was required whenever the image was further distributed to a distinguishable or different audience. This is, of course, not beyond the bounds of what a legal system might require, but it seems a long way beyond what either Article 8 of the Convention or *von Hannover* demand.

---

[80] 'There is little doubt that *Von Hannover* extends the reach of Article 8 beyond what had previously been understood': *McKennitt* v. *Ash* [2006] EWCA Civ 1714 (14 December 2006) para. 37 per Buxton L. J. Note also *Murray* v. *Big Pictures (UK) Ltd* [2008] EWCA Civ 446 (Court of Appeal) confirming that a public figure has no right over his or her own image, while holding that a child of J. K. Rowling, who had been shielded from press attention by his parents, had 'reasonable expectation of privacy' such as to engage Article 8 when being pushed in a pushchair by its parents.)

[81] See e.g. *Stjerna* v. *Finland*, Appn 18131/91 (1997) 24 E.H.R.R. 195, para. 67 (inconveniences were not sufficient to implicate Article 8).

[82] (2005) 40 E.H.R.R. 1, at para. 68; see also para. 59. The argument that *von Hannover* was a special case of persistent media intrusion or harassment was rejected in *McKennitt* v. *Ash* [2006] EWCA Civ 1714 (14 December 2006), para. 41, on the basis that the ECHR had already indicated it involved a principle of general application in *Sciacca* v. *Italy*, Appn 50774/99.

If *von Hannover* does require recognition of image rights, does it also require a general right to 'one's identity'? The statement that 'the concept of private life extends *to aspects relating to personal identity, such as a person's name*, or a person's picture' might suggest so.[83] However, one should be very careful to draw a distinction between the concept of private life in Article 8 and the legal content of the 'right of respect' for one's private life in Article 8. The European Court has happily identified matters such as names,[84] sexual identity,[85] and so on as matters falling within private life. However, just because names come within the idea of private life, and so a person can object when their choice of name is limited in a discriminatory manner, one cannot assume that Article 8 requires recognition of an exclusive right over one's name. The attributes one should be given control over (in preference to the state) are not necessarily co-terminous with those, if any, in which one should be granted exclusive rights.

Some Court case-law does suggest that rights over a person's 'voice' might be included in the content of respect for 'private life'. In *PG and JH* v. *UK*,[86] the applicants (who had been suspected of planning an armed robbery) were recorded while in police custody, in order to compare one

---

[83] (2005) 40 E.H.R.R. 1, para. 50. Note also, *PG and JH* v. *UK*, Appn 44787/98 (25 September 2001) *The Times*, 19 October 2001, para. 56 ('Article 8 protects a right to identity and personal development'); *Bensaid* v. *UK*, Appn 44599/98 (2001) 33 E.H.R.R. 205, para. 47.

[84] Earlier case-law, which has recognized that matters relating to the regulation of names may fall within the concept of private life in Article 8, has concerned administrative regulation of the choice of surname, something quite different from recognition of property in one's name. In those cases the Court has indicated that restrictions on a person's freedom to choose their own name may operate in a way that affects their private life, and be objectionable, in themselves or in combination with the prohibition against unjustified discrimination contained in Article 14. So, for example, a person should not be prevented from changing their name from a name which is humiliating (*Stjerna* v. *Finland*, Appn 18131/91 (1997) 24 E.H.R.R. 195, particularly the Commission decision at para. 64, pp. 205–6), nor should the rules on adoption of surnames after marriage operate to allow only adoption of the name of a particular gender (*Burghartz* v. *Switzerland*, Appn 16213/90 (1994) 18 E.H.R.R. 101; *Unal Tekeli* v. *Turkey*, Appn 29865/96 (2006) 42 E.H.R.R. 53).

[85] *Bensaid* v. *UK*, Appn 44599/98 (2001) 33 E.H.R.R. 205, para. 47 ('private life' is a broad term not susceptible to exhaustive definition. The Court has already held that elements such as gender identification, name and sexual orientation and sexual life are important elements of the personal sphere protected by Article 8); *Van Kuck* v. *Germany*, Appn 35968/97 (2003) 37 E.H.R.R. 973, para. 75 ('a fundamental aspect of her right to respect for private life, namely her right to gender identity and personal development').

[86] Appn 44787/98 (25 September 2001).

of the applicants' voice with that on certain other recordings. He was later convicted of conspiracy to rob Securicor and sentenced to fifteen years' imprisonment. As regards the recordings at the police station, which were primarily for use by experts, the Court held that there was violation of Article 8(1).

2   Why Britain, Europe – and the United States – should think twice before making identity into property

Even if, as I have argued, the UK is not obliged to develop a notion of property in identity, there will doubtless be pressure to do so. Everyone who works in the field of intellectual property law is conscious of the tendency of legal norms to expand and, in areas of harmonization, to gravitate toward the most protective regime. Although there is no international framework that requires harmonization of 'identity-rights' between the UK and US, wherever foreign developments present greater levels of protection, they come to be cited as standards to which domestic law should aspire and models against which it should be judged. The use of the names, images and voices of film, TV and sports stars in advertising and in merchandising is already big business: those who invest in exclusive dealings with these figures, and the celebrities who benefit from such transactions, will doubtless press for the recognition of property in identity.[87]

I am unpersuaded that such recognition would be desirable. For one thing, I share the views of other commentators that the philosophical and policy justifications for such protection have not been made out.[88] Neither arguments based on natural rights, nor those based on economics, which justify protection of intellectual property in intellectual creations, seem to apply satisfactorily to the names, voices or images or individuals.

---

[87] Hazel Carty, 'Advertising, publicity rights and English law' (2004), *I. P. Q*, 209–58.
[88] Michael Madow, 'Private ownership of public images: popular culture and publicity rights', 81 *Cal. l. r.*, 125 (1993); Stacey Dogan and Mark Lemley, 'What the right of publicity can learn from trademark law', *Stan. L. R.* 1161. For other justifications, see Alice Haemmerli, 'Whose Who? The case for a Kantian right of publicity' (1999) 49 *Duke l. j.*, 383; Mark McKenna, 'The right of publicity and autonomous self-definition' (2005) 67 *University of Pittsburgh law review*, 225.

In most cases, one's name, face or voice is not a creation requiring labour, skill, ingenuity or inventiveness. Why then should it be made a property? To echo one English appellate judge,[89] 'monopolies should not be so readily created'.

This is not to say that aspects of identity should never be the subject of legal protection. Misuse of identity can be a vehicle for all sorts of wrongful activities and transactions. A person can defraud another by pretending to be someone else;[90] impersonation can undermine the validity of consent to sexual intercourse;[91] and adopting a person's image in advertising one's goods may deceive consumers into believing that the person featured endorsed the goods.[92] In each case, use of attributes associated with another person is the vehicle for fraud, rape or passing-off. But the wrong, in my view, is not the use of 'someone else's identity' *per se*. Rather it is use of someone else's identity in a way which deceives another person and thereby allows the deceiver to gain something they would not otherwise have achieved (money, sex or custom). Other unauthorized uses of 'identity' may also justify legal intervention under the associated rubric of privacy.

Because the arguments relating to justifications of 'identity-rights' have been rehearsed at length by others (more able than myself) elsewhere, I do not want to interrogate them here. Instead, I want to make two broader points about the suitability of human identities as legal properties – points, I hope, that will make policy-makers and judges think twice before so treating them. One concerns the meaning of 'identity'. The second relates to the coherence of the category of identity.

[89] *Elvis Presley Trade Marks* [1997] R.P.C. 543; [1999] R.P.C. 567, 598 per Simon Brown LJ: there should be no a priori assumption that only a celebrity may ever market his own character.

[90] *R. v. Odewale* [2004] E.W.C.A. 145 (where 'identity theft' is described as 'a particularly serious form of conspiracy to defraud').

[91] Sexual Offences Act 2003, s. 76 (no consent, and thus rape, where the defendant 'intentionally induced the complainant to consent to the relevant act by impersonating a person known personally to the complainant'). In contrast, case-law holds that there is no criminal assault when a person pretending to be a dentist gives dental treatment: a person's professional status or qualifications is not, in general, part of their 'identity'. *R v. Richardson* (1998) 43 B.M.L.R. 21 (Court of Appeal).

[92] See *Irvine v. Talksport*, already discussed above at page 36 and accompanying note 49.

2.1   Definition

My first concern with the idea of giving legal protection over 'identity' is one of definition. To date the United States statutes have mostly talked about 'name, image, likeness', etc.,[93] and it is the commentators,[94] and judges,[95] who have replaced these specific notions with the broader category of 'identity'.[96] In fact, while it seems that Prosser first deployed the notion of identity to limit the scope of protection, stating for example that it was not a name per se which was protected so much as a name as an indicator of identity,[97] the conceptual shift that it inaugurated has resulted in an expansion of protection. The Californian courts, for example, granted protection to Bette Midler when an imitation of her rendition of 'Do You Wanna Dance' was used in an advertisement for the Ford Lincoln Mercury, Circuit Judge Noonan explaining that 'to impersonate her voice is to pirate her identity'.[98] In other cases, the shift to

---

[93]   New York Civil Rights Act, s. 50 ('name, portrait or picture'); Florida Statute s. 540.08 ('name, portrait, photograph or other likeness').

[94]   (1960) 48 *Cal. l. r.*, 383, 403 explained that '[i]t is the plaintiff's name as a symbol of his identity that is involved here, and not his name as a mere name'. At 401, n. 155, Prosser also acknowledged that 'It is not impossible that there might be appropriation of the plaintiff's identity, as by impersonation, without the use of either his name or likeness, and that this would be an invasion of his right of privacy.' See also J. Thomas McCarthy, 'Public personas and private property: The commercialization of human identity' (1989) 79 *Trademark reporter*, 681, 687 (the privacy tort concerns 'damage to human dignity' while the unfair competition action concerns 'commercial damage to the business value of human identity.'); J. Kahn, D. J. Hetzel, Rosina Zapparoni, 'Propertising identity: understanding the United States Right of Publicity and its implications – some lessons for Australia', (2004) 28 *Melbourne University law review,* 690.

[95]   *Motschenbacher* v. *R. J. Reynolds Tobacco Co*, 498 F. 2d 821, 824 (9th Cir. 1974) (Judge Koelsch); *Carson* v. *Here's Johnny Portable Toilets, Inc.*, 698 F. 2d 831, 835 (6th Cir. 1983); *Onassis* v. *Christian Dior New York, Inc.*, 472 N.Y.S. 2d 254, 260 (S. Ct N.Y., 1984) (in a privacy case based on the New York statute which refers to 'name, portrait or picture', the New York Supreme Court explained that '[while the statute may not, by its terms, cover voice or movement, characteristics or style, it is intended to protect the essence of the person, his or her identity or persona'); *White* v. *Samsung Electronics America* 971 F. 2d 1395, 1398 (USCA, 9th Cir. 1992); *McFarland* v. *Miller* 14 F. 3d 912, 919 (USCA, 3rd Cir. 1994) (unauthorized use of an individual's name is nothing short of an 'appropriation of the attributes of one's identity'); *Abdul-Jabbar* v. *General Motors Corp* 85 F. 3d 407, 414 (USCA, 9th Cir. 1996).

[96]   *Carson* v. *Here's Johnny Portable Toilets, Inc.*, 698 F. 2d 831, 835 (6th Cir. 1983).

[97]   (1960) 48 *Cal. l. r.* 383, 403.

[98]   *Midler* v. *Ford Motor Co*, 849 F. 2d 460 (9th Cir. 1988). See also *Waits* v. *Frito-Lay, Inc.*, 978 F.2d 1093 (9th Cir. 1992) cert. denied 113 S. Ct 1047, 122 L. Ed. 2d 355 (1993), where Frito-Lay used an imitator of Tom Waits singing the song 'Step Right Up' to advertise its snackfood 'SalsaRio Doritos' on the radio. Waits had

'identity' has facilitated decisions protecting matter 'associated' with celebrities: an image of a distinctive racing car, normally driven by the claimant;[99] protection to Johnny Carson in relation to his catch-phrase 'Here's Johnny';[100] and, most remarkably of all, to the dress style of a game-show host. In *White* v. *Samsung*, the Court of Appeals for the Ninth Circuit allowed an appeal by Vanna White, hostess of TV game-show *Wheel of Fortune*, against a finding that an action by her against Samsung was bound to fail: Samsung had advertised its video cassette recorder with a depiction of a robot, dressed in a blond wig, long gown and wearing large jewellery designed to resemble White's, standing by a game board instantly recognizable as the *Wheel of Fortune* set and turning over letters. The caption read 'Longest-running game show, 2012 AD', and was designed to suggest that the VCR was so good it would still be in use long into the future. While the Appeals Court agreed that the robot was not a 'likeness' of White, it found that the common law right of publicity encompassed any indicator of 'identity' and that White had alleged facts such that, if proved, could justify a finding of appropriation of her identity.

The shift in language, from protection of 'name or likeness' to 'identity' has gone largely unremarked (though it appears to have been widely adopted).[101] As we have noted, it clearly broadens the potential scope of the action so as to encompass all manifestations of identity. David Westfall and David Landau have suggested that this has occurred because the courts see no principled basis for confining protection to only particular attributes such as 'name' and 'likeness'. Unfortunately, in so doing the

---

consistently refused to do commercials and had rejected numerous lucrative offers. He was awarded $375,000 in compensatory damages ($100,000 the value of his services; $200,000 for injury to peace, happiness and feelings; $75,000 injury to goodwill, professional standing and future publicity value) and $2 million in punitive damages ($1.5 million against Tracy-Locke, the advertising agency, $500,000 against Frito-Lay).

[99] *Motschenbacher* v. *R. J. Reynolds Tobacco*, 498 F. 2d 821 (9th Cir. 1974).

[100] *Carson* v. *Here's Johnny Portable Toilets, Inc.*, 698 F. 2d 831 (6th Cir. 1983).

[101] However, to the extent to which the rights are regarded as exclusively statutory, as in New York, the terms of the statute may be determinative: *Booth* v. *Colgate-Palmolive* 362 F. Supp 343 (SDNY, 1973); *Stephano* v. *News Group Publications, Inc.*, 64 N.Y. 2d 174, 485 N.Y.S. 2d, 474 N.E. 2d 580 (1984); *Tin Pan Apple, Inc. v. Miller Brewing Co.*, 737 F. Supp. 826 (SDNY 1990). See also *Matthews* v. *Wozencraft et al.* (1994) 15 F. 3d 432, 438 (USCA 5th Cir. 1994) (Texas misappropriation law does not give protection to 'general incidents from a person's life').

courts have shied away from providing a firm definition of identity.[102] When is something a manifestation of identity? Is a person's voice, make-up, wedding ring, tattoos, hairstyle, gloves, pet, car, bicycle, part of their identity? Must something be a permanent feature or can temporary attributes be manifestations of identity? Must the feature go to their very essence, or can trivial aspects of a person's appearance be protected? If the legal system is to create exclusive rights in relation to 'identity' it is clearly important that there be some common understanding of what identity is, and when particular manifestations of identity are exclusively owned. The legal system demands, then, a clear definition of subject matter that itself has relatively clear borders.

One way to define identity – previously used in English contract law – would be to distinguish identity (which concerns one's essence) from attributes. In a series of well-known cases, courts have been asked to decide whether misrepresentation by a purchaser as to his name, status, character or address rendered the contract of sale void or voidable.[103] Early case-law suggested that a mistake as to 'identity' means a contract is void, whereas a mistake over the 'attributes' of a person renders the contract voidable.[104] In *Lewis* v. *Averay*, for example, Lewis sold a car to a fraudster X, Lewis believing X to be Richard Greene, a minor television celebrity, and X sold the car on to A. The question arose whether Lewis could recover the car from A. If the contract with X was void, he could

[102] Dissenting in the *Carson* case, 698 F. 2d 831, 837 (6th Cir. 1983), Circuit Judge Cornelia Kennedy would have confined the common law right of publicity to 'an individual's name, likeness, achievements, identifying characteristics or actual performances' but said it could not encompass 'phrases or other things which are merely associated with the individual'.

[103] *J. Cundy* v. *Lindsay* (1878) L.R. 3 H,L, 459 (where L, based in Belfast, believed he was dealing with Blenkiron when he was in fact dealing with Blenkarn, the House held there was no contract for sale of handkerchiefs, the property in which remained with L); *Lake* v. *Simmons* [1927] A.C. 487 (no bailment where jeweller handed over jewels to customer, EE, who tricked him into believing she was Mrs V, and was taking them for inspection to Mr V.); *Ingram* v. *Little* [1960] 1 Q.B. 31 (sale by I of car to X, purporting to be H, void, so I recovered from L to whom X had transferred); *Shogun* v. *Hudson* [2004] 1 A.C. 919 (hire-purchase sale of car to X, believing him to be P, void because no contract existed.

[104] The classic contrast is between *J. Cundy* v. *Lindsay* (1878) L.R. 3 H.L. 459 (mistake as to identity) and *King's Norton Metal Co Ltd* v. *Edridge, Merrett & Co Ltd* (1897) 14 T.L.R. 98 (mistake as to size of defendant's business rendered contract voidable). See *Ingram* v. *Little* [1960] 1 Q.B. 31, 69; *Shogun Finance Ltd* v. *Hudson* [2004] 1 A.C. 919, 931 per Lord Nicholls of Birkenhead (paras 2–5).

do so; if it were only voidable, A would prevail. A argued that, as Lewis had merely been mistaken as to the attributes of X rather than his identity, the contract was not void but voidable, so L could not recover from A. Megaw L. J. agreed, describing L's mistake as being one regarding the credit-worthiness rather than the identity of X.[105] Nevertheless, the judiciary has seemed uncomfortable with drawing such a distinction, recognizing immediately the problem of differentiating between identity and attributes. In the same case, Lord Denning called the purported distinction between identity and attributes as 'a distinction without a difference'.[106] Lord Nicholls recently described the distinction as 'unconvincing', and 'a reproach to the law'.[107] Lord Millett referred to the 'equivocal nature of a person's "identity"', agreeing that 'it is often difficult to say whether [a mistake] should be classified as a mistake of identity or of attribute' and that the consequences of drawing such a distinction for third parties are 'indefensible'. The lesson from English contract law is that, whatever a philosopher might say, the courts are not comfortable drawing a distinction between 'attributes' and 'identity'.

An alternative strategy would be to look outside law, to the social sciences, to locate a definition of identity. The definition of identity employed in social psychology, one of the fields in which more general discourses of identity find their roots,[108] treats identity as equivalent to a person's perception of their own character over time. As Burke says, identity comprises the 'sets of meaning that people hold for themselves

---

[105] [1972] 1 Q.B. 198.

[106] Ibid. at 206. 'A man's very name is one of his attributes. It is also a key to his identity . . . These fine distinctions do no good to the law.' Most commentators have tended to agree: Glanville Williams, 'Mistake as to party in the Law of Contract' (1945) 23 *Can. b. r.*, 271 ('If every "thing", and therefore every person, can be reduced verbally to a bundle of attributes, it follows that "error of identity" (i.e. error of person) can be reduced verbally to error of attributes; also error of personal attribute can be reduced verbally to error of person.'); Treitel, G. H. *The Law of Contract*, 11th edn, (London: Sweet & Maxwell, 2003) (a person may be identified by any one of his attributes, if a mistake is made as to that attribute there can then be a mistake of identity); Karen Scott, 'Mistaken identity, contract formation and cutting the Gordian knot' (2003) *Lloyds maritime and commercial law quarterly* 292, 294 refers to the distinction between identity and attributes as 'illusory' and 'specious'.

[107] *Shogun Finance Ltd* v. *Hudson* [2004] 1 A.C. 919, 931 per Lord Nicholls of Birkenhead (paras 2–5). See also Lord Millett (para. 59).

[108] Stryker and Burke, 'The past, present and future of an identity theory' (2000) 63 (4) *Social Psychology Quarterly,* 284.

that define "what it means" to be who they are as persons, as role occupants and as group members'.[109] Such a definition of 'identity' seems to get to the very nub of what social psychologists are interested in: why do persons behave as they do? Why do they have the attitudes they do? How far are behaviours and attitudes related to concepts of the self? And, applying their insights, what possibilities are there to make them feel happier? Such matters might be relevant, too, to questions that call for decision in courts. A court might well take notice of the importance accorded by psychologists to a name as a key factor in identity-formation.[110] But it is quite a different thing to suggest that a person's beliefs about their own 'selves' can become property. The social psychologist's understanding of identity is too elusive, fluctuating and subjective to constitute the basis of a property right which third parties are expected to appreciate and respect.

2.2 The components of identity

Even if the legal concept of identity can be adequately defined, my second concern with its deployment as a legal category derives from the fact that different elements of 'identity' seem to have very different characteristics.

As regards protection for identity under the rubric of privacy, it is easy to see that uses of one's image or name can implicate one's autonomy or dignity (the protection of which constitute the main justifications for privacy laws). But it is not obvious that the use of one's name infringes one's privacy in the same circumstances as use of one's image. One of the chief characteristics of names, that is, that they are rarely unique, means that they rarely refer to a particular person.[111] In contrast, at least on some

---

[109] P. J. Burke, 'Identities and social structure' (2004) 67(1) *Social Psychology Quarterly*, 5.
[110] *In re L* [2007] 1 F.C.R. 804, para. 37 (considering an application to change a child's surname from that of its absent father to its grandparents, the Court of Appeal said it thought the 'identity' of the child would best be stabilized by 'keeping her circumstances as faithful to reality and the truth of her situation as possible.')
[111] As Lord Phillips explained in *Shogun* v. *Hudson* [2004] 1 A.C. 919, 963, '[w]henever a name is used, extrinsic evidence, or additional information, will be required in order to identify the specific individual that the user of the name intends to identify by the name'.

views, one's physical attributes are unique.[112] If a person claims that a photograph of them was featured in an advertisement or commercial publication, it should be possible to tell whether that was so.[113] As a result a law relating to privacy thus needs to establish different criteria concerning when use of a name invades privacy and when use of an image does so.[114] Moreover, while 'names' and 'images' may be uncontroversial subject matter for privacy laws, it is less obvious that look-alikes or sound-alikes,[115] let alone use of associated objects or catch-phrases, involve invasions of privacy or the underlying interests which privacy laws are seen as protecting.

The problem seems more complex still when we consider protection of 'identity' as property. Even the core examples of identity – names, images and voice – present a diversity of qualities that makes me sceptical

[112] In a case awarding Jackie Onassis injunctive relief against Dior with respect to an advert featuring a look-alike, Justice Greenfield observed that 'For some people, even without their American Express Cards, the face is total identification, more than a signature or coat of arms.' *Onassis* v. *Christian Dior New York, Inc,* 472 N.Y.S. 2d 254 (S. Ct N.Y., 1984). Note also Learned Hand J in *Yale Electrics Corp* v. *Robertson* 26 F 2d 972, 974 (2nd Cir. 1928) ('a reputation, like a face, is the symbol of its possessor and creator, and another can use it only as a mask'). Copyright discourse has often alluded to the fact that the expressive form of a literary work reflects the individuality of its author as much as his face: it is, 'as singular as his countenance'. See *Jefferys* v. *Boosey* (1854) 4 H.L.C. 814, 869; 10 E.R. 681, 703; Francis Hargrave, *Argument in defence of literary property* (London: Otridge, 1774) p. 7 (online at L. Bently and M. Kretschmer, *Primary sources on copyright from five jurisdictions,* www.copyrighthistory.org) ('a literary work *really* original, like the human face, will always have some singularities, some lines, some features, to characterize it, and to fix it and establish its identity').

[113] *Cohen* v. *Herbal Concepts, Inc.,* 63 N.Y. 2d 379, 384, 482 N.Y.S. 2d 457, 459; 472 N.E. 2d 307, 309 (C.A. of New York, 1984) (claim under section 51 New York Civil Rights Law objecting to use of photograph of non-celebrity plaintiff bathing nude in advertisement for product to help eliminate cellulite, the photograph having been taken without permission, but revealing only her back. The Court held that the plaintiff must be capable of identification from the objectionable material itself).

[114] *T. J. Hooker* v. *Columbia Picture Industries, Inc.,* 551 F. Supp. 1060 (N.D. Ill. 1982) (professional woodcarver of international renown, specializing in ducks, objected to broadcast of show about fictional policeman in California who was coincidentally named T. J. Hooker, under common law tort of appropriation of plaintiff's name. The claim was rejected because of lack of evidence that there was 'appropriation' or 'piracy of identity'. There was no reason to think that the TV character was the same person as the woodcarver.) See also *John Doe, a.k.a. Tony Twist* v. *TCI Cablevision,* 110 S.W. 3d 363 (Sup. Ct Miss., 2003).

[115] Although the sound-alike cases are based heavily on 'dignitarian' claims, for example, that the singers refused ever to allow their recorded sound to be used in advertisements, it is not obvious why one person's privacy should entitle them to prevent others exploiting what, evidently, are also *their own* attributes.

whether it makes sense to treat them as a single category. One common justification for private property concerns one's natural rights in the products of one's labour: where a person produces something through their own labour, there is a *prima facie* claim to property, as long as the recognition of such property does not diminish the capacity of others to create property through their labour.[116] It is possible that in some circumstances a case can be made out that one's physical appearance, one's image is 'created'. A natural rights argument might justify property in one's tattoos, make-up, hair style and, in extreme cases, other aspects of one's appearance. Given the possibility of voice training, a natural rights argument might justify protection of one's voice (as long as the boundaries of one's vocal property could be clearly defined). However, it is difficult to argue that one's name (as opposed to one's goodwill, or reputation – interest protected by the laws of passing-off and defamation) is a product of one's labour.

Moreover, in each case there are distinct questions outstanding as to whether such property leaves sufficient room for others to create and exploit their own attributes. As long as the attributes being claimed are 'unique', as judges have in some cases held appearance and voice to be,[117] there may be no objection to transforming them into properties. But, given the limited powers of human recognition, one cannot help wondering whether creating property rights in such matters would not, in practice, affect the freedoms of others to exploit their own attributes. As one early Massachusetts case said, when denying a claim to protection of voice, '[w]e might hesitate to say that an ordinary singer whose voice, deliberately or otherwise, sounded sufficiently like another to cause confusion was not free to do so'.[118] Moreover, we know that names are rarely unique: anything approaching a property right in a name needs to be very severely circumscribed to ensure that it does not inhibit the freedom of others to adopt the name, to use it in building their

[116] There is not space in what follows to discuss the application of other theories of property to the various attributes of identity.
[117] *Midler* v. *Ford Motor Co*, 849 F. 2d 460 (9th Cir. 1988) per Circuit Judge Noonan remarking that 'A voice is as distinctive and personal as a face . . . We are all aware that a friend is at once known by a few words on the phone . . . To impersonate her voice is to pirate her identity.'
[118] *Lahr* v. *Adell Chem. Co.*, 300 F. 2d 256 (1st Cir. 1962).

own reputation or practising their own trades. The law of passing-off developed a restricted system of protecting names from misuse in trade that, for more than 150 years has required that the person themselves be a trader, and that the allegedly infringing use of the name damage their trade reputation, particularly by diverting custom. No persuasive case has yet been made that such a restricted view is anything other than optimal.

3   Conclusion

Today, in the writings of legal scholars, the most common use of the term 'identity' is not to refer to potential proprietary interests discussed here, but rather as a rubric under which to describe the operation of various aspects of the law concerning discrimination. Contemporary commentators are concerned with how modern law operates (or fails) to redress centuries of discrimination against particular groups which focused on specific aspects of their identity: most obviously, race, gender, sexual orientation and disability. Some of these commentators are concerned with the way discrimination law itself constructs particular identities and marginalizes others. Drawing on this scholarship, legal anthropologist Rosemary Coombe has expressed real concern over the potential for private, exclusive properties in identity (of the sort discussed in this paper) to limit the ability of marginalized groups to develop and explore their own identities. For example, she observes that 'celebrity images provide the cultural resources which those in marginalized groups use to construct alternative gender identities'.[119] Echoing this, Michael Madow has observed that '[w]hen the law gives a celebrity a right of publicity, it does more than funnel additional income her way. It gives her ... power to deny to others the use of her persona in the construction and communication of alternative or oppositional identities or social relations.'[120]

The extent to which these criticisms are well made depends, of course, on the breadth of any proprietary rights in identity,[121] as well as the

[119] (1991) 69 *Texas l. r.*1853, 1877.   [120] (2004), *I. P. Q*, 145.
[121] It should be recalled that, at least in the United States, the right of privacy and publicity frequently give way to the right of free expression. For an argument that the claims of Coombe, Madow and 'other deconstructionists' neglect important interests in maintaining the stability of meaning of cultural artefacts, see Justin Hughes, 'Recoding, intellectual property and overlooked audience interests', (1999) 77 *Texas l. r.* 923.

manner in which they are policed and enforced. What is useful about these criticisms, however, is that they remind us that we should be careful before giving in to any instinct or intuition that our identities are 'our own' and thus should be regarded as properties. Such property rights may have unforeseen impacts well outside the 'easy' cases of use of name, likeness, voice and imagery in advertising.

Not long after the English courts declined to recognize a property right in a name, the case of *Belisle Du Boulay* v. *Jules Réné Herménégilde du Boulay* came before the Privy Council.[122] In this case, the claimant was a member of a family long resident in St Lucia which for many generations had been known by the name Du Boulay. The defendant was the son of a former slave named Rose, who, on being freed in 1831, adopted the name Du Boulay. The defendant, in turn, on attaining the age of sixteen, began using the same surname. The claimant called on the defendant to abandon the use of its surname. The claimant succeeded at first instance (in the Royal Court of St Lucia), the defendant successfully appealed (to the Court of Appeal for the Windward Islands), and the claimant finally sought vindication in the Privy Council. The Council, however, found that, though the law applicable to St Lucia included French law, various French laws concerning names had never been brought into force in the island. Moreover, Sir Robert Phillimore added that 'In this country we do not recognise the absolute right of a person to a particular name to the extent of entitling him to prevent the assumption of that name by a Stranger. The right to the exclusive use of a name in connection with a trade or business is familiar to our Law.'[123]

The case seems to me to furnish a salutary lesson. Property rights in 'identity', unless heavily circumscribed, have the potential to curtail the liberties of those who wish to build their own identities, in whatever way, and for whatever reason. The English legal system should think very carefully before recognizing a property in name, likeness or other aspects of identity.[124]

---

[122] (1869) L.R. 2 P.C. 430.   [123] Ibid.
[124] For helpful conversations, my thanks go to Robert Burrell, Bill Cornish, Jennifer Davis, Michael Einhorn, Justin Hughes, Joanna Kostylo, Kathy Liddell, Clair Milligan and Timo Ruikka; for research assistance to Doug MacMahon; and for funding that research assistance to the Herchel Smith fund, Emmanuel College, Cambridge.

3 Species-identity

PETER R. CRANE

May 23rd 2007 saw worldwide celebrations of the tercentenary of the birth of the Swedish physician and naturalist Carl Linnaeus. Born the son of a clergyman in relatively humble surroundings in Småland, southern Sweden, Linnaeus had a remarkable life that established him as one of the great intellectuals of the eighteenth century. He was ennobled as Carl von Linné in 1757. Today Linnaeus is almost an heroic figure, especially in Sweden, where his life and influence are celebrated, and where his face appears on the 100-Kronor banknote. His image has been captured by hundreds of paintings and statues around the world. He is widely recognized as one of the great figures in the history of science.

Linnaeus combined great industry with extraordinary talent. He was an accomplished writer and poet. He was an inspiring teacher. He made important contributions to medicine and he modified the temperature scale developed by Celsius into the one that we use today. Quite clearly, he was also an imposing presence: both at Uppsala University and elsewhere. He helped found The Royal Swedish Academy of Sciences in 1739 and served as its first President. But his real passion was the diversity of life, and he was the first to try to get to grips with it in a comprehensive and scientific way. Many others before him, building on the 'folk taxonomies' of Europe, had sought to name recognizable entities in the living world, but it was Linnaeus who established the essentials of the approach that we still use today, with the identity of species at its core.

Linnaeus succeeded in a remarkable way – at least if success is measured by the extent to which his approach has been widely adopted. Linnaeus'

Identity, edited by Giselle Walker and Elisabeth Leedham-Green. Published by Cambridge University Press. © Darwin College 2010.

work was taken up, not because of some dazzling new theoretical insight, but mainly because it was pragmatic, systematically applied, and in the context of its time it was close to comprehensive. As a result, it was exceedingly useful.

Today, despite many subsequent advances in the life sciences, species still remain the basic currency in our understanding of biological diversity, and the idea of species has become entwined in our lives, and also in our laws, in diverse and complicated ways. When Linnaeus gave specimens of common cultivated hemp the name *Cannabis sativa* he could scarcely have imagined that 200 years later there would be a lively debate in American courts over whether his name was sufficiently 'comprehensive to proscribe all kinds of marijuana'.[1]

The dispute over the plant that has been cultivated for millennia as a source of fibre and oil, as well as for production of hashish, brings into sharp focus some of the problems inherent in establishing species-identity. Is there just a single species of *Cannabis* or are there more? What about the plants named *Cannabis ruderalis* by Janisch and *Cannabis indica* by Lamarck? How do we decide? Only *Cannabis sativa* is mentioned in US legislation. Does this mean that the 'other species' are 'legal'? The fact that during the 1970s different botanical authorities lined up on both sides of the 'one species versus multiple species of *Cannabis*' question, and on occasion even managed to change sides,[2] suggests that there is scope for different interpretations of the same situation in nature. And if that is the case, what can we conclude about the reality of species: especially those that are much less well known?

In this paper I shall outline some of the complexity associated with current ideas of species-identity, focusing in particular on plants. Much has been written on the species concept in biology, especially from the standpoint of theory. It would be redundant here to attempt a detailed review. Instead I begin with Linnaeus and his approach to species. I then touch on both theoretical and practical issues, especially as they relate to species-identity and the use of species as the fundamental units in the scientific study of plant diversity.

[1] E. Small and A. Cronquist, 'A practical and natural taxonomy for *Cannabis*', *Taxon* 25 (1976), 405–35.
[2] Ibid.

Linnaeus' concept of species

Linnaeus is best known for developing a pragmatic approach to naming species using a Latin binomial that includes a generic name (e.g. *Cannabis*) combined with a specific epithet (e.g. *Cannabis sativa*) (Box 1). Latin binomials had been in use, for example by Caspar Bauhin,[3] well before Linnaeus. Bauhin and others had also organized biological diversity hierarchically, but it was Linnaeus who established this approach as standard through its relentless application across the whole of biology. Because the binomials proved more useful than the cumbersome polynomials or phrase names that Linnaeus also used, they were quickly taken up. Nevertheless, while part of Linnaeus' great contribution was popularizing an elegant way of labelling species, and often coming up with memorable names, his influence also had much to do with his energy, industry and scholarship in applying a consistent approach to a near-comprehensive systemization of biological diversity as it was known at the time.

Every species is placed in a genus. There may be one or more species in a genus, one or more genera per family, and so on up the hierarchy. The author who first named the species is indicated after the specific epithet in a standard abbreviated form (e.g., L. = Linnaeus). Each plant species name is linked to a specific specimen, the type specimen, from among the preserved plant material examined by the original author. See Figure 3.1 for the type specimen of *Cannabis sativa* L. In certain special cases an illustration may be accepted as the type if no specimen is available.

Box 1: Species in the hierarchy of plant classification

Kingdom – Chlorobiota (green plants)
Division – Tracheophyta (vascular plants)
Class – Magnoliopsida (angiosperms)
Order – Rosales
Family – Cannabaceae
Genus – *Cannabis* L.
Species – *Cannabis* sativa L.

---

[3] C. Bauhin, Πιναξ [Pinax] *theatri botanici* (Basel: sumptibus et typis Ludovici Regis, 1623).

FIGURE 3.1. The specimen of *Cannabis sativa* L. from the George Clifford Herbarium now preserved in the collections of the Department of Botany at the Natural History Museum, London. This specimen, which is presumed to have been seen by Linnaeus during his time in Holland, has been designated as the type specimen for the species by Stearn (1973). Reproduced with kind permission of the Natural History Museum, London.

Linnaeus was also acquisitive and a master synthesizer. He was interested in the work being done by others and incorporated plants and animals encountered by his contemporaries in his own treatments. Many of his names were also taken from the work of earlier authors. His concept of *Cannabis sativa*, for example, used as the genus name the word used much earlier by Bauhin, Dalechamp and others. And Linnaeus' concept of the plant was based, in large part, not only on specimens in his own collections but on material he saw in the private collections of the wealthy Anglo-Dutch merchant and financier George Clifford (1685–1760). Linnaeus described many new plant species from the living and dried specimens in Clifford's collections during his time in the Netherlands between 1735 and 1737. The specimens of *Cannabis* that Linnaeus very likely saw, and that served in part as the basis for his name, still exist among the specimens in the Clifford Herbarium, purchased subsequently by Sir Joseph Banks in 1791, that are now preserved in the Natural History Museum.

But Linnaeus was also cautious in his scholarship. In his *Systema Naturae* (1758) he included a Class 'Paradoxa', in which he placed many organisms about which he was uncertain. With the benefit of hindsight we now see that some of these, like the satyr, were clearly imaginary. Others were real, but Linnaeus had cause to be uncertain about them. For example, at first he placed the pelican (*Pelecanus onocrotalus* L.) in the Paradoxa because he considered it such an implausible animal. Only later did he feel comfortable including it as a bird.[4]

Linnaeus was also anxious to gather information on new material brought back by collectors from far-flung parts of the world. His widely travelled students, such as Pehr Kalm, Frederic Hasselquist, Daniel Solander and Carl Peter Thunberg were one important source of material, but he also expanded the scope of his knowledge and experience through his travels to Lapland and elsewhere in Scandanavia, exchange of specimens and extensive correspondence with a broad network of contacts.

Through a quirk of history, in part associated with a temporary decline in Linnaeus' reputation at home in the late eighteenth century, the bulk of Linnaeus' specimens, including 14,000 plants, as well as the associated

---

[4] S. Knapp, 'Fact and fantasy: The zoology created by our imagination is far outstripped by that of reality', *Nature* 415 (2002), 479.

animal specimens, library and correspondence, were purchased by James Edward Smith in 1783. They comprise the core of the collections of the Linnean Society of London, which was founded in 1788. Together with Linnaeus' publications, these collections provide the best indication of what Linnaeus actually meant by the names that he used.[5]

Linnaeus was also methodical and scholarly in his approach, which was fundamentally comparative and empirical. Whenever possible he based his ideas on data in the form of reference specimens, previous literature and illustrations, all of which he examined critically in reaching his conclusions. He also set out thirty-eight principles,[6] in effect a research method, outlining how work in natural history should be done. These principles include many practices that are now standard in the study of biological diversity, for example the importance of listing synonyms, providing information on habitats and giving precise locality details. But they also enumerate principles of value in science more generally, such as the importance of comparative methods and complete, careful descriptions. These principles also make it clear that Linnaeus was not just interested in describing and naming, he was also driven by the urge to systematize information. In his view, a proper account of a species should synthesize all that is known about it: from its form and structure to its ecology and use. In this way he established the now self-evident principle that the name of a species is not just a label, but the portal through which we gain access to all that we know about it – in effect its true identity.

Linnaeus' other key contribution was to bring order out of chaos in the naming of animals and plants. Through his energy and scholarship, as well as the global sweep of his work, he effectively drew a line under an important source of confusion created by his predecessors: the use of multiple names for the same species. Others had recognized the plant that Linnaeus called *Cannabis sativa* before he gave that name in 1753 (Figure 3.2). He himself had called it *Cannabis foliis digitatis* in *Hortus Cliffortianus*, while Dalechamp had used the names *Cannabis mas* and *Cannabis femina*. But in

---

[5] See for example C. Jarvis, *Order out of chaos* (London: The Linnean Society of London, 2007).

[6] F. A. Stafleu, *Linnaeus and the Linnaeans* (Utrecht; International Association for Plant Taxonomy, 1971); Uppsala Universitet, *Linnaeus' method*, 2006: www.linnaeus.uu.se/online/history/metod.html.

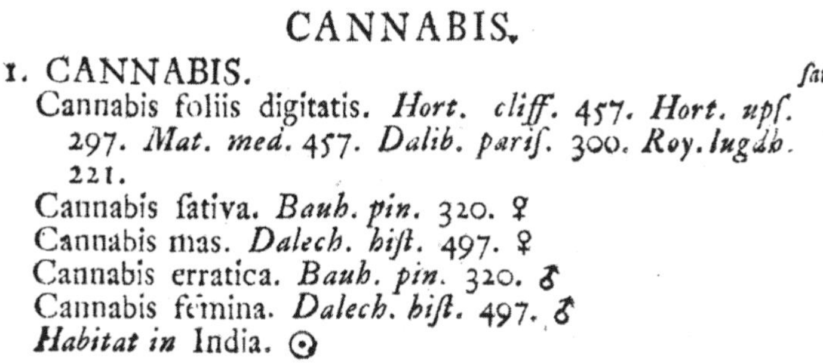

CANNABIS.

1. CANNABIS.   *sativa,*

Cannabis foliis digitatis. *Hort. cliff.* 457. *Hort. upf.*
297. *Mat. med.* 457. *Dalib. parif.* 300. *Roy. lugdb.*
221.
Cannabis fativa. *Bauh. pin.* 320. ♀
Cannabis mas. *Dalech. hift.* 497. ♀
Cannabis erratica. *Bauh. pin.* 320. ♂
Cannabis femina. *Dalech. hift.* 497. ♂
Habitat in India. ☉

FIGURE 3.2. The entry for *Cannabis* in *Species Plantarum* (Linnaeus 1753). Note the inclusion of the epithet *sativa* on the right margin, and the listing of synonyms and previous references to the species. Reproduced with kind permission of the Natural History Museum, London.

his time Linnaeus set a new baseline, and it is for this reason, as much as anything to do with the details of his approach, that *Species Plantarum*[7] is taken as the historical starting point for the scientific naming of plants under *The International Code of Botanical Nomenclature* (Box 2).

It is also clear that for Linnaeus the species had special meaning. At one level species were merely another category in the hierarchy of classes, orders and genera. But Linnaeus also viewed species as real units in Nature waiting to be discovered. For him species were fixed and unchanging. '*Species tot numeramus quot diversae formae in principio sunt creatae*'–'We count as many species as different forms were created in the beginning.'[8]

Changing concepts of species-identity

There are many who helped clear the way for Darwin and Wallace, and their ideas of natural selection and evolution, but among them Linnaeus was one of the more important. Through his work, and through its widespread adoption as a basis for organizing biological diversity, he formalized the idea of species as the basic unit in biology, and by placing species within a hierarchy he showed that there was also a higher

[7] C. Linnaeus, *Species plantarum exhibentes plantas rite cognitas, ad genera relatas, cum differentiis specificis, nominibus trivialibus, synonymis selectis, locis natalibus, secundum systema sexuale digestas* (Stockholm: impensis Laurentii Salvii, 1753).
[8] C. Linnaeus, *Fundamenta botanica* (Amsterdam, 1736); Stafleu, *Linnaeus and the Linnaeans*.

Box 2: The International Code of Botanical Nomenclature

The International Code of Botanical Nomenclature is the formalization of the system that includes Principles, Rules and Recommendations for the naming of plants. In practice, the Code is voluntary but it is enforced by convention in the community of scientists studying and communicating about the diversity of plant life. According to the Code, 'The purpose of giving a name to a taxonomic group is not to indicate its characters or history, but to supply a means of referring to it and to indicate its taxonomic rank.' The 'Code aims at the provision of a stable method of naming taxonomic groups, avoiding and rejecting the use of names that may cause error or ambiguity or throw science into confusion.' It also seeks to avoid the needless creation of new names. The Code is founded on six Principles through which it tries to achieve its objectives. The Principles are, in abbreviated form: 'I. Botanical nomenclature is independent of zoological nomenclature … ; II. The application of names of taxonomic groups is determined by means of nomenclatural types; III. The nomenclature of a taxonomic group is based on priority of publication; IV. Each taxonomic group with a particular circumscription, position and rank can bear only one correct name, the earliest that is in accordance with the Rules, except in specified cases; V. Scientific names of taxonomic groups are treated as Latin regardless of their derivation; VI. The Rules of nomenclature are retroactive unless expressly limited.' Also important is the concept of valid publication, through which names in effect 'qualify' for consideration under the Code.

---

structure in nature. In his *Philosophia Botanica* (1751) he wrote, 'The true beginning and end of botany is the natural system.' Both of these ideas were essential in the subsequent development of an evolutionary view of species. At the same time, Linnaeus' view of 'everyone's war against everyone' included in his *Politia Naturae*,[9] which Darwin read around the time he read Malthus, recalls Darwin's thoughts on the struggle for existence. Linnaeus' perspective on the 'economy of nature' was also important in the subsequent development of ecology.[10]

Darwin had a pragmatic view of species, but his work fundamentally changed the way in which species were viewed, most notably by altering the perception of them as fixed and unchanging entities. However,

[9] C. Linnaeus, *Dissertatio academica de politia naturae*, Dissertation Uppsala, 1760 (also in Linnaeus' *Ammoenitates academicae*, vol. VI (1763)).

[10] Uppsala Universitet, *Linnaeus' ecology and Darwin's evolution*, 2006: www.linnaeus. uu.se/online/eco/darwin.html.

Darwin offered no new practical methods by which species could be delimited. Indeed, he minimized the significance of species, seeing them as part of a continuum from orders, families and genera above the species level to subspecies and varieties below. And, as many have commented,[11] Darwin's impact on the practice of systematics – the science of systematizing biological diversity – as contrasted with the interpretation of its results, was minimal. Darwin was interested in how species came about, but he could not have set out his view of what they represented more clearly: 'I look at the term species, as one arbitrarily given for the sake of convenience to a set of individuals closely resembling each other'.[12]

It was only with the development of genetics fifty years later, followed by the development of the so-called *Modern Synthesis* between about 1920 and 1950,[13] that a new view of species began to emerge. The bringing together of systematics, genetics and palaeontology into a new holistic view of evolution cast species in a new light and brought into focus the two related issues of how species change and how they maintain their integrity. The result was the concept of biological species most frequently linked with the name of the ornithologist Ernst Mayr.

Mayr defined species as 'groups of actually or potentially interbreeding natural populations isolated from other such groups by reproductive barriers'.[14] This defined species by actual or potential internal continuity of gene flow, as well as by barriers to gene flow that exist with other species. It remains hugely influential, especially for concepts of species-identity among birds and other land vertebrates. It has also been applied to plants, and for some it has been considered the decisive criterion in species-recognition.

For example, in the *Cannabis* controversy,

> Aside from some experimentally produced polyploids, all *Cannabis* is diploid (n = 10), and there appear to be no barriers to successful hybridization within the genus. The present pattern of variation is due in large part to the influence of man. Two widespread classes of plant are

---

[11] See, for example, P. H. Davis and V. H. Heywood, *Principles of angiosperm taxonomy* (Edinburgh and London: Oliver and Boyd, 1963).
[12] C. Darwin, *On the origin of species by means of natural selection, or the preservation of favoured races in the struggle for life* (London: John Murray, 1859), 52.
[13] J. Huxley, *Evolution, the modern synthesis* (London: Allen and Unwin, 1942).
[14] E. Mayr, *Systematics and the origin of species* (New York: Columbia University Press, 1942).

discernible: a group of generally northern plants of relatively limited intoxicant potential, influenced particularly by selection for fiber and oil agronomic qualities, and a group of generally southern plants of considerable intoxicant potential, influenced particularly by selection for inebriant qualities. These two groups are treated respectively as subsp. *sativa* and *indica*, of *C. sativa*, the only species of the genus *Cannabis*.[15]

Nevertheless the biological species concept has had its critics. One problem has been a certain circularity in terms of cause and effect. Even in the absence of evidence, reproductive isolation has often been inferred to be the cause of morphological distinctiveness, while morphological distinctiveness has been seen as an effect of barriers to reproduction. There are many examples where it is now known that morphological similarity can be maintained even in the absence of ongoing interbreeding. There are also examples, when selection is especially ruthless, of distinctiveness being maintained despite ongoing interbreeding.[16]

Another problem has been confusion between the criteria used to recognize the species as a group, and the basis for assigning that group to a rank in the classificatory hierarchy. The biological species concept fails to distinguish between these two elements – in effect it does both at the same time. One group of modern critiques asserts that it is insufficiently concerned with the criteria for grouping, and that the question of ranking has meaning only in terms of genealogical relationship.[17]

The problems of grouping and ranking come to the fore in a more recent study of *Cannabis*. Investigation of allozyme variation at seventeen gene loci for 157 diverse *Cannabis* accessions gave two major groupings, with a thinner scatter of intermediate and outlying points. The author opted for a concept of *Cannabis* with three species: *Cannabis sativa*, *Cannabis indica* and *Cannabis ruderalis*.[18]

Over the last fifty years, given how much has been written on the strengths and limitations of the biological species concept, it is inevitable that many other kinds of species concepts have been developed. For

---

[15] Small and Cronquist, 'A practical and natural taxonomy for *Cannabis*', 405.
[16] M. J. Donoghue, 'A critique of the biological species concept and recommendations for a phylogenetic alternative', *The Bryologist* 88 (1985), 172–81.
[17] Ibid.
[18] K. Hillig, 'Genetic evidence for speciation in *Cannabis* (Cannabaceae)', *Genetic resources and crop evolution* 52 (2005), 161–80.

example, the cohesion species concept,[19] the ecological species concept,[20] the evolutionary species concept,[21] and two different formulations of the phylogenetic species concept.[22] In view of the central importance of species identity in biology and in society, such introspection and debate is to be expected. For the specialist, the complexity and contrasting bases of current concepts of species-identity represent a challenge, as well as fertile ground for developing deeper understanding. However, such considerations have had little practical impact on attempts to understand the bulk of plant diversity. This is largely a problem of scale and unevenness in knowledge about plant species.

In the tenth edition of *Systema Naturae* Linnaeus enumerated a little over 17,000 animal and plant species.[23] Modern estimates of the total number of living species of all kinds (eukaryotes excluding bacteria and their allies) place that number as somewhere between 5 and 10 million. Only about 1.5 million of these have been described so far.

In his lifetime Linnaeus recognized about 9,000 species of plants. He thought that the total number of plant species globally might be about twice that. We now know that the total number of described plant species is more likely to be in the range of 350,000 to 400,000 species. Given the daunting practicalities of applying more sophisticated techniques to such a vast number of species, most plant species are defined in much the same way now as they were by Linnaeus and other naturalists of the eighteenth and nineteenth centuries. Despite current knowledge of how species develop through the process of evolution, despite ever deeper insights gleaned from genetics, despite advances in the theory of systematics, and

[19] A. R. Templeton, 'Species and speciation: Geography, population structure, ecology, and gene trees', in *Endless forms: species and speciation* (New York: Oxford University Press, 1998), 32–43.

[20] L. van Valen, 'Ecological species, multispecies, and oaks', *Taxon* 25 (1976), 233–9.

[21] G. G. Simpson, 'The species concept', *Evolution* 5 (1951), 285–98; E. O. Wiley, *Phylogenetics* (New York; John Wiley and Sons, 1981).

[22] Compare D. E. Rosen, 'Fishes from the uplands and intermontane basins of Guatemala, revisionary studies, and comparative geography', *Bulletin of the American Museum of Natural History* 162 (1979), 267–376, and Donoghue, 'Critique of the biological species concept', with J. Cracraft, 'Species concepts and speciation analysis', *Current ornithology* 1 (1983), 159–87, and K. C. Nixon and Q. D. Wheeler, 'An amplification of the phylogenetic species concept', *Cladistics* 6 (1990), 211–23.

[23] C. Linnaeus, *Systema Naturae*, 10th edn (Stockholm: impensis Laurentii Salvii, 1758).

despite the increasingly sophisticated tools of molecular biology now available to us, so far it has not been practical to apply them to all of the vast, and poorly sampled, variety of plant life.

Uneven knowledge of plant species

Plants, like most other groups of non-microscopic organisms, show a characteristic relationship between the number of species and the extent of their distribution. There are relatively few widespread species. Most plant species are relatively restricted in their geographic distribution. It is also the case for plants, as for other major groups of organisms, that the greatest species diversity is concentrated in the tropics. As a result, most of these relatively restricted species are found in the tropics, and most are rather poorly known.

Comparison between the floras of the UK and Madagascar provides an instructive example (Table 3.1). In the UK the flora is relatively depauperate, and has been studied intensively. Many of the individual plant species have been the subject of detailed treatments in the 'Biological Flora' accounts of the British Ecological Society. Some have been investigated from the standpoint of gene flow and breeding systems at a level that provides a deeper understanding of the processes by which species integrity and species differences are maintained.

In contrast, the flora of Madagascar is much more diverse, contains a much higher proportion of endemic species and is very much more poorly understood. Very few plant species from Madagascar have been studied from the standpoint of their population genetics, and many plant species that are new to science continue to be discovered. For example, three recent treatments of important plant families on Madagascar, legumes, palms and orchids, resulted in the description of many new species (Table 3.2). Worldwide, approximately 2,000 plant species are described every year that are believed not to have been recognized previously. Both from Madagascar and elsewhere, most of the newly described species are relatively restricted in their distribution. Our currently relatively poor knowledge of plant species, especially in the tropics, is indicated both by the frequent discovery of new species and also by the relative paucity of information about them. A simple measure is provided by the number of herbarium specimens available for study.

Table 3.1 *Comparison between the floras of the UK and Madagascar*

Vascular Plants	UK	Madagascar
Total number of species	1,403 (+1,600 non-natives)	9,345–12,000
Endemic species	<4%	>80%
Species of conservation concern	Identified	Still to be identified
Population genetic data	Available for species of particular conservation concern	Little data available for any species
Ecology and physiology	Some species known in detail through *Biological Flora* accounts	Known for very few species
Species protected *ex situ* in seed banks	Almost all	<10%
Species inventory	Complete – new species added only rarely (generally aliens)	Incomplete – new species discovered frequently (generally natives)

Table 3.2 *Newly described species of plants from Madagascar for three diverse families of flowering plants based on the recent treatments of Du Puy et al.,* Orchids of Madagascar;[24] *Dransfield and Beentje,* Palms of Madagascar;[25] *and Du Puy et al.,* The Leguminosae of Madagascar.[26]

	No. of described species	No. of newly described species	% newly described species
Orchids	960	103	10.7
Palms	171	70	40.9
Legumes	667	129	19.3

[24] D. Du Puy *et al.*, *Orchids of Madagascar* (London, The Royal Botanic Gardens, Kew, 1999).
[25] J. Dransfield and H. Beentje, *Palms of Madagascar* (London, The Royal Botanic Gardens, Kew, 1995).
[26] D. Du Puy *et al.*, *The Leguminosae of Madagascar* (London, The Royal Botanic Gardens, Kew, 2002).

Most native British species have been collected extensively and are very well represented in many herbarium collections. For Madagascar the majority of specimens are held in herbaria in Antanarivo, the Missouri Botanical Garden, the Royal Botanic Gardens, Kew and Musée national d'histoire naturelle, Paris. Taking legumes as an example: about half of the 435 species recognized so far in Madagascar are represented in these combined collections by fewer than ten specimens each.

Under these circumstances, and especially because plant species diversity is broadly concentrated in those parts of the world where human and institutional capacity for studying biodiversity is not well developed, it is not surprising that most plant species are recognized using an approach that is fundamentally little different from that of Linnaeus. And what is true for plants is true for those other groups of organisms that make up the bulk of global biodiversity. Outside the most conspicuous groups of animals and their most common representatives, the variety of life is vast, poorly sampled and very imperfectly understood.

Are plant species arbitrary?

So does this mean that most plant species are merely arbitrary constructs of the human mind, or do they approximate to fundamental units in nature that have some meaningful evolutionary reality? It is a difficult question to answer, but different approaches suggest that most of the plant species that we recognize by traditional methods do indeed exist independently of our ability to recognize them. A crude indication is provided by considering the fate at the hands of subsequent systematists of the 9,000 or so plant species recognized by Linnaeus. This sample of plant diversity includes the most common plants of Europe, as well as widespread plants from other parts of the world, many of which have since been studied in much more detail. While many species have been reassigned to different genera as ideas about their relationships have changed, and some have been subdivided more finely, relatively few have been synonymized (combined into a single species). The implication is that at least in terms of recognizing the units of plant diversity Linnaeus basically got it right. His species concepts have stood the test of time.

The same picture emerges if one compares floristic treatments of plants from the same area undertaken by different authors, from different research groups, with different backgrounds. Eight or nine times out of ten they come up with the same species.[27] Ernst Mayr, in one of his very few botanical papers, analysed the species of vascular plants of Concord Township in eastern Massachusetts, which was so much admired by Henry Thoreau.[28] He concluded: 'The vast majority, to be exact 616, of the 838 named species of Concord Township, are so well defined that they raise no problems of species identity.' Similarly, in a study of 104 monographs that treated 1,790 plant species, about 80 per cent were described without any indication that they posed a particular problem.[29]

The overwhelming picture that emerges is that most plant species seem to have an identity that can be recognized in a repeatable way. The well-known 'difficult groups' of plants, which result from unusual reproductive situations, such as apomixis (reproduction without fertilization) or hybridization, are in the minority.

A more detailed study of the nature of plant species, albeit based on a very restricted sample, was undertaken by Reiseberg, Wood and Baack, who compared the correspondence between species delimited by traditional means and infrageneric morphological clusters recognized by quantitative methods.[30] They found in the case of both plants and animals that only about half of the clusters corresponded to traditionally recognized plant species. Most of the difference was accounted for by over-differentiation (recognition of more than one species per cluster) by traditional methods. A further analysis, based on a review of crossing analysis data (as a test of post-mating isolation) for species within 114 plant genera representing 1,231 inter-specific cross combinations, indicated that about 70 per cent of these traditionally recognized plant species were likely to reflect reproductively independent lineages. While these results are comparatively crude, for example, in considering only

27 E. Anderson, 'An experimental investigation of judgments concerning genera and species', *Evolution* 11 (1957), 260–3.
28 E. Mayr, 'A local flora and the biological species concept', *American journal of botany* 79 (1992), 222–38.
29 L. A. McDade, 'Species concepts and problems in practice: Insight from botanical monographs', *Systematic botany* 20 (1995), 606–22.
30 L. H. Reiseberg, T. E. Wood and E. J. Baack, 'The nature of plant species', *Nature* 440 (23 March 2006), 524–7.

post-mating rather than pre-mating isolation, they also suggest that traditionally recognized plant species are not entirely arbitrary.

However, while species boundaries may mirror reproductive boundaries the other side of the coin also needs to be addressed: is there sufficient gene flow among conspecific plant populations to unite them as a single evolutionary unit? In many cases the answer is clearly no, and this highlights a further fundamental problem with the biological species concept. It is a description of an idealized situation in the here and now, that takes no account of history. The individual populations may have been united by gene flow in the past, especially perhaps during the crucial phase of their morphological differentiation, but this may no longer be the case. In the same way, the capacity to interbreed may provide a poor indication of genealogical relatedness. If some subgroup of an evolutionary lineage becomes reproductively isolated, it would be quite possible to have some members of the group that has reproductive continuity actually be more closely related to members of the subgroup with which they cannot breed.[31] These are the kinds of arguments that have led some to propose an evolutionary or phylogenetic species concept that takes more account of history and common ancestry.

Are plant species equivalent?

While knowledge of individual plant species is extremely uneven, and while the different situations that they represent in terms of genetic and population-level processes are uncertain, they are still treated operationally as fundamental units of plant diversity that have some basic equivalence. For example, they are routinely counted and used as an overall index of biological diversity in time or in space.

Perhaps the most straightforward application of this approach has been the use of counts of species and counts of endemic species to define biodiversity hotspots, which have then been used as a basis for discussing priorities in conservation. However, it is interesting that conservation biologists have also quickly come to the conclusion that not all species are identical in terms of their significance for conservation. At its

[31] Donoghue, 'Critique of the biological species concept'.

simplest, this idea emphasizes, for example, that in terms of conservation, *Ginkgo biloba*, as the sole living representative of an ancient and once more diverse group of plants and one of only five major groups of living seed plants, is relatively more important, than one of the 300 very closely related species of the neotropical legume tree genus *Inga*.

This idea has been formalized and quantified in a series of papers in which the phylogenetic distinctiveness of species is factored into the development of conservation priorities.[32] And it is interesting that priorities based on pure species richness are not always the same as priorities based on phylogenetic distinctiveness. For example in the Cape region of Southern Africa simple diversity measures based on plants emphasize the conservation significance of the Western Cape, while measures that also factor in the phylogenetic distinctions of species give stronger emphasis to the Eastern Cape.[33] Clearly, individual species do not have equivalence. They vary enormously in the different kinds of evolutionary situations that they represent.

Naming species and stability

A central problem at the core of biodiversity science, which is reflected in different concepts of species identity, is the inherent conflict between its scientific objectives (discovering the fundamental units of biological diversity, understanding the processes that gave rise to them, resolving phylogenetic relationships) and the service function it provides to the rest of science and society. A significant part of its job is to provide a stable and reliable system of names for purposes of unambiguous communication. In an ideal world we would discover the basic units of biological diversity and give them names. But unfortunately studies of biological diversity are rarely so clear cut. What we have instead, as in other areas of science, are successive approximations to the truth. It is in the nature of the way that science works, but it is nevertheless a reality that does not engender stability.

There are two main problems with regard to nomenclatural stability: the curse of synonymy and the inconsistent use of names. With regard to

[32] D. P. Faith, *Conservation evaluation and phylogenetic diversity* (Oxford: Clarendon Press, 1994).

[33] F. Forest *et al.*, 'Preserving the evolutionary potential of floras in biodiversity hotspots', *Nature* 445 (2007), 757–60.

synonymy (the judgement that two different names actually refer to the same biological entity), Linnaeus' work was a breakthrough in terms of tidying up what had come before, but since then systematists have struggled to preserve the order that he was able to create. Given the much larger number of species that we now know to exist, and given the distributed and fundamentally entrepreneurial enterprise of science, it is inevitable that different scientists come to give the same biological entity different names. And while the principle of priority (Box 2) establishes which of these names should be used (given certain rules concerning valid publication) it still has to be applied, and without some form of central register the correct name for a particular species can sometimes be difficult to find. For plants the scale of the problem is considerable. The *International Plant Name Index* maintained by Kew, the Harvard University Herbaria and Australian National Herbarium contains almost a million names. Differences in estimates of the total number of angiosperm species are a result of basically different estimates of levels of synonymy among this single set of names.

It is also unfortunate that questions of synonymy cannot be solved simply by the application of nomenclatural rules. They are also a matter of scientific judgement because of an unfortunate weakness inherent in Linnaeus' binomial system. Uniform application of the binomial approach requires uniform concepts of both genus and species identity. The binomial system, rather unfortunately, intertwines the delivery of straightforward species labels, with the very much more complicated issue of how similarities and differences translate into hypotheses of evolutionary relatedness at the generic level. When generic concepts change, so too can the Latin binomials. For example, the recent discovery of a new kind of conifer in Vietnam led to its description as *Xanthocyparis vietnamensis*. This in turn led to reassignment of the Nootka Cypress, *Chamaecyparis nootkatensis*, to the new genus as *Xanthocyparis nootkatensis*. To a Canadian forester this would be bad enough, but the knock-on effects go further. Because *Xanthocyparis nootkatensis* is one of the parents of the commonly grown hybrid Leyland Cypress its name too has to change: from x *Cupressocyparis leylandii* to x *Cuprocyparis leylandii*. Now it is the gardener, and those who seek to control the planting of this outsized conifer in suburbia, who are upset. The situation will get still worse if *Chamaecyparis nootkatensis* is reassigned to *Callitropsis* as is suggested by a recent study using DNA-based estimates of its phylogenetic position.[34]

Beyond synonymy a further problem has been the inconsistent use of the same name for different biological entities. This issue has been solved by the designation of type specimens: specimens to which a particular name is forever attached, within the framework of rules developed by the *International Code of Botanical Nomenclature* (Box 2). The use of 'types' was introduced in the early twentieth century but like the principle of priority its rigorous application can be time-consuming. To give just one example: Linnaeus did not designate type specimens for the species that he recognized. The type of *Cannabis sativa* was designated much later by Stearn.[35] It has taken a considerable effort, through a long-term joint project undertaken by the Natural History Museum and supported by the Linnean Society, to sift the evidence that Linnaeus considered for all the plant species that he described and therefore (in most cases) to be able to designate type specimens for the names that he used.[36]

So while the systems and processes developed in the *International Code of Botanical Nomenclature* can help systematics toward its goal of stable and useful names, it does not trump systematic judgement and its rules can be laborious to apply. Its rules are also only open to change every six years by vote at a general session of the International Association for Plant Taxonomy. Change, to keep pace with other rapid change in the world, is not easy for such a body to embrace. Radical change is anathema. The result is frustration, so much so that some consider the rules to be as much part of the problem as part of the solution, in urgent attempts to increase the speed and utility of the systems we use to cope with the vast diversity in many groups of organisms.[37]

[34] A. Little, E. Schwarzbach, R. P. Adams and C. Hsieh, 'The circumscription and phylogenetic relationships of *Callitropsis* and the newly described genus *Xanthocyparis* (Cupressaceae)', *American journal of botany* 91 (2004), 1872–81.
[35] W. T. Stearn, 'The typification of *Cannabis sativa* L.', *Botanical Museum leaflets, Harvard University*, 23 (1974), 325–36.
[36] Jarvis, *Order out of chaos*.
[37] H. C. J. Godfray, 'Challenges of taxonomy', *Nature* 417 (2002), 17–19.

Species identification

In addition to a stable and useful system of names, another important function provided by systematics to the broader biological community, and to a wide range of other users in society, is the development of aids to the identification of species. Linnaeus himself was a pragmatist who understood the importance of straightforward species identification. Most obviously, his overtly artificial 'Sexual System' by which he organized his classes, and then within them the finer hierarchical levels of his classification, provided both a useful means of organizing information, and also a means of aiding identification. Linnaeus also used a kind of early dichotomous key, and even up to the present this has been the identification tool of choice among the outputs of traditional systematists.

Dichotomous keys, where one follows a path through a specified series of (usually) bifurcating questions to arrive eventually at an identification, can be organized in various ways, and the writing of a 'good' key has been one of the tests of competence for traditional plant taxonomists. Often, however, their telegraphic brevity, as well as their reliance on technical terminology, makes them difficult for the non-specialist to master and tedious to use. As a result, over the last few decades, there has been considerable interest in more flexible aids to identification, catalysed by advances in information technology. Multi-access electronic keys, supplemented by illustrations and images of specimens, are becoming ever more widespread, and are often available freely over the web. In some groups, but not yet in plants as far as I am aware, there has also been progress with identification based on differences in form that can be quantified and automated.

At different levels, and in many different circumstances, the repeatable identification of plant species is crucial to environmental management. The recent attempt to identify a hundred ecological questions of high policy relevance in the UK emphasizes the broad importance of species as a way to understand and monitor biodiversity.[38] Biodiversity entered into all fourteen key areas identified (Ecosystem Services, Farming, Forestry, Fisheries, Recreation, Urban Development, Aliens

[38] W. J. Sutherland *et al.*, 'The identification of 100 ecological questions of high policy relevance in the UK', *Journal of applied ecology* 43 (2006), 617–27.

and Invasive Species, Pollution, Climate Changes, Energy Generation and Carbon Management, Conservation Strategies, Habitat Management and Restoration, Connectivity and Landscape Structure, Making Space for Water).

At a more detailed level particular species frequently enter into environmental legislation at all levels of Government. At the one end of the spectrum particular species feature in international law, for example the International Treaty on Plant Genetic Resources in Food and Agriculture (ITPGRFA) or the Convention on International Trade in Endangered Species (CITES). More than 25,000 plant species are controlled under CITES. As the UK scientific authority for plants, each year Kew processes more than 5,000 applications under CITES. At the national level individual species may be protected under national or federal legislation such as the Endangered Species Act in the USA. In federal systems individual species may also be protected to differing extents by environmental legislation that differs from state to state.

Similarly, the accurate identification of plants for medicinal purposes was a primary stimulus of early scientific interest in plants. Much of the effort that went into the descriptions and illustrations of the early herbalists was directed toward plant identification. Still today more than 80 per cent of the global population, mainly in the developing world, turns to plants as their primary source of medicines, and in these circumstances correct plant identification is obviously a priority.

Accurate identification is also very much an issue in drug safety in the developed world as attempts continue to properly integrate scientific Latin binomials with widely used pharmaceutical names.[39] This is especially important in Traditional Chinese Medicine (TCM), which is increasingly popular in the UK. TCM uses many tens of plant species, often in different combinations, to treat a variety of ailments. In one case, the use of parts of the rhizome of *Aristolochia manshuriensis* in a medicinal preparation resulted in severe negative effects, including liver failure, for the unfortunate patient. The then Medical Control Agency of the UK Department of Health passed legislation banning the manufacture,

[39] M. H. Farah *et al.*, 'Botanical nomenclature in pharmacovigilance and a recommendation for standardisation', *Drug safety* 29 (2006), 1023–9.

import, sale or supply of any unlicensed medicine in the UK which contained *Aristolochia* or other herbs in the TCM *Mu Tong* group, which includes eight species from four different genera.[40] Increasing effort is being expended, both in the UK and in China, on appropriate standards of plant identification.

Similar kinds of issues frequently arise around the identification of poisonous plant and fungal species that are accidentally or deliberately ingested. At Kew, and at other institutions with professional mycologists on the staff, there is a regular need for fungal identification in cases of accidental poisoning. More than 1,500 calls are made each year to the National Poisons Information Service in London about cases that involve poisoning with plants or fungi. The Nightshade® collaboration is a joint activity between the Medical Toxicology Unit of Guy's and St Thomas' Hospital Trust and the Royal Botanic Gardens, Kew, that brings together botanists, mycologists and toxicologists to work on these kinds of cases. One output of this work has been a simple interactive electronic key for the identification of 229 species of plants and 120 groups of fungi that are either poisonous, or that could easily be confused with poisonous species. These are now found in the Accident and Emergency departments of hospitals throughout the UK and Germany.

The need for improved identification is clear. In a recent survey of suspected plant poisoning cases, of ten cases attributed to 'deadly nightshade' (*Atropa belladonna*) five actually involved *Solanum nigrum* (black nightshade) and two involved *Solanum dulcamara* (woody nightshade): a different genus in the same plant family. The toxins in these species of *Solanum* are glycoalkaloids such as solanine, which have a different toxic action to the tropane alkaloids of *Atropa belladonna*. The other cases involved plants that were still more distantly related to *Atropa*.[41] Species identification based on plant fragments is also of practical importance. For example, tree roots need to be identified to determine the outcome of insurance claims based on subsidence. At Kew, the Anatomy Section routinely identifies plant fragments for a great range of users from antique dealers and furniture restorers, to HM Revenue and Customs.

[40] Leon, personal communication.
[41] Simmonds, personal communication.

There is also a certain amount of forensic work. In the 'torso in Thames' case, one of the very few pieces of evidence as to the background of the victim came from the identification of a fragment of the highly poisonous calabar bean (*Physostigma venenosum*) in the stomach contents by one of Kew's experienced plant anatomists.

Species identity back in time

Another area where the identification of fragmentary plant material is important is in archaeological or palaeontological contexts. One of the great strengths of the Cambridge Botany Department in the 1950s and 1960s was the analysis of the vegetational history of the UK under the leadership of Harry Godwin and others. This led to a greatly improved understanding of the climatic and vegetational history of the UK over the last million years. Such work depends on the correct identification of fragmentary plant fossils with living plant species, and from this, reliable extrapolation to specific climatic and other environmental tolerances. The method is robust and has delivered important new insights, but there is nevertheless a legitimate scientific question as to the limits of this kind of uniformitarianism, especially in 'deeper' time. For example, it is sometimes difficult to get to the correct species identity from plant fossil fragments when evolution and extinction create confusion. For example, in the southern United States, Jackson and Weng showed that a species of spruce, originally identified as the extant species *Picea glauca* (from its dispersed seed cones), was actually an extinct species (which they named *Picea critchfieldii*).[42] It had a combination of morphological features unlike that of any living spruce.

Further back in time these kinds of problems become more severe, causing some to question whether even the most complete fossil evidence provides sufficient basis for the accurate recognition of long-term stasis in form and biology in classic 'living fossils'.[43] Nevertheless, in many cases, the evidence that is available (e.g. for fossil *Ginkgo*) does indeed suggest that some species have remained virtually unchanged over very long periods (tens of million years). Such examples emphasize the reality

[42] S. T. Jackson and C. Weng, 'Late Quaternary extinction of a tree species in eastern North America'. *Proceedings of the National Academy of Sciences* 96 (1999), 13847–52.
[43] N. Eldredge and S. M. Stanley, *Living fossils* (New York, Springer Verlag, 1984).

DNA barcodes: a short cut to species identity?

A recent development with potentially important implications for species-identity has been the possibility of merging improved information technology with molecular biology to revolutionize species identification: a possibility that recalls the hand-held 'tricorder' of *Star Trek* that was used to scan and identify alien life forms.[44] This would be an automated device that could extract DNA from an unknown organism, identify a particular sequence of bases making up part of a particular gene, and then match that sequence to a database of similar sequences to identify or suggest close relatives for the unknown organism.

The great attraction in creating a so-called DNA barcode system for species identification is that it could be automated, and applied to any life-history stage or fragment of an organism. It could overcome, for example, the practical difficulties of identifying tree seedlings in forest plots in the tropics. At the moment this is done based solely on phenotypic characteristics. At the same time it could assist customs officers charged with controlling the flow of plants and plant products across national borders. Such an approach would also find wide application in forensic science.

The barcoding approach has been developed over the past five years and has been applied most enthusiastically to animals. For most animals there appears to be sufficient variation in the mitochondrial gene *cox-1*, which codes for subunit-1 of cytochrome oxidase, a ubiquitous respiratory enzyme in most organisms, to facilitate routine species identification on the discrimination of species or other units of diversity.[45] However, for plants it seems that no single gene is likely to be quite so useful.[46]

[44] V. Savolainen, R. S. Cowan, A. P. Vogler, G. K. Roderick and R. Lane, 'Towards writing the encyclopædia of life: An introduction to DNA barcoding', *Philosophical transactions of the Royal Society B* 360 (2005), 1805–11.

[45] M. Blaxter, J. Mann, T. Chapman, F. Thomas, C. Whitton, R. Floyd, and E. Abebe, 'Defining operational taxonomic units using DNA barcode data', *Philosophical transactions of the Royal Society B* 360 (2005), 1935–43.

[46] M. W. Chase, N. Salamin, M. Wilkinson, J. M. Dunwell, R. P. Kesanakurthi, N. Haidar, and V. Savolainen, 'Land plants and DNA barcodes: Short-term and long-term goals', *Philosophical transactions of the Royal Society B* 360 (2005), 1889–95.

The equivalent botanical barcoding approach currently in development will require the sequencing of several different genes to provide discrimination at different taxonomic levels. Nevertheless, with rapid improvements and increasing sophistication in both molecular techniques and information infrastructure, it is possible that there may be hand-held barcode tools for the DNA-based identification of certain kinds of animals and plants within the next decade.

However, barcoding cannot sidestep various complications and problems that will need to be overcome. A key theoretical decision concerns the kinds of algorithms to be used for 'matching' the sequences of unknowns to the reference database.[47] Especially important will be the development of the reference database itself. One problem in constructing such a database will be whether, even in animals, the single gene *cox-1* will prove to be enough, and also how many individuals of a given species will need to be included. One, or only a few, individuals may not be sufficiently representative for reliable species determination. It seems inevitable that the design of any informed sampling strategy to address such issues will have to draw on existing 'traditional' information about the biology, ecology and distribution of each species.

The kinds of sequences generated using barcoding approaches may also prove valuable as primary information for establishing group membership and defining species boundaries. Combined with high-throughput sequencing, and automated quantitative analyses for determining group membership, such methods perhaps offer the best hope for the rapid construction of a taxonomic framework in poorly understood and hyperdiverse groups, such as certain groups of insects.[48]

Where next with plant species-identity?

During 2007 Linnaeus, and the central importance of his contribution to biology that came from systematizing knowledge of the variety of life,

[47] R. DeSalle, M. G. Egan and M. Siddall, 'The unholy trinity: Taxonomy, species delimitation and DNA barcoding', *Philosophical transactions of the Royal Society B* 360 (2005), 1905–16.

[48] J. Pons *et al.*, 'Sequence-based species delimitation for the DNA taxonomy of undescribed insects', *Systematic biology* 55 (2006), 595–609.

received considerable attention. Much less prominent were the celebrations around another notable tercentenary: the birth of the French cosmologist, mathematician and naturalist George-Louis Leclerc Compte de Buffon (1707–88). Buffon and Linnaeus famously disagreed on many things, not least the basis for discovering the true 'order of nature'.[49] But in many other respects their world-view was remarkably similar. For example, it was Buffon who was perhaps the first to suggest explicitly that the capacity to interbreed should be used as a criterion in species-identity,[50] but Linnaeus also used the same criterion in practice in his treatment of birds.[51] Both also attempted the comprehensive systemization of all life as it was then known. Linnaeus' efforts are contained in *Systema Naturae* and *Species Plantarum*. Buffon's attempt was published in his massive synthesis *Histoire naturelle, générale et particulière*, which ran to forty-four volumes.

Since Linnaeus and Buffon the scale of the task that they set themselves has increased, but nevertheless, in recent years their vision has re-emerged with various calls to complete what they were among the first to attempt: a complete catalogue of life's diversity at the species level. For the most diverse groups of organisms, for example all the major groups of insects, such an effort may still be a bridge too far. It is self-evident that fieldwork, and the associated processing of the material gathered, will be the rate-limiting step in any such undertaking.[52] However, these kinds of calls to action frequently gloss over an important point. There is a big difference between cataloguing all the world's species and systematizing knowledge of all the world's *known* species. The former is open-ended, and is predicated on an enormous effort to explore and sample the natural world. The latter, while daunting, is nevertheless more or less finite. It is a task that mainly involves bringing together and organizing information that, while very scattered, nevertheless already exists.

[49] P. R. Sloan, 'The Buffon–Linnaeus controversy', *Isis* 67 (1976), 356–75.
[50] E. Mayr, *The growth of biological thought: Diversity, evolution, and inheritance* (Cambridge, MA: Belknap Press of Harvard University Press, 1982).
[51] J. M. Diamond, 'Horrible plant species', *Nature* 360 (1992), 627–8.
[52] R. M. May, 'Tomorrow's taxonomy: Collecting new species in the field will remain the rate-limiting step', *Philosophical transactions of the Royal Society B* 359 (2004), 733–4.

Plants present an interesting challenge. On the one hand they are a group of high diversity, at least compared to vertebrates. On the other hand the number of plant systematists compared to the likely number of known plant species is relatively large, the absolute number of species is considerably less daunting than many groups of insects, and a great deal is known about plant diversity already. In these circumstances where does the right balance lie between gathering new information and describing new species, as against bringing together what is already known?

Given the rapid pace of environmental degradation in many of the most biologically species-rich parts of the world, now is not the time to stop collecting. There are many new species of plants still to be described. Most of them will be rare, of very restricted distribution, and of concern in terms of conservation; many of them should also be expected to have valuable properties or to be of great scientific importance. Nevertheless, there is a strong case for balancing targeted fieldwork with a much more concerted effort to bring together, in the same way that Linnaeus and Buffon attempted, all the existing information about all of the world's plant species and thus to establish their identity more clearly. With the informatics tools now available, there is no excuse for perpetuating an unsystematic approach to systematics. Both for users of information on plant species, and for those interested in developing a better scientific understanding of plant diversity, new efforts of synthesis are sorely needed.

There are encouraging indications that this challenge is being taken up. Many individuals and organizations are making good progress in getting the key information about plant species into electronic form and there are some impressive large-scale efforts that have made significant headway towards the development of a central clearing-house for information of all kinds about the variety of plant life. For example, the International Plant Names Index (IPNI, www.ipni.org/index.html), a collaborative project of the Royal Botanic Gardens, Kew, the Harvard University Herbaria and the Australian National Herbarium, contains a list of the nearly one million names of individual plants, while the Global Checklist programme underway at Kew and elsewhere has made excellent progress with the problem of synonymy to reduce this list to a list of plant species. Similarly, the TROPICOS system of the Missouri Botanical Garden (mobot.mobot.org/W3T/Search/vast.html) now holds information associated with more than a million plant species names, including images, and very nearly half a million pages of the original pertinent literature.

Most recently, there has been the launch of the *Encyclopedia of Life* project with substantial support from US Foundations to follow the vision of E. O. Wilson and develop a webpage for every species. There is much for this effort to draw upon. For example, a massive collaborative initiative (African Plants Initiative of ALUKA, www.aluka. org) involving more than fifty institutions in Africa, Europe and the United States has made available over the web images of approximately 230,000 specimens, including the type specimens that form the basis for the names of almost all the approximately 60,000 plant species of Africa. This initiative, funded by the Andrew W. Mellon Foundation, went from inception to completion in a mere five years. It was launched in late February 2007 at a meeting in Yaounde, Cameroon. It shows what can be accomplished by focused effort driven by adequate funding. And speed is important, because this effort will feed back into the more efficient discovery, description, conservation and use of the plant diversity of Africa.

Darwin's view of species[53] is perhaps even more applicable today than when he wrote it: 'No one definition [of species] has yet satisfied all naturalists; yet every naturalist knows vaguely what he means when he speaks of species'. But Darwin also understood the practical importance of this widely used, but sometimes elusive, unit of biological diversity. In 1881, in a letter to the executors of his will, Charles Darwin wrote of his wish to provide funds to Joseph Dalton Hooker, one of my predecessors as Director of Kew, 'for the formation of a perfect M.S. catalogue of all known plants'.[54] Through the *Global Strategy for Plant Conservation* the world governments have asked for the same thing. It is important to deliver that and more. The diverse efforts now underway

[53] Darwin, *Origin of species.*
[54] Cambridge University Library MS DAR 161:80. See www.lib.cam.ac.uk/ Departments/Darwin/.

in many different places are encouraging first steps to provide not just a list, but a twenty-first century manifestation of what Linnaeus and Buffon had in mind 250 years ago: a meaningful summary of the identity of all the world's plant species so far discovered, through a near complete, widely accessible, enumeration that also includes all that we know about them.

4 Mathematical identity

MARCUS DU SAUTOY

Throughout history, mathematics has been producing language to be able to articulate the fact that objects have identical structures. From the simple act of counting to the sophisticated techniques of topology, mathematicians have been developing ever more interesting ways to perceive the world around us and understand when two very different structures are expressions of the same mathematical identity.

Numerical identity

The very concept of number illustrates the power of the human mind to abstract mathematical identity from physically very different settings. In fact we seem genetically programmed to be able to detect when things are numerically identical or not. The decision to fight or fly in the face of the enemy depends on an assessment of whether the number in your pack is bigger or smaller than the number in the opposition. Those that can count, survive.

This ability of animals to detect numerical identity has been identified in many species. Monkeys, cats and dogs count their young to check they are all there; coots can identify when the number of eggs in their nest has increased, indicating someone has added a parasite egg; babies as young as five months can tell when dolls are taken away from a pile. Even dogs seem to be able to tell that something fishy is going on when experimenters try to trick them into thinking that $1 + 1 = 3$. But it is humans who have given names to these numerical identities.

Identity, edited by Giselle Walker and Elisabeth Leedham-Green. Published by Cambridge University Press. © Darwin College 2010.

Some tribes have only produced names for the first few numbers, lumping together anything too large under the heading 'lots'. But even without names for numbers, such tribes are able to compare wealth. The tribe who has numbers 'one, two, three, lots' can still say when one member of the tribe has more 'lots' than another. If chickens are a mark of wealth then by pairing chickens up we can tell whether one person's 'lots' is bigger than another's.

This idea of comparison led to mathematicians in the nineteenth century realizing that even in our more sophisticated mathematical tribe we could actually compare infinities and say when two infinite sets are identical in size or not. Prior to the nineteenth century this idea of different sizes of infinity had never been considered. In fact, when the German mathematician Georg Cantor proposed the idea in the 1870s, it was considered as almost heretical, or at best the thoughts of a madman.

Using the idea of pairing objects, Cantor was able to propose a way of declaring when two infinite sets were numerically identical or not. For example, one might be tempted to declare that there are half as many even numbers as compared to all numbers. However Cantor showed there is a way to line up both sets of numbers so that each number has its pair. For example 1 gets paired with 2, 2 with 4, 3 with 6, and n with 2n. So these two sets have the same size. The tribal member with even-numbered chickens is as wealthy as the tribesman with chickens numbered with all whole numbers. These infinite sets are identical in size.

You have to be slightly more ingenious to see how to compare all whole numbers against all fractions and prove that both sets are identical in size. At first sight this looks impossible. Between each pair of whole numbers there are infinitely many fractions. But there is a way to match the whole numbers perfectly with all fractions so that no fractions are left unmatched. The procedure starts by producing a systematic way to make a table containing all the fractions. The table has infinitely many rows and columns. The nth column consists of a list of all the fractions $^1/n, ^2/n, ^3/n, \ldots$

How then do you pair up the whole numbers with the fractions in this table? The trick is to wend a snake diagonally through the fractions in the table as illustrated below. The number 9 for example gets paired with ⅔, the ninth fraction that one meets as the snake slithers through the table of fractions. Since the snake covers the whole table, every fraction will get paired with some whole number.

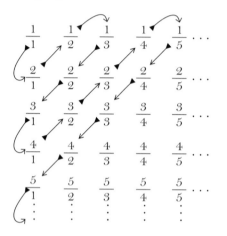

This is beginning to look as if all infinities are identical in size. Perhaps once a tribal member has infinitely many chickens he won't get beaten by anyone else's collection. Now enter the new big cheese whose chickens are labelled with all the possible decimal expansions there are of numbers. Will the tribal member whose chickens are labelled just with the whole numbers 1, 2, 3 . . . up to infinity be able to pair his chickens up with this new big cheese? He might start by matching his first chicken with chicken $\pi = 3.1415926 \ldots$, then the second with $e = 2.7182818 \ldots$

Why can we be sure that, however hard he tries to match up chickens, we can always guarantee an irrational chicken unaccounted for? Let's take one of his attempts to match his chickens with the irrational chickens belonging to the big cheese.

$$1 \leftrightarrow 3.1415926 \ldots$$
$$2 \leftrightarrow 2.7182818 \ldots$$
$$3 \leftrightarrow 1.4142135 \ldots$$
$$4 \leftrightarrow 1.6180339 \ldots$$
$$5 \leftrightarrow 0.3331779 \ldots$$
$$\ldots$$

We are going to build a number with an infinite decimal expansion such that the corresponding irrational chicken has not been paired up with one of the whole numbers. Each decimal place is a number between 0 and 9. In the first decimal place, we choose a number which is different from the first decimal place of the number paired with chicken number 1. In the second decimal place choose a number different from the second decimal place of the number paired with chicken number 2. For example, the irrational chicken with number starting 0.28518 . . . is not paired with the first five whole numbers. In this way we can build up a number labelling a chicken which hasn't been paired up with any whole number. If someone claimed it was the chicken paired with, say, chicken number 101, we could simply say: 'Check the 101st decimal place: it's different from the 101st decimal of this new number.'

There are a few technical points to watch in building this number, for example you don't want to produce the number 0.9999 . . . because this is actually the same as the number 1.000 . . . But the essence of the argument suffices to show that there are more numbers with infinite decimal expansions than there are whole numbers.

The great German mathematician David Hilbert recognized that Cantor was creating a genuinely new mathematics. Hilbert declared Cantor's ideas on infinities to be 'the most astonishing product of mathematical thought, one of the most beautiful realisations of human activity in the domain of the purely intelligible . . . no one shall expel us from the paradise which Cantor has created for us.'

Cantor's illumination of the different mathematical identities hiding inside the idea of infinity lead to a question that would reveal how subtle numbers are. Cantor wanted to know whether there are sets of numbers which are bigger in size than whole numbers but small enough that they can't be paired with all infinite decimal expansions. In other words can there be a tribal member with numbered chickens that is richer than the man with chickens labelled with whole numbers but poorer than the big cheese with chickens labelled with every possible infinite decimal expansion.

The answer to this problem, which finally arrived in the 1960s, rocked the mathematical community to its foundations. Paul Cohen, a logician at Stanford, discovered that both answers were possible. Cohen proved that one couldn't prove from the axioms we currently use for mathematics whether or not there was a set of numbers whose size was strictly between the number of whole numbers and all real numbers. Indeed he produced two different models which satisfied the axioms that we are using for mathematics and in one model the answer to Cantor's question was 'yes' and in the second model the answer was 'no'.

Before Cantor, all infinities had been lumped together under one heading. But Cantor was able to distinguish different sizes of infinities. This feature of mathematics – to distinguish different mathematical identities – is very much a product of a nineteenth-century movement in mathematics towards looking for abstract mathematical structures underlying physical reality.

Another nineteenth-century success story was the ability of mathematicians to articulate the idea of symmetrical identity.

Identical symmetry

There is one place for me that captures the story of symmetry more than anywhere else: the Alhambra. Sitting like a jewel atop the hills that make up the Andalusian town of Granada, it is one of the most beautiful palaces built by the Moors in Spain. What draws most visitors to the Alhambra is the elaborate stucco decorations that adorn the walls of the palace.

Although each room provides the artist with yet another canvas to express his art, the writings of the Muslim *hadith*, which interpret the Koran, have put some limitations on the artist. It is forbidden under Muslim law to depict the image of any living creature. So instead the artist has been forced to express the majesty of creation through more geometric games. And that is what makes the Alhambra such a feast for a mathematician making the journey to southern Spain.

To innocent eyes the different games that the artist can play with the symmetrical pieces look unlimited. But a mathematician stares at these walls through very different glasses from the average visitor. For instead of the infinite complexity of the different tiles and colours, the mathematician sees just seventeen different symmetrical games being played by the artists.

Although two walls may be adorned with very different pictures, the mathematics of symmetry is able to articulate that these two walls have identical symmetries. This is the power of the mathematical language.

But what exactly is symmetry? How can we give meaning to the question: 'Do these two objects have identical symmetries?'

Just as we seem genetically programmed to count, evolution has also primed us to respond to symmetry. For the bumble bee in the garden, symmetry signifies sustenance in the shape of a flower. In the jungle, symmetry in the undergrowth is something you could eat or something that might eat you. When choosing mates, animals are attracted to symmetry as an expression of good genes. Anyone who can waste resources making themselves symmetrical must be fit. Indeed animal rights activists have highlighted the unsymmetrical nature of battery farm eggs as an indication of the trauma these hens suffer.

In contrast, for many artists, symmetry has been a symbol of death. In *The Magic Mountain* Thomas Mann talks about the symmetry in a snowflake but 'shuddered at its perfect precision, found it deathly, the very marrow of death'. But for a mathematician, symmetry is full of movement and energy. Symmetry can be described as the actions that I perform on an object which leave it looking as it did before I moved the shape. For example, consider the symmetries of the six-pointed starfish and the equilateral triangle depicted here.

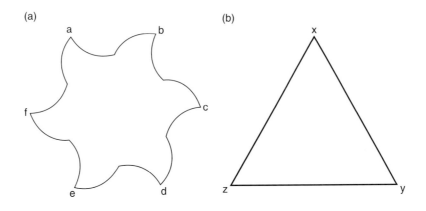

To try to identify the symmetries of each object, we can draw an outline around the shape and then ask: how many different ways can I pick up the shape and place it down inside its outline? So a symmetry is essentially a move that I can make whilst your back is turned which you can't detect when you look around again. I like to describe each symmetry as a 'magic trick move'.

The six-pointed starfish has lots of rotational symmetry because there are lots of ways I can spin the object which fit it back inside its outline. There are five different rotations that I can make of the starfish. Using the letters attached to the tentacles I can articulate these symmetries via a language for symmetry. For example the rotation that moves tentacle **a** to tentacle **b** we will call B. The rotation that takes tentacle **a** to tentacle **c** we will call C. The five rotations therefore have the names B, C, D, E and F. There is one additional symmetry that mathematicians include. If symmetry consists of the things that I can do to an object which make it fit back inside its outline, then actually leaving the object where it is also deserves to be included. So we shall call this rotation A because it sends tentacle **a** to **a**.

These six symmetries A, B, C, D, E and F are all the symmetries of the starfish. By putting a twist on the tentacles I have destroyed what most people commonly identify as symmetry, namely reflectional symmetry. The equilateral triangle on the other hand does have this more obvious reflectional symmetry. There are three lines of reflectional symmetry. For example I can pick up the triangle and flip it over so that point **y** and **z** exchange and **x** stays where it is. Similarly the other two reflectional symmetries fix **y** and **z** respectively whilst exchanging the other two vertices.

Again we can give these reflectional moves names. The reflection fixing **x** we call X. The reflection fixing **y** we call Y and the reflection fixing **z** we call Z.

In addition to these three reflectional symmetries we have two rotational symmetries. One spins the triangle by a third of a turn anti-clockwise. Call this symmetry move U. The other spins the triangle clockwise by a third of a turn. Call this symmetry move V. As with the starfish, there is an additional symmetry which consists of just leaving the triangle where it is. Call this symmetry I.

Both objects have six symmetries. The symmetries of the starfish consist of the six rotations called A, B, C, D, E and F. The symmetries of the triangle we have named I, U, V, X, Y and Z. So given that these two objects have the same number of symmetries, should we say their symmetries are identical?

The language to express the idea of symmetrical identity was only formulated in the nineteenth century and has its origins in one of the most romantic, yet tragic, stories in the mathematical history books. Evariste Galois was killed in a duel over love and politics at the age of twenty. He had already led a turbulent life, having been arrested and imprisoned for several months for revolutionary political activity following the Paris revolution of 1830. But it was the revolutionary mathematics that Galois had produced in his teens that would be his lasting legacy.

What Galois understood was that the essential characteristic of symmetrical identity is how the individual symmetries interact with each other. Interestingly, Galois formulated the language of symmetry, called 'group theory', whilst answering a completely unrelated problem concerning solving equations. It would take several generations before his ideas were recognized and fully appreciated.

One of those who revealed the power of this new language to articulate symmetrical identity was an English barrister called Arthur Cayley, who was practising in Lincoln's Inn Fields at the end of the nineteenth century. He had studied mathematics at Cambridge and been elected to a fellowship at Trinity College but the fact that he was unwilling to take holy orders meant that he had to resign it after a few years. (He was to return to Cambridge as the first Sadleirian Professor of Mathematics in 1863.) Meanwhile he decided instead to apply his analytic skills to practising law. He was called to the bar in 1849. But his legal activities were just a means to support his true passion: mathematics. During his legal career he published more mathematical papers than most mathematicians do in a lifetime of professional work. It was while exploring Galois' papers that he recognized that there was a grammar hiding behind the geometry that expressed each object's individual symmetrical character.

One of the interesting features about the idea of symmetry as the 'magic trick moves' is that, if I perform one move followed by another, it gives a third 'magic trick move'. So, for example, if I perform rotation B then combine it with rotation C that actually is the same as rotation D. Cayley realised that one could define a sort of multiplication expressing the way these symmetries interact. So, for example, one could write the observation about how these symmetries combine as an equation:

$$\text{B} * \text{C} = \text{D}.$$

Given that the starfish has six symmetries, Cayley realized one could record in a 6 × 6 table the different ways that all the symmetries interact. Here is Cayley's table for the interactions between the rotations of the starfish:

*	A	B	C	D	E	F
A	A	B	C	D	E	F
B	B	C	D	E	F	A
C	C	D	E	F	A	B
D	D	E	F	A	B	C
E	E	F	A	B	C	D
F	F	A	B	C	D	E

So the entry in the ith row and jth column of the main table shows the name of the symmetry you get by doing the ith symmetry followed by the jth symmetry. It is this table describing the grammar of the interactions of the symmetries which captures the identity of the symmetry of the starfish.

By comparing this table with the table for the six symmetries of the equilateral triangle we can finally reveal the different symmetrical identities of the two objects. Here is Cayley's table expressing the symmetries of the triangle:

*	I	U	V	X	Y	Z
I	I	U	V	X	Y	Z
U	U	V	I	Z	X	Y
V	V	I	U	Y	Z	X
X	X	Y	Z	I	U	V
Y	Y	Z	X	V	I	U
Z	Z	X	Y	U	V	I

Mathematicians now had a way to say that two objects had the same - symmetries. If there was a dictionary that translated the names A, B, C, D, E, F for the symmetries of the starfish into the names of the symmetries I, U, V, X, Y, Z of the triangle such that the two tables were identical, then we say the symmetries of each object are identical.

In this case there is a way to reveal that such a dictionary is impossible. In the table for the starfish the grammar has a symmetry. It does not matter in which order you do the symmetries, the answer will be the same. For example

$$\text{C} * \text{D} = \text{F} = \text{D} * \text{C}.$$

We say in this case that the group of symmetries of the starfish are 'commutative'.

But this is not true for the symmetries of the triangle. Now it is very important in what order you perform the symmetrical moves. For example

$$\text{U} * \text{X} = \text{Z}$$

whilst

$$\text{X} * \text{U} = \text{Y}.$$

Or, in other words, if I rotate the triangle anticlockwise, then reflect in the vertical line through the triangle, this combination leaves the triangle in a different position than if I had first reflected the triangle and then spun it.

It is the language of group theory first developed by Galois in the depths of revolutionary France that enables modern scientists to articulate the concept of symmetrical identity. It is with this language that mathematicians at the end of the nineteenth century were able to express the fact that these two designs found in the Alhambra, although physically very different, have identical symmetries.

(a)   (b)

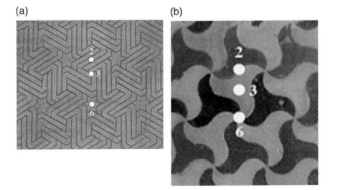

Once again, symmetry consists of the ways in which I can lift these tiles, move them and place them back down again so that they fit perfectly in the original outline. In each picture there are points around which I can spin the image by a sixth of a turn and see all the tiles magically align up. There are other points around which I can make a third of a turn and a half-turn and see the images lining up. Examples of these points are marked in both designs. Neither wall contains reflectional symmetry. So although the images used by the artist on each wall are very different, mathematicians can identify the symmetries as identical. The name for this symmetry is 632.

Just as the number 'three' captures the identity of a collection which has three objects, whether it be three apples or three kangaroos, the naming of the symmetry 632 has abstracted the symmetrical identity shared by these two walls in the Alhambra.

One of the special features of these walls is that they have translational symmetry whereby I can move the wall up or down, left or right, and match up all the tiles. It was the nineteenth-century language of group theory that revealed that there are only seventeen different identities that the symmetries on these walls can have. Any attempts by the medieval artists to conjure up a new symmetry were doomed to failure. Whatever games they played, the wall would have symmetry identical to one of the seventeen in the mathematicians' list.

Topological identity

What makes two shapes identical? For the ancient Greeks, geometric identity meant objects with equal measurements or proportions. Geometry, meaning 'measuring the earth', was primarily concerned with shapes whose measurements were the same. Two triangles were identical if the lengths of the sides of the triangles were identical. That meant that one triangle could be placed exactly on top of the second.

Euclid's *Elements* discuss at length when you can deduce that two triangles are identical. How much do you need to know about a triangle to determine its shape? Are two angles and the length of one side enough? From the axioms Euclid laid down at the beginning of the *Elements*, Proposition 26 of Book 1 proves that two triangles sharing two angles and a length in common will be geometrically identical in the sense that one triangle can be moved so that it sits exactly over the other triangle. Such triangles are called congruent.

The nineteenth century again heralded a different way of interpreting identity of shapes. In some mathematical problems the physical dimensions of a shape might be irrelevant. Instead the way the shape is connected together might be of primary importance. A classic example of this is the iconic London Underground map developed by Harry Beck in 1933. A physical map showing the geographic locations and routes on the London Underground is not a very helpful picture to negotiate your way around London. Instead Beck's map isolates the way the network is connected together whilst ignoring physical dimensions. The fact that the same length of line is used to represent the connection between Covent Garden and Leicester Square as that between King's Cross and Caledonian Road does not mean the distances are the same. For a commuter knowing there is such a connection is much more important than knowing the distance between stations.

Similarly, many mathematical problems become much simpler once this new form of identity of shapes is used. It reflects the fact that sometimes too much information can be a bad thing. Perhaps the first example of this new view on the world is the famous problem of the Seven Bridges of Königsberg.

The seventeenth-century residents of the Prussian town of Königsberg used to entertain themselves of a weekend by playing a game. The town was divided into islands by the river Pregel, which ran through Königsberg. There were seven bridges that connected different bits of the town. The game was to find a way around the town so that you crossed each bridge once and once only.

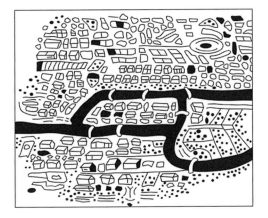

However hard they tried, the residents always were left with one bridge they could not cross. But no one was sure whether there might be an alternative route that would solve the puzzle. The solution to this problem arrived when the Swiss mathematician Leonard Euler brought his mathematical perspective to bear. Instead of the map of Königsberg with all its intricate detail one can analyse an alternative map which picks out the essential qualities of the problem. The Problem of the Bridges of Königsberg can then be identified with the problem of drawing the new map without taking your pen off the paper and without running over a line twice.

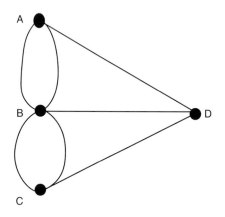

Just as with the map of the London Underground, the graph crystallizes the essential information that is needed to solve the problem. One then observes that in any network, except for your initial and final location, every node in the graph must have an even number of edges emanating from it if a path is possible. So if it is possible to find a path round Königsberg to solve the residents' game, there must be at most two nodes with an odd number of edges. The graph of the Bridges of Königsberg has four nodes with an odd number of edges so it is impossible to navigate the town crossing each bridge once and once only, just as the residents discovered by trial and error.

The geometrically accurate maps of the London Underground or Königsberg can be continuously morphed into the simpler maps without cutting any of the connections. This provides a new way of identifying shapes and it initiated a new branch of mathematics called 'topology'. Two shapes are topologically identical if one can be continuously mapped into the other without tearing the objects. So we can twist and stretch but not cut.

For example a circle and an ellipse are topologically identical because one can be stretched into the other. Similarly a football and a rugby ball are identical because one can be morphed into the other. If you take a bagel or one of Homer Simpson's doughnuts (or what mathematicians call a torus) then this can be morphed into a coffee cup. But it turns out that the hole in the cup's handle or the bagel is a defining feature of this shape, capturing its identity. A torus and a sphere are not topologically identical. There is no way to morph one into the other without making a cut.

If you take a two-dimensional surface, what are the different ways it can be wrapped up in such a way that it is finite yet without edges such that the orientation on the surface is preserved? The condition of being orientable means the surface has an outside and an inside so that there is a way to put two ants walking on either side of the surface such that they cannot meet. At the beginning of the twentieth century, the French mathematician Henri Poincaré recognized that the number of holes in a shape essentially captured the identity of the shape. Poincaré proved that the sphere, the torus with one hole, two holes, three holes or any finite number of holes are the only orientable two-dimensional topological shapes possible.

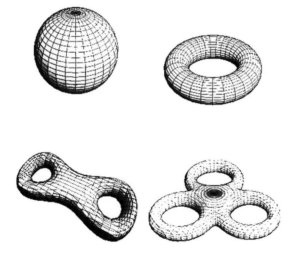

The number of holes – what mathematicians call the genus – characterizes the shape. So however complicated a shape might be, it must be topologically identical to one of these shapes. For example, whilst a tea-cup is identical to the bagel, a tea-pot is identical to the pretzel with two holes in it. It is perhaps more challenging to understand why this shape can be morphed into the two-holed pretzel.

After all, with the bagels interlocked, it looks as if you would have to cut the shape to morph it successfully. At the end of the chapter you will find a smooth deformation involving no cuts which moulds this shape into the two-holed pretzel.

What different characteristics of a shape determine its particular identity? For example if you are a flatlander stuck inside the two-dimensional universe and unable to fly off the surface to see the hole in the middle, are there ways you can identify the nature of the shape you are living in? Poincaré's concept of homotopy-theory gave a mathematical way to identify the topological identity of a shape. For example, one of the characterizing properties of a sphere is that, if you draw a closed pathway on a sphere, there is always a continuous deformation of that path so that it contracts to a point. Or, in more concrete terms, if you tie a noose round a sphere and pull the noose tight then it will always be possible to pull the noose tight so that the hole vanishes.

Poincaré proved that any shape having the same property must be topologically identical to a sphere. This property characterized the identity of a sphere. In contrast there is a way to draw a path on a torus such that it cannot be smoothly deformed to a point, namely the path in and out of the hole at the centre. A noose tied through the hole of the bagel cannot be pulled tight so that the noose disappears.

The concept of the paths in a space turns out to characterize the topological identity of all these two dimensional surfaces. But one of the biggest challenges of the last century has been determining whether the same is true for higher-dimensional shapes.

Just in the same way that a two-dimensional surface can be wrapped up in different ways, mathematicians began to investigate the different possibilities for the different shapes of three-dimensional space. The different ways of wrapping up three-dimensional space are called closed 3-manifolds. In particular Poincaré was interested to know whether there were any closed 3-manifolds in which all paths were contractible but which nevertheless was topologically distinct from the hyper-sphere, the higher dimensional version of a ball.

In 2002 Grigori Perelman announced the answer to Poincaré's question: just as in two dimensions, the identity of a hyper-sphere is characterized by the fact that all paths are contractible, so any closed 3-manifold in which paths can always be contracted to a point can be morphed into a hyper-sphere. Perelman's proof was declared one of the major advances of the last decade and in 2006 earned him a Fields Medal, the Nobel Prize of mathematics. However Perelman made international headlines by being the first mathematician ever to refuse to accept the award.

But Perelman's proof goes further than pinpointing the identity of the hyper-sphere. He also identified what other topological shapes 3-manifolds can assume. In 1982, Bill Thurston made a conjecture for the building blocks of 3-manifolds. In 2-manifolds all the shapes can essentially be built by glueing together copies of a torus. In three dimensions things become more interesting. Called the Thurston Geometrization Conjecture, it proposes that there are essentially eight different shapes from which you can build 3-manifolds. The challenge is to prove that there are not any shapes with a topological identity which are missed by Thurston's classification. It looks possible that Perelman's methods also prove Thurston's conjecture.

Mathematical equations

Most people's impression of mathematics is that it is a matter of equations. The very essence of an equation is an expression of some mathematical identity. Some equations are mundane identities expressing something of little surprise. But the best equations are those that show that two seemingly very different ideas are in fact identical.

A mathematical identity often picks up the abstract structure of the grammar of mathematics which underlies some pattern observed in numerical identities. For example, 5×5 is one more than 4×6. 7×7 is one more than 6×8. Whatever number you start with, say X, the square of that number is one more than multiplying together X-1 and X+1. This numerical pattern is picked up by the algebraic identity: $X^2 = $ (X-1) $\times$ (X+1) +1.

The grammar of algebraic manipulation allows one to elaborate on simple identities like this to build up ever more surprising equations. One of the earliest examples of a surprising mathematical identity was discovered by the seventh-century Indian mathematician Brahmagupta.

Brahmagupta was one of the first to show why zero has a mathematical identity. The idea of 'nothing' as an important mathematical concept developed much later than the other numbers. Indeed, even in medieval Europe, the concept of zero was viewed with much suspicion for centuries. But it was Brahmagupta's investigation of the algebraic rules which govern adding, subtracting, multiplying and even dividing by this new number which led to zero assuming a mathematical identity alongside the other numbers.

This power to do algebraic manipulation led to Brahmagupta's discovery that, if you add two square numbers like $4 + 16$ and multiply that by the sum of two other square numbers like $9 + 25$, then the answer can also be expressed as the sum of two square numbers, in this case $14^2 + 22^2$. In fact Brahmagupta discovered that it can be written as the sum of two squares in two different ways. An alternative in this case is $26^2 + 2^2$. This is a particular realization of the following mathematical identity:

$$\left(a^2 + b^2\right)\left(c^2 + d^2\right) = (ac - bd)^2 + (ad + bc)^2$$
$$= (ac + bd)^2 + (ad - bc)^2$$

The algebraic manipulation behind proving such an identity is rather like playing around with a Rubik's cube. You start with all the colours aligned with a certain pattern then by taking the Rubik's cube through a series of moves you arrive at another arrangement of the cube with a beautiful pattern. In some sense there is an important role that aesthetics plays in singling out those identities which are worthy of note from among the plethora of mundane tautologies. One can simply apply the rules of algebraic manipulation to churn out strings of mathematical identities, but just as in turning the Rubik's cube, there are some arrangements of the pieces which are particularly appealing. Brahmagupta's identity has that quality because of the surprising reappearance of squares on the right side of the equation.

The importance of Brahmagupta's identity also derives from its key role in uncovering even more unexpected properties of numbers. For example, it is a key ingredient in Euler's proof of Fermat's beautiful discovery that every prime number that leaves remainder 1 on division by 4 can be expressed as the sum of two squares. For example:

$$5 = 1+4, 13 = 4+9, 17 = 1+16, 29 = 4+25, 37 = 1+36, 41 = 16+25.$$

It is an amazing property. There are infinitely many primes which leave remainder 1 on division by 4. But however large such a prime you take, Fermat proved that it can be written as the sum of two squares. For example

$$3141592653589793238462643383279502884 1 =$$
$$3684758713859920604^2 + 4223562448517994405^2$$

A further development of Brahmagupta's identity by Euler showed why sums of four squares also could be multiplied together to give sums of four squares. This identity was used in Lagrange's proof that every number can be written as the sum of four squares, the first case of Waring's Conjecture. At the beginning of the nineteenth century Degen proved a similar identity for sums of eight squares but this is as far as these identities go. If you multiply together the sum of two lots of sixteen squares, you won't always be able to write the answer as a sum of sixteen squares.

The power to manipulate equations and uncover surprising mathematical identities was taken to a new level by another Indian mathematician. Brahmagupta's mantle was picked up by the untrained genius Srinivasa

Ramanujan in the early twentieth century. He had an extraordinary intuition for manipulating equations to pull out some unexpected relationships between numbers.

The Rogers-Ramanujan identities, for example, relate different ways that you can partition numbers. A partition of a number is a way of writing a number as sums of positive whole numbers. For example I can write 6 as $5 + 1$ or $4 + 2$ or $1 + 1 + 1 + 3$. (Note writing $6 = 6$ is also considered a partition of 6.) The partitions of 6 are essentially all the different ways I can divide 6 stones into separate piles.

The identities that Ramanujan discovered showed why the number of ways I can partition a number where the numbers in the sum differ by at least 2 is actually the same as the number of partitions where the numbers in the sum leave remainder 1 or 4 on division by 5. For example, there are three ways that I can partition 6 such that all the numbers differ by at least 2:

$$6, 5 + 1 \text{ and } 4 + 2$$

On the other hand, there are also three different ways I can partition 6 such that the numbers in the sums leave remainder 1 or 4 on division by 5:

$$6, 4 + 1 + 1 \text{ and } 1 + 1 + 1 + 1 + 1 + 1.$$

At first sight it doesn't seem at all clear why these two different ways of partitioning numbers should be related. But Ramanujan's mathematical identities reveal why these two different ways of partitioning numbers are two sides of the same equation.

Ramanujan had an incredible nose for these mathematical identities but lacked the formal education often to provide rigorous mathematical proofs for his claims. When questioned how he arrived at such extraordinary relations, he claimed that his family goddess Namagiri delivered the mathematical revelations in his dreams. Quite often this talk of revelation accompanies many mathematicians' descriptions of their mathematical discoveries although perhaps not so colourfully illustrated with the accompaniment of a family goddess.

These identities arise from algebraic manipulation of equations. But the nineteenth century is responsible for the discovery of equations which reveal very surprising identities across different bits of the mathematical opus. The proof of an equation in general involves something rather similar to the process of morphing one object topologically into another. Instead of geometric objects, it is logical steps which are being used to morph one side of the equation into another. For example the German mathematician Lejeune Dirichlet discovered an equation called the class number formula. In all its gory detail it says that, if K is an algebraic number field, then

$$\lim_{s \to 1} (s-1)\, \zeta_K(s) = \frac{2^{r_1} \cdot (2\pi)^{r_2} \cdot h_K \cdot \mathrm{Reg}_K}{w_K \cdot \sqrt{|D_K|}}$$

On the right-hand side of the equation is information about the way a number field factorizes, something essentially algebraic. The number h_K, called the class number, records information about how many different ways a number might decompose into primes. In normal numbers there is only one way. For example $105 = 3 \times 5 \times 7$. I can't write 105 as a different combination of primes. But in more general number fields there can be several different ways to decompose numbers into primes.

On the other side of the equation is information about the analytic behaviour of a special function called the zeta function of the number field K. At first sight there seems no reason why an algebraic concept like the class number should be identical to an analytic one. These are two very different areas of mathematics. But Dirichlet's proof shows why one is identical to the other.

Modern mathematics is full of theorems which express these surprising mathematical identities. The Atiyah-Singer Index Theorem shows why the number of solutions to differential equations is related to the underlying geometry of the surrounding space. Analysis being identified with geometry. The Birch Swinnerton-Dyer Conjecture hypothesizes that the number of solutions of an elliptic curve can be identified from the output of the zeta function of the elliptic curve at one particular value. Number theory being identified with analysis. Borcherds' solution of Monstrous Moonshine shows why there is an identity between the characters of the Monster simple group and modular functions. Group theory being identified with number theory.

Mathematics is so rich because of these strange connections that permeate the world of mathematics. Each new equation is like a new tunnel linking what had previously seemed like isolated bits of the mathematical warren. But if I was asked to take one mathematical identity away with me on a desert island it would be Bernhard Riemann's extraordinary identity for the primes.

It was probably Dirichlet's interest in the zeta function which was the catalyst for Riemann's discovery of an equation which revealed an extremely surprising identity between prime numbers and zeros of the zeta function. The zeta function that Riemann studied is defined as the sum of the powers of the harmonic series. In particular if x is a (generally complex) number then $\zeta(x)$ is defined by the following formula:

$$\zeta(x) = 1 + \frac{1}{2^x} + \frac{1}{3^x} + \frac{1}{4^x} + \frac{1}{5^x} + \frac{1}{6^x} + \cdots$$

Riemann's supervisor Gauss had started to understand primes by enumerating them. He defined a new function $\pi(N)$ which counts the number of prime numbers less than or equal to N. For example $\pi(10) = 4$ since there are four primes less than 10, namely 2, 3, 5 and 7. Hidden inside this function is precise information about the primes. For example, the fact that $\pi(100) = 25$ whilst $\pi(101) = 26$ tells us that 101 is a prime.

By analysing the analytic behaviour of the zeta function, Riemann discovered a formula which showed an identity between prime numbers and the points at which the zeta function outputs zero.

$$\psi(x) = x - \sum_{\rho} \frac{x^\rho}{\rho} - \ln(2\pi) - \frac{1}{2}\ln(1 - x^{-2})$$

The function on the left-hand side is a variant of Gauss' counting function called the *summatory Von Mangoldt function*. On the right-hand side the summation is over all the complex numbers ρ which are zeros of the Riemann zeta function, i.e. $\zeta(\rho) = 0$.

This identity completely transformed research on prime numbers. Since the discovery of Riemann's equation, mathematicians have been trying to understand the zeros of the Riemann zeta function rather than directly studying the primes.

Rather fittingly, Riemann published his breakthrough in 1859, the same year as the publication of Darwin's *On the origin of species.* Riemann's identity captured instead the Origin of the Primes, the numbers from which the whole of mathematics are built. Indeed mathematical identities, in all their different guises, can be regarded as the mathematician's attempt to recognize when two different structures are in fact expressions of the same mathematical species.

Postscript: how to topologically morph two interconnecting rings into a double-holed torus.

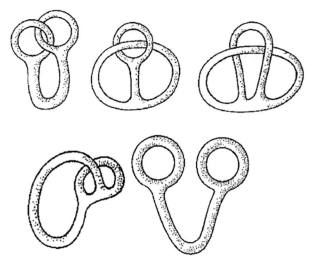

5 Immunological identity

PHILIPPA MARRACK

All creatures have to defend themselves against other organisms. To manage this, two processes are needed: each creature must have mechanisms they can use to destroy or inactivate invaders but first, and crucially, they must have a process that helps them to distinguish the invader from themselves. All the defence-mechanisms one could imagine would be at best useless, and at worst destructive, if they did not distinguish between self and everything else.

During the several thousand million years that life has been present on earth, organisms have evolved many methods to manage this feat. Many of these processes have been inherited by human beings and other mammals and are used by our immune system to help it ignore us and attack everything else. Some of these processes are very old, inherited from ancestors that are common to us, invertebrates such as insects and even, to some extent, plants. Others are newer in evolutionary terms, and first appeared more than 250 million years ago in an organism that was the common ancestor to all vertebrates from fish to reptiles, birds and mammals. Not much has happened since then; on the whole the immune system in human beings distinguishes self from everything else in pretty much the same way as that in the trout.

Given that, it is not a surprise that the immune system in human beings uses several methods to identify self, and recognize other, with varying degrees of sophistication and varying consequences for its host. The variety of these methods is reminiscent of the ways we use to distinguish ourselves as individuals from other people. For example,

Identity, edited by Giselle Walker and Elisabeth Leedham-Green. Published by Cambridge University Press. © Darwin College 2010.

football teams identify members of the opposition in three ways: by the fact that the opposition is wearing a uniform with certain colours and characteristics, by the fact that their own team is wearing uniforms which are all the same, and by identifying characteristics of individual members of the opposition, the colour and length of their hair, the number and name on the back of their shirt. This analogy will be used here although, like all analogies, it is less than perfect in many respects.

The opposing team's uniform is different: The immune system recognizes generic features of invading organisms

All organisms distinguish themselves from everything else by enclosing themselves in some way, to demarcate the boundary of the individual. Vertebrates, for example, coat themselves in a tough skin. In fact this boundary is a valuable defence against invasion, not easily breached unless it is scraped or cut. Bacteria also enclose themselves in tough walls and membranes to maintain their integrity and protect themselves against biological and chemical damage. Because bacteria have to live in many different environments, and because these outer casings have several different tasks to perform, these casings have properties that are common to many different bacterial species. Gram-negative bacteria, such as *Escherichia coli* or *Salmonella typhi*, for example, have a compli- cated structure in their outer membranes called lipopolysaccharide. This structure is unlike anything made by multicellular organisms such as human beings or fruit flies. Multicellular organisms such as ourselves have therefore developed receptors, which appear on the surfaces of their cells, which indirectly recognize the appearance of lipopolysaccharide in the body and orchestrate a response which helps to get rid of the infection. Amazingly the receptors and signalling pathways that respond to lipopolysaccharide are very similar in human beings and flies, indicat- ing that this mechanism of recognizing non-self is evolutionarily very ancient and very important to our survival. We would not have been able to live without it.

In fact invaders have several generic features which distinguish them from us. Gram-positive bacteria have complicated polysaccharide cell walls. Many bacteria can swim, using flagella which are made up of a

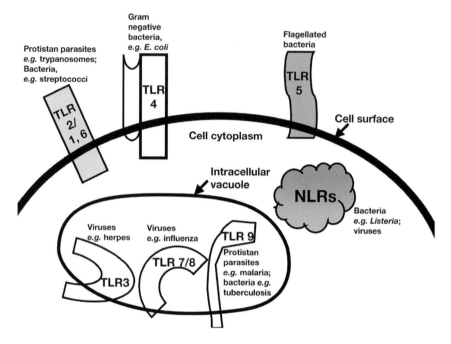

FIGURE 5.1. The location and specificity of innate immune receptors. Toll-like Receptors (TLRs) and Nod-Like Receptors (NLRs) bind features that are common to many different organisms. The location in or on the cell and some of the organisms bound by these so-called innate receptors, is shown.

protein called flagellin. Viral DNA and RNA have properties which are different from that of our own nucleic acids. These generic features were collectively and rather inelegantly called 'pathogen-associated molecular patterns' by Dr Charles Janeway, one of the first people to realize that this kind of feature is an important stimulant for our own immune system.

Human beings and mice have a number of proteins which detect these generic differences between invaders and us. Some of these proteins are related to each other and are called 'Toll-Like Receptors', or 'TLRs', after Toll, the first protein of this kind that was discovered, in fruit flies. The TLRs are placed on the surfaces of cells, or on membranes inside the cell, where they react with the invaders. Different members of the TLR family recognize different aspects of invaders, illustrated in Figure 5.1.

TLR4, for example, indirectly recognizes bacterial lipopolysaccharide. TLR7 binds to single-stranded RNA, a feature of some viruses. The location of TLRs is tailored to optimize detection of the foreign material that is their target. TLR4 is on the cell surface, where it is most likely to encounter its target, bacterial lipopolysaccharide; whereas TLR7 is inside cells, where it is most likely to encounter single-stranded RNA produced by viruses consumed by cells.

When they bind to their invading targets, TLRs deliver signals to the cells bearing them, causing the cells to begin responses which will help to get rid of the invader. Different TLRs are expressed on different cells which, in turn, have different functions. TLR7, for example, is in plasmacytoid dendritic cells, which are designed to produce massive amounts of type I interferons, proteins which act to suppress viral growth. When TLR7 binds to viral RNA inside the plasmacytoid dendritic cells, they make interferon and thus prevent spread of the virus.

The immune system has other kinds of protein that can also help in this type of recognition. These include the NOD-like receptors (NLRs), which exist inside cells and help to recognize invaders such as viruses and bacteria (like *Mycobacterium tuberculosis*) which can live in that location.

Among humans, there are variations in the genetic sequences of many of these proteins. Many of these variations are quite common and have consequences for their hosts. For example, a polymorphism in TLR4, one of the proteins involved in recognition of gram-negative bacteria, in pregnant women infected with malaria, is associated with recurrences of the disease in pregnancy, and with lower birth-weights for their children. A genetic loss of function in one of the NLR proteins, NOD2, is highly associated with an intestinal inflammation, called Crohn's disease. NOD2 is part of the system that recognizes muramyl dipeptide, a part of gram-positive bacterial cell walls. In its absence, greater inflammation occurs in the gut, where many such bacteria exist, leading to gut damage and disease. The fact that many of these polymorphisms are quite common in man suggests, however, that under some circumstances they may be advantageous to their hosts.

Our team has a uniform: The immune system is inhibited by self

The constant battle between invading organisms and their hosts has caused the evolution by invaders of methods that dampen immune responses. The smallpox virus, for example, produces proteins that interfere with inflammation. HIV infects and destroys the very cells, CD4+ helper T cells, which govern immune responses. Other viruses, such as those related to herpes, have invented another means of avoiding T cell attack: making proteins which inhibit the activity of a group of host products called class I major histocompatibility complex (MHC class I). MHC class I is present on the surface of all normal host cells and stimulates immunity by binding fragments of invaders in a way that makes the fragments recognizable by T cells. T cells which interact with the combination of invader fragments and class I on the surface of the host cells then kill those cells, thereby destroying invaders, such as viruses, which might be concealed within the cell. The viruses that can inhibit class I function thus avoid such attack.

The immune system has found a way to circumvent this problem, however, by developing a special set of cells, called Natural Killer cells (NK cells) which, if unchecked, would kill other cells. Their murderous activity for normal cells is inhibited by reaction of specialized proteins on the surface of the NK cells with MHC class I on the surface of potential target cells. This reaction inhibits killing by the NK cells. Cells which are infected with herpes viruses, and therefore express only low levels of class I on their surfaces, can no longer inhibit the action of NK cells and are therefore killed. The upshot of all this is that it is difficult for viruses inside cells to escape the immune system. If they allow the cell to bear MHC class I, normal T cells (see below) can detect fragments of the virus bound to MHC class I and kill the cell. If the virus inhibits T cell-killing by blocking production of MHC class I, then the cell containing the viruses becomes a target for NK cell-killing. Either way, the immune system is able to detect and eliminate virus-infected cells.

The unexpected ability of NK cells to detect absence of self (that is, absence of self MHC class I) is illustrated in Figure 5.2.

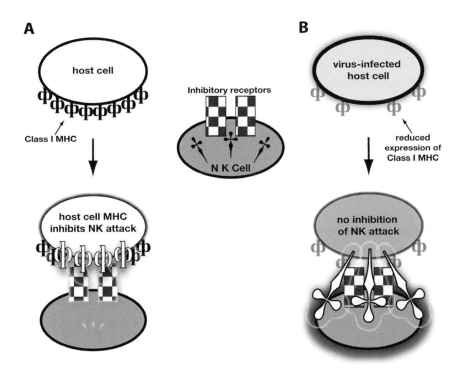

FIGURE 5.2. Natural Killer cells kill targets that lack self class I.
A. Natural Killer (NK) cells contain cytotoxic proteins (shown as daggers), which,
if unchecked, the NK cells fire at target cells. Natural killer cells bear special proteins
(inhibitory receptors), shown with a checkerboard fill. These receptors bind class I major
histocompatibility complex proteins on other cells, and this binding causes a signal to be
transmitted to the NK cell. The signal prevents release of the cytotoxic proteins.
B. Viruses infect cells, and when this happens many viruses reduce the amount of
class I on the cells they infect (shown as washed-out class I). Consequently inhibitory
receptors on NK cells are not fully engaged by class I on the virus-infected cell, the
intrinsic killer activity of NK cells is unleashed, and the virus-infected cell is killed, thus
preventing further proliferation and spread of the virus. Note that the NK cell will thus
be allowed to kill the virus-infected cell and not bystander uninfected cells.

There is good evidence that this process is very important for our
ability to control virus infections. For example, a gene which allows NK
cell activity is present on the X chromosome, occasionally in a mutated,
inactive form. Some boys inherit a mutant form of the protein from their
mothers and thereby lack proper NK cells. Consequently these individuals cannot deal properly with infections by common viruses related to

herpes, in particular the Epstein Barr Virus, which causes infectious mononucleosis and infects almost all humans.

Natural Killer cells have another function. Immunologists have long been interested in the idea that the immune system is designed, or could be trained, to attack cancers. The idea is that cancer cells are by definition different from self, in that they are being allowed to divide uncontrollably, unlike normal tissue. Therefore they must be expressing some factor which allows them to divide, which is not expressed in normal tissues and which therefore should be a target for immunity. In fact the idea came up that the appearance of tumours represented a failure in what came to be called 'immune surveillance'. Years of research have confirmed that in some cases this may be true, although the real story is turning out to be much more complicated than we might have expected thirty years ago.

Tumour cells are not the same as normal cells. They usually have increased production of proteins that are needed for cells to be activated and divide, such as the cyclins, or of proteins which are peculiar to cell type of the tumour, such as the melanin made by normal melanocytes and melanomas. Since the immune system is sensitive to concentration, these changes could be detected. Tumour cells also often produce mutated versions of normal proteins. For example, mutations in a protein called Ras, which is involved in cell activation, are often found in cancers.

The immune system could, and in fact often probably does, detect these mutations as foreign. However, tumour cells continue to mutate after they have begun dividing and the mutants are selected for survival in the teeth of immune attack. One common mutation results in lower expression by tumour cells of class I MHC, a phenomenon which allows the tumour's cells to hide its mutated proteins from T cells, but which now makes the tumour sensitive to attack by NK cells.

Members of the opposing team have identifying numbers on their backs

About 250 million years ago, the beginning of vertebrate evolution appears to have coincided with the development of a method that allowed its host to tell the difference between different invaders accurately. Because of this system our bodies can distinguish between staphylococcal and streptococcal bacteria, between different strains of influenza virus or between extremely closely related chemicals, trinitro- versus dinitro-phenol, for example, which differ by only one side chain. For years scientists have been thrilled by this ability and worked hard to understand how this is achieved.

The system operates by creating a very large collection of proteins, receptors, each of which is different from the others. Human beings contain about 10^{12} of these proteins. Each protein is displayed on the surface of a different lymphocyte and each lymphocyte has about 30,000 copies of the receptor it has chosen on its surface. When an invader appears in the body, the receptors on a few of the lymphocytes can bind the invader. Engagement with the invader leads the receptors to deliver a proliferation signal to the cells bearing them. Because the descendants of the dividing cell bear the same receptors as their parent, the number of lymphocytes that can recognize the invader is rapidly converted from a frequency of about one in a million to a number that can be as high as one in three: for example, in human beings infected with influenza, about 3×10^{11} lymphocytes are all dedicated to reacting with the virus about 7 days after the infection began. The daughter cells differentiate at the same time as they are dividing, and, unlike their mother, produce chemicals that destroy the invader. This process is called the 'clonal selection theory' because the antigen selects the clone of cells that is best able to bind to it and organize an immune response against it (the antigen). The clonal selection theory is illustrated in Figure 5.3.

As every parent knows, small children catch all kinds of colds and other infections while they are growing. If all the lymphocytes created to get rid of each infection were to survive, the child would rapidly be overwhelmed, not by the invaders but rather by the trillions of lymphocytes it created. Therefore, most of the lymphocytes made during each infection die. However, after each infection a few lymphocytes, called memory cells, survive. They are greater in number and better equipped to deal with the invader than their mother-precursors were and it is these memory lymphocytes that protect the child against a second infection by the same invader (Figure 5.3).

Philippa Marrack

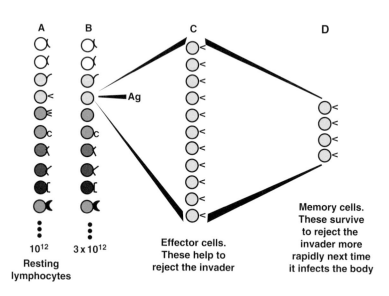

FIGURE 5.3. The clonal selection theory. (A) Lymphocytes bear receptors for antigen. When lymphocytes are created, each bears an antigen-receptor that differs from those on other lymphocytes. Each lymphocyte bears 20,000 to 40,000 copies of its chosen receptor. Once the lymphocytes have matured they migrate around the body in blood and lymph and find their way to the peripheral lymphoid organs, the lymph nodes and spleen. There they exist as resting, non-dividing lymphocytes, with a turnover time of one to two months. (B) When foreign invaders enter the body, the receptors on a few lymphocytes are able to engage the invader. Usually about one in a million of all lymphocytes has the right receptors. (C) The binding reaction causes the engaged receptors to transmit a signal into the lymphocyte carrying them. This signal induces the lymphocyte to divide rapidly and many times, thus creating, within a few days, as many as one in three lymphocytes-bearing receptors with the same abilities to recognize antigen as that of their mother. The daughter lymphocytes also have various functions, all of which help to kill or inactivate the invader. (D) When the invader is killed and disappears from the body most of the lymphocytes created to deal with the infection die. A few survive, to form a pool of memory lymphocytes with the same specificity and functions as that of their mother. Usually the number of memory cells that survive is much greater than were present as naive cells before the infection occurred. The memory cells also respond more rapidly and powerfully than their naive precursors do. Thus the memory cells, by their numbers and speed of response, effectively and rapidly protect their hosts against secondary infections. Vaccines are designed to generate memory lymphocytes.

118

The receptors that recognize individual features of invading organisms are created by random combinations of small genetic elements

Clonal selection depends on the ability of the child to create a very large number of receptors, each different from the others.

We now know that human beings and other vertebrates have fewer than 30,000 genes altogether, so clearly the receptors cannot each be coded for by a different gene. In fact, the 10^{12} or more different receptors for antigen are created by combinations of relatively few genes and a couple of small stretches of completely random DNA, a process originally discovered by Dr Susumu Tonegawa and his colleagues some thirty years ago.

Lymphocytes are created from precursor cells, found mostly in the bone marrow of adult animals, but also present in the blood, spleen and, in newborns, the cord blood of the placenta. Precursor cells can differentiate into one of three different kinds of lymphocyte, called B cells, $\alpha\beta$T cells or $\gamma\delta$T cells. B cell development occurs in the bone marrow of adult mammals. Most T cells, on the other hand, develop in the thymus, a two-lobed organ found under the chest wall and above the heart and lungs. The receptors for antigen on B cells are specialized antibody molecules. Antibodies are made up of two polypeptide chains, called light and heavy chains. Each of these chains is coded for by a number of different segments of DNA. Heavy chains bound to resting naive B cells, for example, are made up of two so-called constant regions, μ and δ, which are the same on all B cells. Several other genes contribute to the fully formed heavy chain gene. Each B cell has a choice of one out of about six so-called J_H region genes, one out of about twenty D_H region genes and one of about fifty V_H region genes. The exact number of choices depends on the species. As the developing B cell makes its choices the chosen gene segment moves, or rather intervening DNA is removed, so that the chosen DNA now lies next to the other choices, as illustrated in Figure 5.4.

The choices listed above for antibody heavy chains allow a total number of combinations of $6 \times 20 \times 50 = 6{,}000$. In fact the total number of heavy chains an individual can make is much higher, because special

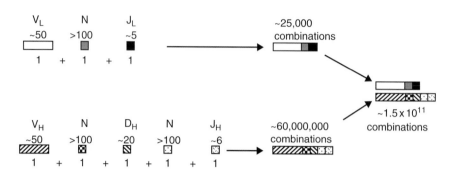

FIGURE 5.4. Lymphocytes receptors for antigen are created from a few genes by a combinatorial process. Lymphocyte receptors are made of two polypeptide chains. Each chain is coded in the host's DNA by two or three elements, and for each element the lymphocyte has a number of choices. For example, one of the chains for antibody molecules, on B cells, is made up of genetically inherited V_L and J_L regions. While it is developing, each B cell precursor selects one of about 50 V_L genes and one of about five J_L genes to code for the light chain of its receptor. The choice involves movement of the chosen V_L gene to lie next, in the DNA of the B cell, to the chosen J gene. Additional diversity comes from the fact that at the point where the V_L and J_L genes lie next to each other, DNA bases can be added and/or removed to create what is called the non-germ-line-encoded N region. A similar process, using a different set of V, J and, additionally, D region genes, leads to the creation by B cells of the gene which will code for the other polypeptide of antibodies, the heavy chain. The use by B cells of these combinatorially selected light and heavy chain elements allows the host to create more than 10^{11} different antibody proteins from fewer than a thousand genetic elements. Similar processes, using different sets of genetic elements, lead to the creation of receptors for antigen on αβ or γδ T cells.

processes allow removal or addition of DNA bases at the joining points between DNA segments (shown as 'N' regions on Figure 5.4).

The three sets of receptors, antibodies and αβ and γδ T cell receptors have different properties and different functions in the immune system. The system is very powerful. Its random libraries of receptors allow vertebrates to anticipate, without any preconceptions, almost any invader.

New infections cannot evade clonal selection, even if they have properties that are entirely different from any the host has encountered before. However the system has its disadvantages. The DNA rearrangements that are required to create the random libraries of receptors cause the genomes of lymphocytes to be a little unstable. Mistakes are made (fortunately rarely) as the DNA coding for the elements of the receptors are moved around, and these mistakes can lead to lymphocyte cancers. More importantly, because lymphocyte receptors are created randomly, they can recognize anything, and anything includes pieces of their own host. It is estimated, in fact, that more than 50 per cent of the lymphocytes we make bear receptors that can react with us. These so-called auto-reactive cells, if unchecked, would attack our tissues just as their virus-specific counterparts attack and destroy external invaders.

The immune system destroys auto-reactive lymphocytes (clonal deletion)

The threat of autoimmunity drove the immune system to develop many methods of destroying or inactivating potentially auto-aggressive cells. The first method to be fully understood depends on the fact that the individual is always present, but the invader is only intermittently around. Ray Owen was the first to realize that constant presence was crucial, and he demonstrated this accidentally in some studies on cows. Cows are often twins, in fact farmers encourage twinning in cows, it increases the yearly yield of animals. However, in the 1930s it was realized that twinning is not always a good idea, because female cows that have a male twin are often infertile. Such females are called free-martins. Dairy farmers can waste a lot of money raising twinned females only to find that some of them never yield milk. Not all female cows with male twins are infertile: it turns out that it is only the females that share placentas with their brothers *in utero* that have this problem. Sharing placentas causes the female foetuses to be exposed to male hormones during development and the male hormones make the female calves infertile. In the 1940s, dairy farmers in the USA asked Ray Owen to develop a test to distinguish normal females from free-martins early in their lives. Owen was, and is, an expert on cow blood types. He tested the blood cells of twinned female cows and discovered that the blood cells of free-martins were actually a mixture of their own cells, and cells from their brothers. The sisters and brothers were certainly not genetically identical, in fact, in some notorious cases, the twins were not even sired by the same father, and yet the free-martin females did not reject their brothers' blood cells. Instead, they remained within them over the course of many years. Owen realized that this occurred because the immune system in the female cows had been constantly exposed to its brother's antigens and, in fact, could not distinguish between self, the female host's cells, and the brother's cells. Constant exposure to the brother's antigens had taught the immune system of the female cows that the brother was self.

Years later we were the first to do an experiment to account for this phenomenon. We showed that, while lymphocytes are developing, their receptors are checked for reaction with anything that is around at the time. If the receptors on the developing lymphocyte can react with anything in their environment, the developing lymphocyte dies and its receptor disappears with it. The idea is illustrated in Figure 5.5. It is estimated that more than 50 per cent of the lymphocytes we create can react with us, and are eliminated by this process.

The antigens of the host are always around. Therefore developing lymphocytes are always checked for reaction to self, and those that react are killed. Foreign invaders, such as chickenpox or polio virus, are only present after an infection occurs. At that time, developing lymphocytes that can recognize the invader are killed. However, the host is saved by the lymphocytes that have developed and turned into mature cells before the invader arrived. It is these mature lymphocytes that expand clonally and protect their host.

To understand these ideas it is important to realize that lymphocytes are being produced constantly in our bodies. Although production falls off as we get older, our bodies are still capable of producing new cells. Once the lymphocytes have passed the test of reaction with their environment, they are released to circulate around the body, looking for invaders, and turn over rather slowly, with a half-life of a month or two.

Thus we can explain the phenomenon of Ray Owen's cows. The female and male cows shared circulation *in utero* and exchanged blood-cell- and lymphocyte-precursors. As lymphocytes developed in each twin, they were checked for reaction with their environment, which, in this case, contained lymphocytes from both foetuses. Lymphocytes in the female that could react with their brother's cells therefore died, allowing the brother's red blood cells and lymphocytes to survive in the female, and

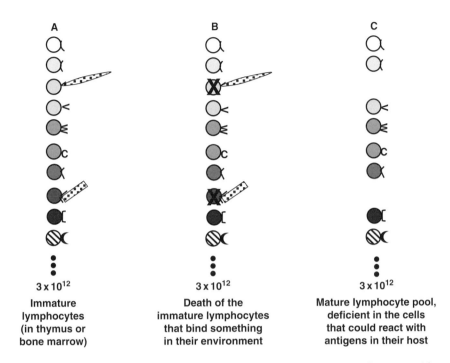

A	B	C
3 x 10^{12}	3 x 10^{12}	3 x 10^{12}
Immature lymphocytes (in thymus or bone marrow)	**Death of the immature lymphocytes that bind something in their environment**	**Mature lymphocyte pool, deficient in the cells that could react with antigens in their host**

FIGURE 5.5. Developing lymphocytes-bearing receptors that react with something in their environment die. When the developing lymphocyte first expresses its receptor for antigen (Figure 5.4) the antigen may be able to bind material in the host at the time, shown as hatched material in the figure. If this happens, the lymphocyte self-destructs. If the receptor on the developing cell does not engage anything, the lymphocyte matures and, once maturation is complete, engagement of the lymphocyte's receptor no longer makes the cell die, but rather causes the cell to divide rapidly, as shown in Figure 5.2. Because material from the host is always present, all developing lymphocytes are checked for their ability to react with self, and thus most potentially auto-reactive cells are eliminated. Invading organisms, on the other hand, are only intermittently present, so the host can build up a pool of lymphocytes able to react with and eliminate invaders before the invasion has occurred.

vice versa in her brother. Had the cows not shared placentas, their developing lymphocytes would not have been exposed to the antigens on the other twin's cells, and would therefore have killed such cells, had they been transplanted in later on.

These thoughts illustrate a crucial feature of the immune system. The specific immune system distinguishes between self and everything else because self is always present and invaders are only intermittently around. Self-reactive lymphocyte-precursors are constantly being killed off, and lymphocytes that can react with invaders survive to help get rid of infections.

Clonal deletion is not enough: there are other means of maintaining tolerance to self

It turns out that not all lymphocytes that can react with self are destroyed during development. Those that react poorly can survive. Likewise, cells that can react with self antigens which are sequestered from the rest of the body, such as the antigens of the eye, brain and joints, sometimes survive. These could pose a threat to the health of their host were they unchecked. Evolution has, of course, anticipated this problem, and many processes in addition to clonal deletion control these potentially damaging cells. One of those most intensively studied at the moment involves a specialized kind of lymphocyte called regulatory T cells. Regulatory T cells appear to react with self, but instead of attacking their host they produce a collection of immunological hormones and perform other functions which inhibit the response of other lymphocytes attacking self. At the moment we do not understand exactly how regulatory T cells are created for their job or how they function. Suffice it to say, these cells are very important to our health and in their absence human beings and mice suffer terrible autoimmune consequences.

Nevertheless, some people acquire autoimmune diseases

In spite of clonal deletion, regulatory T cells and the other safeguards against attack by our own lymphocytes, our T and B cells do sometimes turn on us and recognize and destroy our own tissues. The problems caused by such mistakes are called autoimmune diseases and include multiple sclerosis, juvenile diabetes, rheumatoid arthritis and lupus. In many of these diseases the lymphocytes target a particular tissue: the brain in multiple sclerosis, the beta cells of the pancreas in juvenile diabetes and the joints in rheumatoid arthritis. This suggests that autoimmunity is caused by T and B cells that bear receptors that can react with antigens of their host that are particular to the target tissue.

Thus autoimmunity may have been caused by lack of exposure of developing lymphocytes to these tissue-specific antigens, and/or failure of the regulatory T cells that are responsible for protecting that particular tissue. In any event, there is currently an intensive search for the lymphocytes and host antigens that drive these diseases, in the hope that such knowledge will lead to more effective treatment. At the moment physicians and patients are left with therapies that target the immune system in general, turning down the ability of T and B cells to attack targets and thus alleviating autoimmunity and simultaneously reducing the ability of the individual to prevent attack by infectious agents.

Summary

Just like a sports team, the immune system recognizes the individual that supports and contains it in many ways, most of which were unanticipated by those of us who study lymphocytes. The immune system has general methods of recognizing invaders, exemplified by Toll-Like Receptors, inherited from our remote invertebrate ancestors. The immune system has methods of recognizing its own host and preventing attack against the host, exemplified by NK inhibitory receptors and regulatory T cells. The immune system has methods, via lymphocyte receptors, of recognizing and remembering individual invaders. These methods allow the immune system to produce memory cells, which act more effectively and in greater numbers than their precursors, and which prevent us from getting the same infection more than once. This last method has a built-in problem, however, if not well controlled it allows recognition and attack of its own host. Apparently the autoimmunity generated by such cells is rare enough, or frequently arises late enough in life (i.e. after reproduction) not to have been eliminated by natural selection.

The brief review presented here doesn't begin to do justice to the complexity and beauty of our immune systems. Many aspects have been omitted. For example, not included in this paper are discussions of complement, the many receptors on many types of cells which react with polymerized sugars and clear organisms bearing them and the major histocompatibility complex, the collection of proteins that governs recognition of antigen by $\alpha\beta$T cells. The interested reader is referred to any of the many excellent new textbooks on immunology for further reading, but should beware: the complications and nomenclature can be quite intimidating.

Most importantly, the immune system recognizes self and establishes immunological identity by the fact that self is always around and others, like our mothers, are only intermittently present.

FURTHER READING

Bancroft, G. J., 'The role of natural killer cells in innate resistance to infection', *Current Opinion in Immunology* **5** (1993), 503–10.

Delbridge, L. M., and M. X. O'Riordan, 'Innate recognition of intracellular bacteria', *Current Opinion in Immunology* **19** (2007), 10–16.

Hoffmann, J. A., and J. M. Reichhart, 'Drosophila innate immunity: An evolutionary perspective', *Nature Immunology* **3** (2002), 121–6.

Hozumi, N., and S. Tonegawa, 'Evidence for somatic rearrangement of immunoglobulin genes coding for variable and constant regions' (1976), *Journal of Immunology* **173** (2004), 4260–4.

Janeway, C. A., Jr, 'How the immune system recognizes invaders', *Scientific American*, **269**(3) (1993), 72–9.

Janeway, C. A., Jr, and R. Medzhitov, 'Innate immune recognition', *Annual Review of Immunology* **20** (2002), 197–216.

Marrack, P., and J. W. Kappler 'How the immune system recognizes the body', *Scientific American* **269**(33) (1993), 81.

Ochs, H. D., S. F. Ziegler, and T. R. Torgerson, 'FOXP3 acts as a rheostat of the immune response', *Immunological Reviews* **203** (2005), 156–64.

Prud'homme, R., Interview with Ray Owen, http://oralhistories.library.caltech.edu/123/.

6 Visualizing identity

LUDMILLA JORDANOVA

Around the time I turned forty-four I noticed that objects at a distance appeared a bit blurred: it's a common enough experience. Since then I have worn glasses for driving, watching films and looking at slides. As a result of these changes to my vision, I started to pay careful attention to how distinctive each person is in terms of their gait, their proportions and overall shape. It is possible to develop some quite precise visual skills that help to identify someone at a distance without resorting to spectacles – comparing height and bodily proportions, the shapes of heads and hair, for example. At the same time, such devices are hardly foolproof, and emotional intensity, in my experience, easily throws them off balance. As the sought-after individual comes closer, the mind undertakes a series of adjustments: these refine the skills involved and enhance a sense of the particularity of the individual.

Such mundane observations can, I hope, serve to ground the arguments that follow. They suggest that elaborate visual skills are possessed by the vast majority of the population, only becoming noticed when necessity dictates. These skills serve to tell people apart, and as a result they are closely bound up with the constellation of issues that the word 'identity' evokes. It follows that 'identity', and especially 'visualizing identity', are insinuated, lived experiences, present, in one form or another, in virtually every aspect of contemporary life as they were in the past. It is thus more appropriate to think of processes and practices than of static traits and fixed images. Human minds, in other words, through the senses, register and process individual particularities in the

Identity, edited by Giselle Walker and Elisabeth Leedham-Green. Published by Cambridge University Press. © Darwin College 2010.

bodies of others; 'identity' is not a mechanical assemblage of such particularities, but a subtle, shifting ensemble. I am noting that specifically *visual* identity is central to the ensemble. I suspect there are few people who do not feel a slight unease about the pictures on their passports, library cards and other documents used to ascertain identity. If those checking that identity are feeling playful, they can make remarks like 'it doesn't do you justice', and in the process acknowledge both how much we care about how we look, and how often the frozen image fails, and thereby undermines the whole project of identifying individuals accurately by taking a picture of them.

The range of skills and experiences I have just mentioned are mostly taken for granted, left unremarked upon. They spring into focus, however, when the specialized institutions, occupations and technologies that visualize identity on behalf of others are considered. I suggest that making, selling, copying, disseminating, collecting, displaying, cataloguing and analysing portraits are just such special and specialized processes and that they give privileged access to the theme of identity. Furthermore, precisely how they do so is a matter of considerable complexity. The example of documents used to identify individuals draws attention to the representation of the face; if we compare a number of such documents belonging to the same person, it is evident how different the same face can easily look. These differences derive from quite distinct factors: there are aspects of appearance of which subjects are in charge – hair-style, make-up, clothing and jewellery, for example. Expression also has a lot to do with it, and the sitter may not be fully in command of that. The situation in which the picture is taken, whether in a photo booth or in an office, may not be conducive to a relaxed look. By contrast the point about most portraiture is its specialness, particularly the distinctive relationships that are built up in the process. I would say that the financial transactions involved, and time expended, far from detracting from the special qualities of a portrait, actually serve to heighten them. I have come to believe that this specialness is exceptionally elaborate and multi-faceted, and that those who study portraiture are only beginning to unravel it. In my own thinking on the subject, talking to those with direct experience of sitting for and making portraits has been particularly useful, and I note that they generally take the experience as one which prompts reflection upon the theme of 'identity'. In the tiny number of cases where a sitter keeps the artist at a distance, the artist invariably comments on the fact, and finds their work impeded as a result. Such an intimate blending between portrait-artists and their subjects constitutes, then, a major source of insights into 'identity'.

This approach has the effect of focusing on the figure depicted rather than on any accoutrements present in a portrait. It is extremely common, especially among those who are interested in early portraiture, to focus on the objects included as a way of deciphering the image in question. This is compelling when the human figure itself is iconic, but it can encourage a deciphering mentality which, although it remains attractive, easily impedes deeper engagement with the nature of 'identity'. It is true that accoutrements are used by some contemporary artists. For example, Pembroke College, Cambridge recently commissioned Tom Phillips, arguably Britain's most original and thoughtful portrait painter, to depict the distinguished scientist Sir John Sulston. The exquisite result is, like so many of Phillips' works, full of details that are meaningful to and for both him and the sitter. Such details are best seen as extensions to the main attraction – the sitter's body. There have indeed been important historical changes in this aspect of portraiture, which bear directly on the theme of identity. But accoutrements are nonetheless a limited, and sometimes mechanistic, way of focusing on the insights concerning identity that portraiture can unfold. For example, when in the mid-1780s Sir Joshua Reynolds painted the surgeon John Hunter, who was famously gauche, he put some quite striking accoutrements in the picture. Yet Reynolds' depiction of John Hunter himself is far more important: the two men moved in overlapping social circles and, by placing Hunter in a thoughtful, almost visionary position, Reynolds was able to endow him with a useful politeness some contemporaries claimed he did not possess. Many derivative prints were made, including the highly esteemed one engraved by William Sharp in 1788 (Figure 6.1). It is worth noting that by this time, it was not uncommon for portraits to have no objects or even background details in them at all. Much, then, is carried, subtly, in the body of the sitter by virtue of the portrait-maker's skills.

JOHN HUNTER.

FIGURE 6.1. John Hunter, line engraving by William Sharp, 1788, after a painting by Joshua Reynolds, *c.* 1786, courtesy of the Royal College of Surgeons, London. The original hangs in the Royal College of Surgeons, London. John Hunter is their key founding father, and remains central to their collective identity.

So it appears that a vital part of visualizing identity is the deliberate process of taking a picture of someone. What a very revealing notion 'taking' is, with its connotations of ownership, possession, and now freighted with the complex history of photography, with the sense of grabbing appearances by mechanical means. But the basic idea of capturing a likeness (and 'capture' too has a grabby feel to it) is hardly new.

Discourses concerning likeness are very old indeed; they fascinate in part because they can never be fully resolved and accordingly facilitate potentially infinite conversations about the relationships between persons and representations of them. The impossibility of resolution is a product of the large number of necessarily subjective judgements involved. In fact, there are two distinct issues here. One is about human action and agency, the other about the apparently static objects themselves. The first opens up questions about how representations are *made*, that is to say fabricated, to resemble their originals and *taken* to do so by viewers. The second focuses on the resulting representation, examining its constituent elements, frequently divorced from the many contexts in which portraits can be placed. In talking about most forms of visual identity, the second is frequently privileged over the first, a privilege that is neatly revealed when, in displays of portraits the name of the sitter is given, but not that of the artist, who is perhaps the most important agent involved. So the sitter's name acts as a tag – both name and person are still; the maker(s), the dynamic forces, have been put aside. In colleges, learned institutions and libraries this practice of identifying sitters more consistently than artists is surprisingly common; Cambridge University Library is a case in point. Exceptions tend to occur when the recognition factor of the artist's name is unusually high.

I have moved from mundane experiences to a highly specific form of visual representation, namely portraiture. While there certainly is a significant category-distinction to be made, the blurrings are also noteworthy. In the formal setting of an art gallery or a country house, visitors are prone to speak about those depicted in the portraits before them as if they were known to them personally, simply presuming their own access to the character of sitters. Often this is couched in terms of liking – 'she looks nice' or 'I don't like the look of him'. This is simply to express a preference, precisely the type of preference that may in everyday life lead to intolerant, even cruel, behaviour. Again, none of this is new. The phenomenon is, however, of considerable anthropological interest, if I may put it that way, since viewers of *portraits* 'know' perfectly well that they have limited access to the lives – and especially to the experiences – of sitters, yet behave and speak as if they do. It suggests that visualizing identity involves fluid 'transferable skills', in this case between seeing and judging people in everyday life and viewing portraits on display in formal settings. The role context plays in both cases is fascinating. In some settings, where items categorized as portraits are put on public display, viewers possess tacit permits to do what as children we are told is rude, that is to say, to make personal remarks about another person. Indeed without the ubiquity of such permits, the genre of portraiture simply could not function.

Thus a type of art, portraiture, has emerged that at specific times and places and by common consent mediates identity by making it visible. The careful attention paid by rulers and politicians to their portraiture constitutes sure recognition of the point. Yet the precise nature of that identity remains underdetermined, inviting debate and conversation, demanding viewers' engagement: they bring their emotional intelligence and all their everyday experiences with them – baggage as well as skills. This engagement is a complex mixture of both aware and unselfconscious responses. Conversation can help to shape, to bring to the fore, reactions that are as much somatic as they are mental. For example, the scale of a portrait, the disposition of figures and their poses, may touch viewers more or less instinctively because their own bodily habits have allowed them to make associations between sensations, moods, feelings on the one hand, and expressions, stances, body parts on the other. This is why I stress the importance of the figure depicted rather than the accoutrements. Details of texture and hue, whether in skin, hair or dress, are there to be noted, although not necessarily consciously.

To appreciate the somatic effect of portraits in scale, pose and hue, a comparison between two portraits in London's National Portrait Gallery is instructive. First, Captain Cook, painted three years before his death. He was little depicted in his lifetime, but is portrayed in a small, plain painting by a man he knew well, John Webber, the artist on his ship. The image of Cook's head and shoulders measures 43 centimetres by 35. By way of contrast, the second is a full-length painting of the much-depicted Prime Minister and philosopher Arthur James Balfour, executed by John Singer Sargent in 1908. This is a huge canvas, 260 centimetres by 150, six times as high as Cook's portrait. Balfour stands on a patterned carpet, in a classicized interior, his right arm resting on a ledge. Sargent was wearying of his portrait practice around this time. It is impossible not to struck by the size of the canvas, by the languid pose and the anatomically problematic right arm, by the grand if enervated beige setting. Viewers readily register a marked contrast between these two depictions, and in the process experience differences that are about social hierarchies, for example, mediated through paint.

Portraits by definition trade on the ability of viewers to use their visual skills. The genre of portraiture takes for granted that what we now call 'identity' may indeed, somehow, be inferred from an image. By consent, portraiture mediates 'identity', even as the precise nature of that identity is underdetermined. While by no means all cultures are so obsessed with portraits as the English-speaking world appears to be, those that are admit an intricate, intimate relationship between portraiture and identity and have done so for centuries.

It is worth holding two ideas in mind: first that visualizing identity is one of the most common practices in the world, and second that in many contexts there are specialists who earn their living by building on those practices; they possess a distinctive type of agency when it comes to visualizing identity. In saying this I have in mind particularly artists who produce portraits, but not only them. Clinicians are constantly mobilizing skills that serve to 'visualize identity'; the notable propensity of the medically trained to be interested in, and practitioners and active patrons of, the visual arts might be understood as indicative of their concern not just with how patients present themselves, but with transforming their perceptions into a coherent account – a representation – of an individual's state of health. Thus, case-notes are indeed a type of portraiture. Indeed the term 'portrait' is most commonly used to mean a detailed description, an account of the character of something, such as a place or an age, as simple searches of book titles in library catalogues reveal.

These two ideas neatly illustrate a challenge that is constitutive of portraiture. As I have suggested, a portrait invites responses that are in many ways quite ordinary; they arise from a jumble of experiences, feelings and reactions that can be as much somatic as they are mental. Yet artists, like scholars, necessarily operate differently. Artists channel and refine their skills, energies and insights; they mentally process questions of identity, of pre-existing portrait models, of conventions and their adaptability. It could be argued that these are largely intuitive processes – nonetheless they are *un*likely to be a jumble, if artists are to meet, and modify, the needs of sitters, patrons and institutions. However, those who make portraits are not *required* to write or speak about what they do, although many have done. Yet words are the primary tools of scholars who want to understand the phenomenon of visualizing identity through portraiture. That is to say, an analytical vocabulary is constantly in the process of being refined and elaborated to do a job that is totally different from the casual comments about people that characterize everyday life. This is why, if you show someone a portrait out of the blue, they are just as likely to get it completely wrong as to perceive accurately what is going on. I have no intention of being harsh towards such spontaneous responses; they give pleasure and have their value, but they should not be confused with arguments that probe the complex issues raised by the term 'identity'.

It is true that direct evidence about how identity works in a given portrait is sometimes sparse or even non-existent, but the circumstantial evidence is generally extensive. Direct evidence can be enormously revealing, but, where it is thin or absent, scholars can examine earlier images that act as sources, contemporary images, other images of the same or a comparable person, and by the same or a comparable artist. Derivatives, such as prints and medals, and copies, also provide revealing evidence. I would argue that personal relics – we might think of hair, spectacles, clothing and personal possessions – bear significant testimony to the processes through which identity is visualized in portraits. For instance, the Royal College of Surgeons in London owns a lock of hair from John Hunter's elder brother William.[1] Encased in a box recording its provenance, and laid on a bed of satin, surrounded by velvet, its value is made manifest. But this material evidence, like comparative visual evidence, does not solve the problem of how to speak and write about images of people. What, then, are the languages of 'visualizing identity'?

It might seem that they fall into three broad yet overlapping types: the languages that participants themselves use, for example, in diaries and

---

[1] Ludmilla Jordanova, *Defining features: Scientific and medical portraits 1660–2000* (London: Reaktion Books and the National Portrait Gallery, 2000), 80.

memoirs; those that are organized around notions of likeness, which are taken to be both unproblematic and revelatory of the identities in question; and those that strive for a more explicitly analytical purchase on how a portrait may visualize identity, which include artists such as Joshua Reynolds, who sought to elevate the status of portraiture, as well as distinguished contemporary commentators such as Marcia Pointon.[2] Perhaps we might also include art criticism under this heading. In fact, there is a fourth type – creative literature. I would argue that scholars need to take all of them into account, if in rather distinct ways. Thus there are many languages of visualizing identity, and in understanding those of earlier generations as well as in forging our own understanding now, I believe we do well to notice how poets, novelists, writers of plays and short stories have developed them in the past. These genres are certainly quite distinct from those adopted by early twenty-first-century commentators. But because they express what might be called the *emotional* dimensions of 'visualizing identity', they reveal to scholars precisely those complexities to which their own, very different, accounts need to do justice.

I shall discuss two examples, and in doing so I partly seek to establish that 'identity' is best taken as a piece of convenient current shorthand for an array of concerns that have certainly existed for as long as the idea of portraiture itself. We might express these concerns in the form of questions – what is transferred between person and representation, and how? How, then, are the original and image connected? How is it most plausible to conceptualize and speak of the dynamics between a human being, a depiction of them and other viewers of that depiction. It strikes me as no coincidence that so many writers have reached for languages of magic, for a sense of religious or quasi-religious awe and reverence.

I am not in fact thinking here of Oscar Wilde's *The picture of Dorian Gray*, first published in 1891 (Figure 6.2). In this novel, it was Dorian's own wish that triggered the portrait's capacity to show its subject's character and life experience, allowing the man himself to remain preternaturally youthful:

---

[2] Marcia Pointon, *Hanging the head: Portraiture and social formation in eighteenth-century England* (New Haven and London: Yale University Press, 1993).

FIGURE 6.2. Oscar Wilde, photographed in 1891, by W. and D. Downey.
© The National Portrait Gallery, London.

> How sad it is! I shall grow old, and horrible, and dreadful. But this
> picture will remain always young ... If it were only the other way!
> If it were I who was to be always young, and the picture that was to
> grow old! For that – for that – I would give everything! Yes, there is
> nothing in the whole world I would not give! I would give my soul
> for that![3]

It is certainly true that Wilde explores an exceptionally intense
relationship between sitter and artist, but his deployment of Dorian's
quasi-Faustian pact, keeps 'the young man of extraordinary personal
beauty' centre stage.[4] Wilde's novel is primarily about the sitter. My
theme is the artist as agent, as the conduit through which identities are
made visible; while Wilde certainly touches on this issue, there are better
and earlier examples to be considered. I constantly wonder how best to
speak of the embodied agency of artists, which blends together visual
intelligence, manual skill, psychological penetration and social commentary. While I recognize the responsibility to find the forms of expression
that are apt for our digital times, in which the 'war on terror' and the
phenomenon of identity fraud give fresh resonances to 'visualizing identity', I want to be attentive to historical and literary modes of expression.

This is because I value an approach that is akin to the 'grounded
theory' of sociology, not least because it helps in resisting the reification
of identity that is currently so common. In grounded theory, the
conceptual framework and the materials it is designed to illuminate
are kept in constant conversation with one another – it is what many
historians do without naming their practices as such. Here, then,
I allow ways of thinking about 'identity' and portrait practices to
inform each other. The following examples, whether literary or visual,
are designed to reveal how quite specific aspects of 'identity' have been
mobilized. I am after particularity, demonstrable associations and palp-
able links, which can be found in abundance in past times. Perhaps the
understanding of such affinities can spawn more satisfactory ways of
thinking about identity.

[3] Oscar Wilde, *The picture of Dorian Gray* (Oxford University Press, 1981), 25–6.
[4] Ibid., 1.

My first literary example is the poet William Cowper (1731–1800) for a perfectly simple reason: he wrote poems and letters about his experiences of portraiture in a context where the social networks that underpinned portrait practices and uses were dense with significance and where his mental fragility was an issue (Figure 6.3). Cowper wrote two poems about being portrayed himself, an experience he did not enjoy. He was depicted by Lemuel Abbott in 1792, and by George Romney in the same year at the instigation of William Hayley, a recent friend and later the biographer of both artist and sitter. The four-line verse prompted by Abbott's artistry was included in a letter to Hayley of 15 July 1792 (Figure 6.4).

> Abbott is painting me so true,
> That (trust me) you would stare;
> And hardly know, at the first view,
> If I were here, or there.[5]

As he enthused, perhaps a touch ironically, in a letter to his cousin Lady Hesketh six days later:

> My Pourtrait [sic] is nearly finish'd. An excellent one in my mind
> and in the opinion of all who see it, both for drawing and likeness ...
> I shall keep it a short time ... that my 2 or 3 friends in this
> neighbourhood may be gratified with a sight of it ... Should it be
> your wish to view it, you will then have an opportunity [in London],
> and trust me I think it will afford you as much pleasure, nay even
> more, than a sight of the Original myself ... whether I live or die,
> while this picture subsists my charming lineaments and proportions
> can never be forgotten.[6]

This enchantment with likeness – we might say identity, since one of its meanings is 'absolute sameness' – is echoed in the inscription on the back of the canvas: 'The Author of the Task etc. in the sixty first year of his age represented with astonishing likeness by Lemuel Francis Abbott who painted this portrait in the month of July 1792 at Weston Underwood in Buckinghamshire according to the engagement of its highly gratified

---

[5] William Cowper, *The complete poetical works* (London, New York and Toronto: Oxford University Press, 1907), 634.

[6] James King and Charles Ryskamp (eds.), *The letters and prose writings of William Cowper*, 5 vols. (Oxford: Clarendon Press, 1979–86), IV, 152.

FIGURE 6.3. William Cowper, stipple engraving by William Blake, 1802, after a drawing by Thomas Lawrence, executed in 1793, and used as the frontispiece to Hayley's *Life ... of Cowper*, volume II. © The National Portrait Gallery, London.

Ludmilla Jordanova

FIGURE 6.4. William Cowper, oil on canvas, by Lemuel Francis Abbott, 1792, 127 cm × 101.6 cm, purchased by the National Portrait Gallery in 1935. © The National Portrait Gallery, London.

possessor John Johnson'. Johnson was a relative on Cowper's mother's side, who became very close to Cowper in the poet's declining years. Fusing the identities of owner, sitter and painter, the inscription, like the poem and

140

letter, expresses not only an awe for artistry that uses familiar notions of likeness, but also projects Cowper and his writings into the future. While it is plausible to link the theme of time to portraits, the central idea articulated so crisply here, that a visualized identity can be thrown into times yet to come, is striking and invites further consideration.

Cowper's portrait by Romney raises more complex issues of visualizing and articulating identity (Figure 6.5). Here is the poem, addressed to the artist and written a few weeks later:

> Romney! Expert infallibly to trace,
> On chart or canvas, not the form alone,
> And 'semblance, but, however faintly shown,
> The mind's impression too on ev'ry face,
> With strokes that time ought never to erase:
> Thou hast so pencil'd mine, that though I own
> The subject worthless, I have never known
> The artist shining with superior grace.
> But this I mark, that symptoms none of woe
> In thy incomparable work appear;
> Well! I am satisfied it should be so,
> Since, on maturer thought, the cause is clear;
> For in my looks what sorrow could'st thou see
> When I was Hayley's guest, and sat to thee?[7]

It is not necessary for readers to be acquainted with Cowper's long history of mental anguish, profound melancholia and religious doubt, for them to perceive the concern with what precisely *is* visible in the face as mediated by the artist, himself a melancholic. This concern was resolved by Cowper with characteristic sweetness and grace – this was, after all, a man who gardened with his pet hare – by a compliment to both his host, for whom he felt like a brother, and the artist. That Romney's portrait touched some raw nerves is clear from the correspondence of Cowper and his close associates. Even if sitting was a 'pennance' [sic], Cowper himself was positive up to a point: 'Romney has drawn me in crayons, and in the opinion of all here, with his best hand and with the most exact resemblance possible.'[8] But the poem, which took him longer than

---

[7] Cowper, *Works*, 419.
[8] King and Ryskamp, *Letters*, IV, 182, cf. 186–7, 200, 222–3, 225–6.

FIGURE 6.5. William Cowper, pastel, by George Romney, 1792,
57.2 cm × 47 cm, purchased by the National Portrait Gallery in 1905. It was engraved by
William Blake as the frontispiece to the first volume of Hayley's *Life ... of Cowper*.
© The National Portrait Gallery, London.

anticipated to compose, implies the portrait is 'not him'. Cowper avows
that he is unable to fully recognize himself in the portrait, despite its
resemblance. His cousin, Lady Hesketh, preferred a privately circulated
print by Bartolozzi based on the Lawrence drawing. In general she
feared for his reputation, and specifically the merest hint that he could
be deemed 'a Visionary! an Enthusiast! or a *Calvinist*!' (emphasis in

original).[9] A later commentator was quite blunt about what was visible in Romney's portrait: he saw its specialness residing in the shared madness of sitter and artist.[10] John Johnson found 'a world of character and Poetic fire in the Countenance'.[11] It is illuminating to compare Romney's fêted depiction of Cowper with his extraordinary unfinished self-portrait, which was bought by the National Portrait Gallery in 1894. It probably dates from 1784 and was also painted while the artist was staying with Hayley, to whom he gave it. This picture was in the house when Romney was working on Cowper.

The medium of Cowper's portrait – pastel on paper – was unusual for Romney and he was apparently exceptionally pleased with the result. He sent Cowper his portrait of William Hayley at the sitter's behest, an act which also provoked a poetic response, and tightened the visual dimensions of this friendship network – a network through which participants forged and reforged their identities. In the sonnet to Romney, the theme of capturing Cowper naturally comes up. It is possible to reflect on the agency of the artist, about his role as a visualizer of identity by giving some thought to the ways Cowper evokes Romney's artistry. It is not surprising that the verbs associated with Romney suggest both the physical acts of making the image and the importance of sight and light: to trace, to show, to pencil, to shine, to see. The verbs concerning Cowper are more static – to own, to know, to be satisfied. Cowper's idea that Romney 'shin(es) with superior grace' is particularly striking; indeed, he is presented in transcendent, possibly quasi-religious, terms. Yet there is another agent here – time, which Cowper was playing with in his letters about Abbott's image. In this respect, Cowper's sonnet for Romney picks up themes explored in an earlier and more famous poem – 'On the receipt of my mother's picture out of Norfolk. The gift of my cousin Ann Bodham', written early in 1790.[12] Since his beloved mother had died when he was just six, it is hardly surprising that being reunited with an image of someone so close to him whom he

[9] Catharine Bodham Johnson (ed.), *Letters of Lady Hesketh to the Rev. John Johnson, LLD* (London: Jarrold and Sons, 1901), 114.
[10] John Ingamells, *National Portrait Gallery Mid-Georgian portraits 1760–1790* (London: National Portrait Gallery, 2004), 128.
[11] Johnson, *Letters,* 19.   [12] Cowper, *Works,* 394–6.

adored and lost acted as a powerful trigger of memory and of reflections upon 'time'. Cowper insists on the verisimilitude of his mother's portrait, later engraved by Blake, and treats the picture as a relic, a substitution for her, by kissing it,[13] but in the poem he generalizes the point to the genre of portraiture, '(the art that can immortalize, / The art that baffles time's tyrannic claim / To quench it)'.[14]

Cowper may have been one of the most popular and admired poets of the late eighteenth century and the first half of the nineteenth, but these sentiments, if eloquently expressed, are unexceptional. Portraits are endowed with significance precisely because they seem to distil something special about a person – we might say, their identity – into a (potentially) permanent, visible form. The person who performs this feat is the artist. Anne Cowper's portrait is a 'mimic shew' [sic] that retains the power to soothe her anguished son.[15] I take the term 'mimic shew' literally: the portrait *simulates* his mother, and hence has peculiar power. In some contexts, then, 'likeness' means not a literal, empirical verisimilitude but the capacity to evoke the spirit and personal qualities of the sitter. In affirming the value of the portrait, Cowper is acknowledging and celebrating the capacity of the painter to come close to revivifying his mother, thereby defying 'time'.

My second literary example is the novelist and short-story writer Nathaniel Hawthorne (1804–64). Hawthorne was interested in portraiture throughout his life; his spare intense tales offer insights both rich and raw. I am thinking particularly of his short story *The Prophetic Pictures*, published in 1837, which describes a highly esteemed artist whose portraits are capable of exceptional psychological penetration: 'he catches the secret sentiments and passions, and throws them upon the canvass [sic] ... It is an awful gift.'[16] The unnamed painter produces portraits of Walter and Elinor, a couple about to be married, and discerns something not perceptible to others. Although he warns Elinor by letting her see a 'prophetic' sketch, she pays no heed and some time later is about to be stabbed by her husband when the artist intervenes to save

---

[13] King and Ryskamp, *Letters*, III, 349.   [14] Cowper, *Works*, 394.
[15] Ibid., 396.
[16] Nathaniel Hawthorne, *Tales and sketches* (New York: Literary Classics of the United States, Inc., 1996), 456.

her. There is, as commentators have noted, a Gothic dimension to the
story, which the theme of portraiture facilitates, but I want to point out
Hawthorne's attentiveness to key issues both in the artist's agency and in
the expectations of sitters and viewers.

Hawthorne's painter possesses three further attributes: he is deeply
learned and widely travelled; he is an outsider; he is like a magician. The
story is set up so that his agency is continually affirmed. For example, he
selects his sitters, not vice versa, and in doing so he does not follow but
ignores social hierarchies. Having created these 'splendid' portraits,
'reckoned ... among the most admirable specimens of modern
portraiture',[17] he offers a way out, and finally interposes himself physically between man and wife in order to save her life. Immediately before
he does so, 'A strange thought darted into his mind. Was not his own the
form in which that Destiny had embodied itself, and he a chief agent of
the coming evil which he had foreshadowed?'[18] His power is not only
presented to the reader by the author, but Hawthorne shows it to be
sensed by the artist himself. In a story less than thirteen pages long – a
sustained exploration of wonder, penetrating sight, power, pictorial skill,
awe, magic, intensity, possession, and prophecy – Hawthorne hints that
artistic wizardry has a hubristic side. And he plays, as Cowper did, with
the interchangeability between people and their pictures, that is, he
assumes that art can capture, even create, identity. Not any old art,
naturally, but exceptional art, where, in the case of portraiture, 'the
whole mind and character were brought out on the countenance, and
concentrated in a single look, so that ... the originals hardly resembled
themselves so strikingly as the portraits did'.[19] I am not suggesting that
we now deploy ideas such as magic and prophecy in discussing the
visualization of identity, only that we respect, and meditate upon, the
phenomena these archaic terms imply.

Hawthorne deploys polarities – mind and body, inside and outside, for
instance – that are familiar in studies of portraiture and identity. While
they possess their compelling aspects, they may be misleading in some
respects. For example, they tend to reinforce the idea that interiority has
been a leading theme within Western cultures, perhaps since the

[17] Ibid., 464.   [18] Ibid., 468.   [19] Ibid., 458.

Renaissance and certainly since the eighteenth century. Master narratives about the self reinforce it. Histories of portraiture often follow this account. The history of self-portraiture seemingly confirms it. But why should the idea of visualizing identity be so securely locked into these stories of selfhood and individualism when so much evidence tells us that identity has resided in kinship groups and friendship networks, in corporations, occupational associations and other institutions? Rather than burrowing into the soul, which is simply one trope, the visualization of identity radiates outward – as Hawthorne himself realized in another short story, *Edward Randolf's portrait*, first published in 1838, where he links an old dark image to the growing discontent with British rule over the thirteen colonies in the eighteenth century. The portrait, in other words, acts as a figure for a specific political style, which is coming under attack. This is an abstract proposition and should alert us to the possibility that portraiture is also about ideas, organizations and groups, including polities. Portraiture is about them because it can *embody* them.

It is possible to illustrate this point through the portraiture of an illustrious Cambridge alumnus, William Harvey (1578–1657), a subject to which Geoffrey Keynes, surgeon and scholar, made an important contribution.[20] Surviving and well-authenticated portraits from Harvey's era tend to be in short supply. Hence as Keynes, who was chairman of the Trustees of the National Portrait Gallery in London, pointed out, there was a strong desire to find portraits of such a heroic Englishman even if it meant suspending critical judgement in the process (Figure 6.6). Keynes' own scholarship on Harvey, whom he regarded as 'the greatest of British Physicians', was particularly attentive to issues of authenticity. The point to note is how many people and organizations laid claim to actually owning or desired to own an image of him. We might say that this has little to do with Harvey the man, and everything to do with the *idea* of Harvey as a great member and benefactor of the Royal College of Physicians in London, as a great mind especially in relation to comparative anatomy and physiological experimentation, as a Royalist, as one of the main medical figures who can be securely linked to

[20] Geoffrey Keynes, *The portraiture of William Harvey*, rev. edn (London: Keynes Press, British Medical Association, 1958).

FIGURE 6.6. Cover of Kenneth Franklin's book, published by MacGibbon & Kee, which uses the famous painting in the Royal College of Physicians, London.

the Scientific Revolution. There exist elaborate emotional, intellectual and institutional investments in Harvey for which his portraits stand. Sometimes, of course, literal investments were involved. Harvey portraits have become a focus for those groups and organizations who invest in him, and in the process they become symbols, relics, icons.

A well-authenticated portrait of the young Harvey now hangs in the National Portrait Gallery (Figure 6.7). The identity of the artist is not known with certainty, nor is the precise date of production, but the portrait possesses special significance by virtue of the fact that it is likely to have been executed around the time Harvey published *De Motu Cordis*, 1628, in which he announced his discovery of the circulation of the blood. The picture was exported illegally in 1961 and a case was brought against the dealer and the exporter. In early 1977, the portrait was returned to the United Kingdom after an impassioned campaign in which Geoffrey Keynes was active. A great deal of money was paid to the North American medical practitioner who had purchased it in good faith, yet I can find no evidence that, once he knew of the deception, he did anything at all to facilitate the portrait's release and return. Described as the most significant breach of the law in the eighteen years of the Reviewing Committee on the Export of Works of Art's existence, it became something of a *cause célèbre* in certain circles; a question was asked in Parliament in 1971, as we know from the papers in the National Portrait Gallery's Heinz Archive, which are extensive and revealing. They neatly show which groups had invested what in 'Harvey', and more particularly, how prominent a player the Royal College of Physicians was in the process, for example. There was considerable debate about who should acquire the portrait if and when it was returned. The Royal College of Physicans owns a simply magnificent collection of portraits, including the portrait of Harvey, by an unknown artist, that graced the cover of Franklin's book.[21] The College is not open to the public on a routine basis. Yet the decision for the picture to go to the National Portrait Gallery was not straightforward, as the archival evidence reveals. The simple image of a younger Harvey, originally one of a suite

[21] Kenneth J. Franklin, *William Harvey Englishman* (London: MacGibbon & Kee, 1961).

148

FIGURE 6.7. William Harvey, oil on canvas, attributed to Daniel Mytens, *c.* 1627, 72.4 cm × 61 cm, purchased by the National Portrait Gallery in 1976 with help from the Department of the History of Medicine, University of British Columbia, Jacob Zeitlin and Gonville and Caius College, Cambridge. © The National Portrait Gallery, London.

of family portraits, has been made to do an extraordinary amount of cultural work in being asked to represent a number of collective identities on behalf of highly interested parties.

Actually, there has been a continuous history since Harvey's time of valuing highly – even fetishizing – images of him. For example, the physician Richard Mead FRS, who was born in 1673 and hence did not know Harvey personally, had an intense feeling for medical history. Mead himself was portrayed many times, for example in about 1738 by Jonathan Richardson, who was also a connoisseur, collector and art writer. Mead's collections were stupendous and included portraits of those, living and dead, who were important to him. He owned a painting of Harvey by von Bemmel. It was used as the template for a print, issued by Thomas Birch, a close associate of Mead's and Secretary of the Royal Society, as part of his *Heads of Illustrious Persons of Great Britain*, published in collected form in 1743 and 1756 and juxtaposing biographies with the prints. Harvey was thereby yoked to a national history; the portraits in Birch's collection are mainly political and presented in chronological order. Harvey was also yoked to Mead, well known as a successful medical practitioner, a Newtonian, and a leading Fellow of the College of Physicians, since his name appeared on the print as the owner of the painted original. This was bought after Mead's death by another famous medical man and collector, William Hunter, whose hair was mentioned above. The print was used and modified by others as this rather crude version shows (Figure 6.8). The same painting was used as the basis for a bust of Harvey, which Mead commissioned from Peter Scheemakers to give to the College of Physicians, which had lost its Harvey statue in the Great Fire. It is currently set into the wall of the entrance hall of the magnificent building Denys Lasdun designed for the physicians in Regent's Park. Lasdun created a building in which portraits are unusually prominent. It might be said that Harvey represents the collective identity of physicians, not only through the bust but also through the painted portrait, relics and regular events that keep Harvey 'in mind'.

I have mentioned only a tiny selection of the ways in which the identity of 'William Harvey' remains alive in a number of forms, and have sketched in the central role that portraits play in keeping his identity or rather identities fresh in a number of contexts. But to say 'his' in this context is quite misleading: identity does not belong to him; it is not a species of private property; it is created through social interactions. Because of their visual qualities, and the languages associated with them, portraits make a central contribution to the task

FIGURE 6.8. William Harvey, line engraving, by unknown engraver, precise date of composition unknown, 1750s–1770s. © The National Portrait Gallery, London.

of keeping identities active – we might say 'in play' – a task in which audiences and viewers necessarily participate.

It is hardly surprising that in institutions with long continuous histories, organizational identities and those of its prominent members virtually merge – Newton and the Royal Society of London, for example – and that portraits are the place where they do so. I have experienced this phenomenon myself in a rather unexpected form. When I told people I was associated with Downing College, Cambridge, they would look at me knowingly and say, 'Ah, Leavis' college' (Figure 6.9). While Frank Raymond Leavis (1895–1978) had been an undergraduate at Emmanuel, he was associated with Downing from 1932 until he resigned his honorary fellowship in 1964. The previous statement is, of course, quite wrong! Leavis will be 'associated with' Downing for as long as people remember the link and for as long as his 1961 portrait by Peter Greenham hangs in a prominent position where members of the College and visitors are likely to see it (Figure 6.10). I was struck by it as soon as I saw it. How could I not be, with that open-necked shirt, wiry torso, and slightly defiant casualness? It is an extremely unusual portrait of an academic. The artist, Peter Greenham, already an admirer of his sitter, noted his 'magnificent face ... noble expression ... [and] small tense body'.[22] The link between Leavis and Downing is indeed profound. This is partly because the college was so intimately bound up with his teaching, which was deeply personal, although that is hardly an energetic enough way of expressing the point – it has been called charismatic. Michael Baxandall, the great art historian, was taught by Leavis and spoke about the impact Leavis' teaching had on him in terms of its 'moral' effect.[23] Feelings about Leavis still run deep: this example shows both how tentacular identity is, not least in its visual forms, and how a portrait functions as a material deposit of social relationships, to adapt Baxandall's phrase.[24]

---

[22] Ian MacKillop, *F. R. Leavis: A life in criticism* (London: Allen Lane, 1995), 6.
[23] Ibid., 9.
[24] *Painting and experience in fifteenth-century Italy*, rev. edn (Oxford University Press, 1988), 1.

FIGURE 6.9. Frank Raymond Leavis, charcoal, by Robert Sargent
Austin, 1934, 35 cm × 27.3 cm, bequeathed to the National Portrait Gallery
by the sitter's widow, Mrs Q. D. Leavis, 1981. © The National Portrait Gallery,
London.

Conclusion

I shall now take a step back and pay some attention to the two more
or less parallel paths I have followed so far. You have been reading
words off a page, which have, I hope, problematized the terms in
which visual identity in general and portraiture in particular are
imagined, experienced and discussed. At the same time, you have been

FIGURE 6.10. Frank Raymond Leavis, oil on canvas, by Peter Greenham, 1961, 90 cm × 69.5 cm. Courtesy of the Master and Fellows of Downing College, Cambridge.

looking at a succession of images, which bear a number of distinct relationships to those words. Sometimes the images are those discussed in the text. But at other times, for example when Oscar Wilde was mentioned, there was a photograph of him on the page. He was evoked in two modes simultaneously as if this were perfectly normal. And in many ways it is, but by convention rather than by meticulously considered argument.

The use of portraits as decorative items is common, that is, as a supplement of something else, generally a text. From a publisher's perspective, and also from a reader's, they offer some visual variety. Portraits might be understood to provide 'human interest' in a wide range of settings. They can be seen as tags, rather like an identity card, a quick and handy reminder of the person under discussion. Hence, in a certain restricted sense they serve, precisely, to visualize identity. I have argued, however, that in this sense 'identity' becomes a rather limited phenomenon, an aid to identification like an illustration in a naturalist's guide. Such uses of portraits efface the processes that went into their creation; they generally remain silent on medium and scale, and ignore their life histories. A reproduction of a portrait becomes a bit like a snapshot – of passing interest but not for lingering over. It is the job of writers of many different kinds to give back to portraits their life histories, to engage with their visual properties, and to offer coherent accounts of the processes by which they were made. Visualizing identity is active and complex, possibly one reason why in many societies the privilege of generating portraits is given over to specialized groups. Their skills, procedures and products should be scrutinized in the search for the meanings of 'identity', however defined. Yet this is not enough; vocabularies, ways of thinking, analytical tools, robust conceptual frameworks are also needed. Thus 'visualizing identity' is hardly the prerogative of a single constituency but something in which many, if not all, participate. The model for 'identity' is not the generation of a fingerprint but the yet messier process of making, reproducing, adapting, disseminating, viewing and conversing about portraits. The study of portraits has a great deal to offer those who seek to unravel identity, but only if our own habitual uses of them are thoughtfully interrogated.

FURTHER READING

Hayley, William, *The life and posthumous writings of William Cowper*, 3 vols. (London: J. Johnson, 1803).

Hayley, William, *The life of George Romney* (London: T. Payne, 1809).

Jordanova, Ludmilla, *Defining features: Scientific and medical portraits 1660–2000* (London: Reaktion Books and the National Portrait Gallery, 2000).

Jordanova, Ludmilla, 'Portraits, people and things: Richard Mead and medical identity', *History of Science*, **41** (2003), 293–313.

Kidson, Alex, *George Romney 1734–1802* (London: National Portrait Gallery, 2002).

Pointon, Marcia, *Hanging the head: Portraiture and social formation in eighteenth-century England* (New Haven and London: Yale University Press, 1993).

Reynolds, Joshua, *Discourses on art*, ed. Robert A. Wark (New Haven and London: Yale University Press, 1975).

Reynolds, Larry J. (ed.), *A historical guide to Nathaniel Hawthorne* (Oxford University Press, 2001).

Woodall, Joanna (ed.), *Portraiture: Facing the subject* (Manchester University Press, 1997).

FURTHER LOOKING

National Portrait Gallery, London: www.npg.org.uk.

Royal College of Physicians, London: www.rcplondon.ac.uk and go to Heritage Centre.

Royal College of Surgeons, London: www.rcseng.ac.uk/museums.

7 Musical identity

CHRISTOPHER HOGWOOD

'Music begins where words leave off,' Heine reminds us.[1] Many people would also consider that music, rather like the brain, still largely begins beyond the reach of science and technology. It is therefore a somewhat daunting honour to contribute to this series of essays, since I will surely be less scientific and my opinions more subjective – and in the end, I suspect (by the nature of the subject) less prescriptive – than most of the other approaches to identity in this volume. However, no formulae and few charts will be invoked, and only a minimum recourse to notation will be used in evidence. This would today seem a necessary precaution. The British Library, about to launch a nationwide tour of a newly acquired music manuscripts, recently discovered that 97 per cent of the British public cannot read music. Happily, although I am saddened to learn of such widespread illiteracy,[2] there is no defensible theory that the identity of a piece of music resides in its notation, nor, in fact, in any academic knowledge of its origins or context.

---

[1] A search for the exact source of this well-known quotation produces an immediate identity crisis: in English-speaking countries it is commonly attributed to Heine (without reference), but in Germany the credit goes to E. T. A. Hoffmann, mentioning his review of Beethoven's Fifth Symphony (*Allgemeine musikalische Zeitung*, 4 and 11 July, 1810). Richard Wagner appears to have quoted it in 'Ein deutscher Musiker in Paris' (1840/41): '*Es bleibt ein – für allemal wahr: da wo die menschliche Sprache aufhört, fängt die Musik an*', and dangerously similar sentiments have been located in the writings of Hans Christian Andersen, Thomas Carlyle and Gustav Mahler. Current status: origin unproven.

[2] This applies, of course, only to the *reading* of music; we must remember that a considerable proportion of the audience that first heard Sophocles (or, for that matter, Shakespeare) in the theatre would not have been able to read the text.

Identity, edited by Giselle Walker and Elisabeth Leedham-Green. Published by Cambridge University Press. © Darwin College 2010.

There is, it seems, a certain pleasure to knowing music without knowing a thing about it: Charles Rosen, after a lecture on romantic piano music, asked his audience for questions; a lady who had followed the whole discourse of tonality and form, poetic influence, *Sturm und Drang* and so forth, raised her hand and admitted that one detail still puzzled her: 'What *are* Brahms?'

Should such a lack of factual knowledge blunt our instinctive response to a work of art? And if so, why is our first need so often a hunger for biographical rather than, say, analytical detail? Why do a composer's love-affairs always win out over questions of sonata exposition, and misdemeanours always upstage harmonic progressions? We will come later to the way we create our own context for musical experience, but for the moment I shall start from a 'What are Brahms?' stance, with a couple of definitions of identity.[3]

Definition 1: The collective aspect of the set of characteristics by which a thing is definitively recognizable or known. This clearly means the establishment of 'uniqueness', the 'true essence' and, we hope, the indubitable means of distinguishing this item from any other. But, as all classicists will quickly point out (my start in Cambridge, I must confess, was as a classicist), the root of the word, the Latin *idem*, 'the same', leads us to:

Definition 2: The quality or condition of being the same as something else. This appears to contradict the 'uniqueness' demanded by Definition 1, and proposes a process of noting similarities as a means of including something in a larger group – leading possibly to a formula for repetition, reproduction and eventually (horror!) mass-production. In the arts this has encouraged a grouping of works into schools and periods, with prizes then awarded to the best in each class like a flower or dog show. And, inevitably, a view of history is generated that produces the Top Ten – Most Famous Englishman and Most Important Medical Discovery were two recent categories – but also Best Symphonist, Greatest Fugue, World's Favourite Song, Fastest Trill, Loudest Tenor, etc.

This I would term 'The Danger of Looking Only at Mountain Tops', and it is not limited to music. A training in classics inclines one to think

---

[3] These come from the *American heritage dictionary* (Boston: Houghton Mifflin Company, 2000); no two dictionaries agree on a wording.

of all art in terms of the 'classics' it contains, and a similarly graded approach has been adopted by each of the fine arts. In music, by concentrating on a select diet of 'nothing but the best' we therefore never come across the repertoire that provides the bridges between the famous names that are so often needed for proper understanding of context. The CD-age, although opening some unexpected doors, has dangerously homed in on the 'great men' theory (a pernicious methodology much promoted by Friedrich Rochlitz in the 1820s). Simply because the unique concentration of great composers in the period we have dubbed 'classical' can never be repeated,[4] there is an understandable tendency for musical scholarship to consider only the peaks – 'the classics' rather than 'the classical period' – inevitably distorting the broader musical landscape. Carl Dahlhaus pointed out that 'we involuntarily hesitate to classify Pleyel, Koželuch and Gyrowetz alongside Haydn and Mozart as Viennese Classic composers, even though they were active at the same time'; yet of those names the most 'popular' composer in Vienna at the end of the eighteenth century was actually not Mozart or Haydn, but Leopold Koželuch. When did you last see or hear *his* music? It is important to ask how we can be expected to recognize and prize the special if we are never given a chance to hear the ordinary; thoughts of musical identity have to be equally applicable to (and derived from) the work of the lesser masters, the lower slopes and indeed even the valleys of music.

But when an actual work is named, what is it that we mentally grasp to 'represent' the piece? At the words 'Eroica', or 'Yesterday' or 'Dies Irae', a paradigm of a piece forms in our mind, but a paradigm with a halo.[5] Lutoslawski once pointed out that a piece of music exists on a number of different levels: as a live, real-time experience; as something which can be remembered in real time; and as an essence, which can be recalled in an instant. The first of these is a once-only event, since every succeeding listening contains a remembering, and is building on our first experience to create an ever-growing composite of repeated hearings. The third

---

[4] For statistical proof see Stephen Jay Gould, *Life's grandeur* (London: Jonathan Cape, 1996), 77ff.

[5] The American conductor Robert Spano recently surprised us with the statement that 'There's no such thing as Beethoven's Seventh. It's only a hypothesis' (*The New Yorker*, 21 August 2006).

form, the essence, will rarely relate to any one specific performance, but it will certainly come complete with a halo of uninvited and often unconscious associations, an aura of special 'identities'.

One very common component of the aura is the apparent need to have a biographical connection with the person behind the art (hence so many popular extravaganzas on the lines of *The agony and the ecstasy,* and so many *Amadeus* myths). When the facts are scanty (as, for instance, with Handel, who left very little evidence of his private life), we invent and embellish them. When there are no real facts (as with Okeghem or Giles Farnaby, or Skalkottas – and certainly the prolific Anon.) or when there is general ignorance of any evidence, it is hard for people to spot a fake, but also hard for them to engage with the art. Hildegard von Bingen is a created musical character, providing what the late twentieth century wanted to find in a twelfth-century musical saint, and I suspect none of us would be able to identify the alien bits if Christopher Page or Emma Kirkby inserted a few notes of their own into the transcriptions and performances. How can we be sure we are not dealing with the musical equivalent of Sir Arthur Evans' 'recreation' of Knossos?

The musical canon offers us no guidance of what is proper for the true believer and what is out of bounds. We lack an *Apocrypha* or *Index librorum prohibitorum* and so we are left to make our own judgements and refine our idea of a particular musical identity by a curious process of selection and categorization. Alfred Einstein pointed to several works which were accepted until recently as being by Mozart: 'the unity of style that prevailed in the galant period is so striking that until the work of discovery by Wyzewa and Saint-Foix, it was possible to recognize four concertos (K. 37, 39, 40, 41) as genuine Mozart'.[6] In fact, they are all simply arrangements by Mozart of published keyboard sonatas by Eckard, Honauer, Raupach and Schobert, plus one movement by C. P. E. Bach.

[6] *Mozart: His character, his work*, tr. A. Mendel and N. Broder (New York: Oxford University Press, 1945), 291.

We adopt certain facets of music as 'indicators' and ignore others; a musical idea shorn of its rhythmic nature, for instance, may rarely be recognized by its harmonies alone. For example, these two chord progressions might not summon up a piece to your mind:

But if I linger on them and dress them up in a specific rhythmic figuration, they are instantly recognizable to the ear as the first prelude of Bach's *48*:

Such an arpeggiated prelude was often left to the performer's extempore instinct in the eighteenth century; in other hands it might have also been delivered as:

Would that have changed its identity? Or, if its identity resides in that particular arpeggiation, will the same figuration work in slightly different harmonic country?

Only a triplet figuration renders this sequence of harmonies familiar – but with quite a different identity: Beethoven's 'Moonlight' Sonata. Without the Bach model there would surely have been no 'Moonlight' Sonata; but take its added melody separately from the atmospheric accompaniment and you find something very basic:[7]

Going back to the first prelude of Bach's *48*, we also have to contend with variants. Unless the edition on your piano at home is rather recent, the chances are that you will be playing one bar more than Bach wrote. C. F. G. Schwencke (a pupil of Bach's son, Carl Philipp Emanuel) made one of the first editions of *Das wohltemperierte Klavier* (Bonn, 1801), adding an extra bar to this prelude to sweeten what he thought was a 'difficult' or, some would say, illegal sequence of harmonies:

---

[7] The anecdotal connection between the 'Moonlight' Sonata and John Lennon's 'Because' has been shown by Tim Crawford's computer-analysis to involve the final movement of the sonata, not the 'quasi una fantasia' opening; see 'After the search is over . . . the work begins', http://drops.dagstuhl.de/opus/volltexte/2006/747. He also mentions the known indebtedness of Chopin's Étude op. 10, no. 1 to Bach's first prelude.

This survived for more than a century and a half, accepted as Bach (check your edition and if you have thirty-seven bars, cut out bar twenty-three). But by the strictest definition of musical identity, this extended prelude is a new piece. Nelson Goodman – famously the inventor of the theoretical colour 'grue' – claimed that a single wrong or changed note in a performance rendered it a different piece (the logical chain is that by repeating this process an indefinite number of times a Beethoven symphony could become 'Three blind mice').[8] In terms of plagiarism (to which we will turn later) this 'would entitle the note-changer to present the result under his own name as a new artwork'.[9] Even the lawyers agree that this is 'too extreme for practical legal purposes',[10] and certainly under such a rule a great many imperfect musical performances and home renditions would qualify as premieres.

But into what category should we then place Gounod's *Ave Maria*? In its vocal form he called it *Mélodie religieuse adaptée au 1er prélude de J. S. Bach*, although it had first been issued as an instrumental piece for violin or cello (plus organ and an optional second cello) with the title *Méditation*. We may categorize this as a Gounod song, but because of its dependency on Bach (including Schwencke's extra bar) it registers as 'less original' than many of his other vocal works. And has the 'identity' of the underlying Bach prelude changed, or simply been veneered? Is this change structural or simply cosmetic? Does it have the honourable status of collage or the disgrace of lamination?

Finally, to illustrate how it is possible for the halo to subsume the piece, I should mention one particular recording of that *Ave Maria* which is valued not for the composers' contributions at all, but for the evidence it gives us of a lost vocal world – the art of the castrato singer. Alessandro Moreschi, born 1858, recorded the Gounod in 1913, and the identity of this artefact is now as a piece of archaeological evidence in the museum of performance studies rather than a musical work per se.

---

[8] Nelson Goodman, *Languages of art*, 2nd edn (Indianapolis: Hackett, 1976), 186–7.

[9] Aaron Keyt, 'An improved framework for music plagiarism litigation', *California Law Review*, 76(2) (March 1988), 435–6.

[10] Ibid., 436.

[Here a recording of *Ave Maria* made by Alessandro Moreschi in 1913 was played: Pearl 9823.]

The identity or essence of the original Bach we can hear is not the melody (there is none), nor the rhythm (it can be adapted), nor the drama or programme (there are no tempo, dynamic or expressive markings of any sort). It must be solely the harmonic progression. So can this be treated as exclusive? Remember the recent court case when the former keyboard player of Procul Harum, Matthew Fisher, sued for rights on the chord sequence of the 1967 hit 'A whiter shade of pale'. Many people asked, was it not derived from a sequence of harmonies taken from Bach's *Air on the G string*, or a half-remembered extract from the cantata *Wachet auf*?[11]

Personality

Are we really interested in the 'identity' of music per se or is it a human identity behind the piece that we are looking for? Many music-lovers feel the need for biographical bolstering before they are comfortable with a musical work; they need Bach and his twenty-two children, his religion and his wig, or Beethoven and his deafness and his temper, or fictions of Mozart's silliness or Rossini's appetite – some element of the irrational and personal to balance the unacceptable impersonality of academic analyses. (Such mental pictures may be more important to many of us than we imagine; can you easily picture Beethoven *with* a wig? Or Bach *without*? Or Schubert *without* glasses, but Mozart *with*?)

Musicians tend to be as attached to 'their' picture of a composer as they are possessive in their attitude to music – the familiar critic's category of 'Brendel's Mozart' quickly becomes the personal 'my Mozart', etc. – no doubt as a means of asserting the necessity of their input. And most people, even non-performers, cherish moments in their favourite pieces which need to be turned as they would do it or at least as they have

---

[11] Buddy Holly and the Teddy Bears' hit 'To know him is to love him' was also quoted in court as a source, although the connection was not convincingly demonstrated.

grown up to expect it to be done to make a performance acceptable. Sometimes an outside ritual may take over from the actual music, the peripheral displacing the integral, like the traditional encores in Gilbert and Sullivan without which many supporters are scandalized. Some very regular concert attendees in America refused to come to *Messiah* when I performed it because I discouraged the audience from the anachronistic nineteenth-century tradition of standing during the Hallelujah Chorus; the disruption of a ritual was to them more upsetting than missing the complete musical work.

So in differing contexts, that one Bach prelude could be represented by:

- the manuscript,
- the print,
- the first individual performance we each heard (remembering one can never step into the same river twice),
- the amalgamation of several remembered performances,
- a favourite CD (a repetition of identical performances),
- an imaginary performance (Tomas Blod,[12] a notorious invention of the 1960s, performed well-known piano solos with full gestures on the 'pianoforte dolce' – a soundless instrument),
- the 'instant recall' (Lutoslawski's 'essence'),
- an arrangement (not necessarily as remote as the Gounod),
- the historical remnant,
- the surrounding myth.

It is, I feel, worth mentioning the arrangement as a valid aspect of identity. Today we regard the CD recording as 'the piece' but not the piano duet; our grandparents would have thought the opposite. Music is simply the construct of emotive sounds and symbols that we refit to suit an acquired set of standards and expectations. So the satisfaction of our personal needs is involved in the creation of an acceptable performance manner or style: for some the piano duet version gave the necessary personal connection; more recently the Historically Informed Performance movement, beginning as a minority cult, led to commercial exploitation because it was different, and satisfied fashionable appetites

---

[12] Impersonated by Gabor Cossa, a well-known dancer and Cambridge antique dealer, in a Wigmore Hall recital organized by Jonathan Routh.

for renditions that were fresh, pure and (falsely) 'as the composer heard it'. (In fact there is no such thing as HIP performance, merely HIP preparation.)

These revisionist calls for freshness show that the general public now realizes that identity is not the same thing as familiarity. Familiarity can easily blur precise and authentic identity, and in fact can almost remove the first of the stages of meeting a piece that Lutoslawski identified. Just as you can never see Venice or the Pyramids for the first time because the images have always been with us, so you can never hear Mozart's G minor symphony K550 for the first time, since it has seeped into our consciousness via innumerable arrangements and advertising jingles, its identity stolen by ring-tones and signature tunes. Will Chopin's 'Minute' Waltz ever be able to clear its image of the radio quiz-show *Just a Minute* and the superimposed voice of Nicholas Parsons?

We certainly don't require a complete work to experience either a response to the familiar or a sense of identity. One phrase, even four notes of a popular melody ('Summertime', 'Lara's theme' from *Dr Zhivago*, 'Somewhere over the rainbow') is all the DNA we need. In some cases we may not even know the remainder of the sample – who, after all, can hum the continuation of *The Archers'* signature tune once its first section has faded? Here identity is simply our recognition of the amount of incipit the indexer needs to catalogue the piece, or the judge to condemn plagiarism.

Interpretation

Interpretation is not the piece, although the word calls up immediately that ambiguous term 'style', which can be either the manner of writing or the manner of performing. In extreme cases (jazz, for example, or highly embellished baroque arias) the performing style can virtually conceal the original structure – like the obligatory ivy shrouding the Gothic tower. Often our ability to appreciate, even recognize, music is affected by how it is performed, as we have seen with the Bach prelude and the 'Moonlight' Sonata.

Dolly Parton famously demonstrated in a plagiarism case how 'you can make things sound like other things': by singing the Ray Charles song 'I can't stop loving you' in the same style as '9 to 5' (the song of hers at issue) she created, at least to the judge's satisfaction, a different piece. But an 'authentic' style of performance might therefore also have the same effect. The concept of 'authentic' style is as modern as any other performance fad, but it prided itself on making the music sound different; the difference, however, was *revealing*, not changing, its identity, implying that it had been masquerading in camouflage before.

Recreative performance (or should that be 'creative'?)

There has always been a debate as to whether the practical consider-ations of musical performance should have a bearing on our idea of a work's identity: an incorporeal abstract was preferred by many commen-tators, feeling it was better to learn from the score than from the concert hall. In the kitchen, of course, such niceties have never been considered: theoretical cooking is as unthinkable as theoretical football or motor racing – the performance is what decides it.

'Cooking is the transformation of uncertainty (recipe) into certainty (the dish) via fuss,' according to Julian Barnes.[13] But the Earl of Chester-field expressed a view common to the eighteenth-century upper class when his son was considering learning to play the violin (certainly *not* a gentleman's occupation): 'By all means eat meat, but don't be your own butcher.' You can avoid the fuss by having others do it, although this, on investigation, can seem a rather wasteful process: the gathering of players, soloists, conductor, music, organizing the venue, the music stands, the chairs – all this in order to present a performance of what is, for many people, simply a repeat of a work for which they already possess a firm imprint in their mind's ear.

What we as a general public are lacking is 'listening practice' as opposed to 'performing practice', something equally powerful for shaping our ideas of identity, to help distinguish the interpretation that is being offered.[14] For example, if one simply assessed a Corelli violin sonata from the notated page, it would be a very skeletal version of the

---

[13]   Julian Barnes, *The pedant in the kitchen* (London: Atlantic, 2003), 94.
[14]   See the November 1997 issue of *Early Music*, 591ff, devoted to 'Listening practice'.

embellished performance he is known to have expected. Indeed, to the listener the piece authentically decorated could well be unrecognizable, and we have a conundrum (often uncomfortable for literal-minded modern musicians) where neither the conception nor the realization are truly represented by the notation:

What we are aware of here is the performance and the performer rather than the piece, just as we experience when listening to much jazz. Should identity imply the possibility of repeatability? If so, then not only does jazz lose out, but so does a truly improvised Mozart cadenza or a freely decorated baroque aria.

At the opposite end of the doctrinal spectrum, in the colourful fields of 'less than authentic' performance, does a change of sonority and style (Jacques Loussier's Bach, for example) change the identity? A saxophone playing eighteenth-century music carries – whether we like it or not – alternative connotations of a different century and certainly a smokier atmosphere which may well override the original expectations. Such transfers of medium may be cosmetic (the MJQ and the Swingle Singers varying *Dido's lament*), or they may involve more substantial shifts – a change from voices to instruments, as in Peter Lichtenthal's fine arrangement of the Mozart *Requiem* for string quartet, or the additional (and unforgettable) pictorial associations offered by Walt Disney in *Fantasia*.

In the case of a small historical shift, such as harpsichord music transferred to the piano, the usual argument is that it thereby becomes more immediate, modern and 'relevant'. One wonders whether the use of an original eighteenth-century sonority is widely construed as a drawback in modern times, rather like an enthusiasm for eighteenth-century plumbing. Certainly the medium can be misplaced: a clavichord in a cathedral is as ineffectual as a deodorizer in a pig farm.

In addition to 'authentic' or 'inauthentic', there is, in theory, a third category of an 'absence of interpretation', which some would say gives a stronger identity to the music per se: plainchant and Palestrina would be immediate candidates, but the marching band and other ceremonial music should be there, and even Stravinsky with his disavowal of performer interference could be included.

Notation, although an inconvenient hurdle for late entry to music (there will hardly be a composing Grandma Moses), is neither prescriptive (*pace* Stravinsky) nor compulsory. Notation, as we mentioned at the outset, is not the piece, and in fact in many performances a larger number of musical signs set down by the composer are ignored or contradicted than are audibly implemented. Almost no musical work for orchestra is played today with the bowings of the composer (even when the composer was a violinist, such as Mozart). The same goes for dynamics, articulation and, in vocal music, language; no pianist ever plays with Chopin's pedalling for the simple reason that it has not been thought worth indicating in any modern edition.

On the other hand, the expected opportunities for *ad libitum* improvisation in earlier music are usually left unfilled (often following a misguided notion of 'purity'). Mozart's *ad libitum* fermatas, implying a short extemporized link, are overlooked as often as Corelli's embellishments are notable by their absence. In fact, in most performances of baroque and classical music the only element *not* adapted, the written note-heads, is the one element that the composer *had* expected to be altered in performance.

Not only the immediate flow of the music but also the overall architecture can be affected by such ignorance or omission: the most frequently forgotten musical sign in modern performance is the repeat mark. In a minuet and trio to ignore the *da capo* minuet repeats gives the effect of a triptych with one of the three panels presented in postcard format; and to remove the repeats in a sonata movement can often reduce the scale of the piece by fifty per cent. No other art (and certainly no business other than the *Readers' Digest* company) would countenance such shrinkage.

All these criteria, together with other personal accumulated ideas, create the halo and colour the identity of most composed music. It is hard to identify some musical 'item' which simply has essence, but one suggestion might be:

This very slight musical piece, although complete with beginning, middle and end, suffers from being small and therefore unnamed (like the @ sign in e-mail addresses); it has no title, number, author, no progeny, no specific scoring. I am not even sure whether it is published, since it cannot be looked up. It is about as abstract a complete musical specimen as you could find, and yet it is known to almost everyone and carries a very specific meaning (dismissive finality). There is very little difference between its essence and a complete mental performance in real time. We can't add a picture of a composer to the image – though there is a textual point for the academics to worry over (is the fourth note A flat or A natural?)[15] It probably originated as part of another work (a music-hall

---

[15] An audience survey decided that the flattened sixth was most usual, although the major sixth was also admitted.

song? A Tom and Jerry sequence?), but we must not assume it is by Anon. Take warning from Stravinsky and the organ-grinder tune he quoted in *Petrushka* under the impression that it was 'traditional': in a hotel in Tunbridge Wells I once met the amiable old gentleman who had later come forward as the composer of that number, and lived happily on royalties ever after. Even 'Happy birthday to you', said to be the most well-known melody in the world, was written in 1893 as a school song, 'Good morning to you'; the copyright first rested with the Hill sisters, who had devised both the words and the music, and since 1998 has been in the possession of Time Warner, who receive about $2 million a year from its use. As we will examine later, royalties need to be paid if an extract is long enough to be legally identifiable.

Identity does not always lead to identification

What about listeners with 'face blindness' – never recognizing the composer but hearing the notes – the 'What are Brahms?' syndrome? I was taught that Haydn and Mozart are indistinguishable. Many people unversed in a specific culture would say the same about Gregorian plainchant or bluegrass singing or Indonesian gamelan music or Italian *secco* recitative. There will always be variables in performance – we are trained to be alert to some and to ignore others; if we were the product of a different musical culture we would, for instance, register the slightest variation in pitch not as simply playing a little out of tune, but as a deliberate microtonal variant, and presumably construe it as a different piece.

Sometimes recognition will involve what scientists would call a 'lock and key' principle; you need extra information to turn the key in the problem, but after that it is open. Just as understanding the gesture of a tennis service relies on having seen a tennis match, Tesco's 'You shop, we drop' as a slogan needs prior knowledge of the phrase 'shop till you drop' as a recognition test before the humour is apparent. This 'prior recognition' factor, interpreted in strictly musical, usually melodic, terms is the basis of most 'music appreciation' courses.

The vital key may well be a non-musical fact. Musical codes may involve musical alphabetization (signatures based on the names of notes, like BACH, DSCH, etc.), or familiarity with the well-worn contrapuntal tags that give us such timeless themes as the opening of the 'Jupiter' finale. The *Dies irae* chant was once known to all Catholic churchgoers and would have been recognized when quoted by Rachmaninoff. The way in which recusant virginalists popped concealed quotations from Marian ballad tunes into their works was only an undercover version of Wagner's overt use of leitmotivs. Hollywood has now much broadened the range of meanings that can be ignited purely by association – harp glissandi heard in the cinema today easily translate into 'memories of childhood' – or maybe 'medication taking hold' – and the trombone chromatics that warn 'Dracula round the corner' are perhaps a distant relative of the horn fanfares in Bach's first *Brandenburg Concerto*, automatically recognized by its original audience as announcing the morning reveille.

Classification

I have presented a mixed bundle of factors that might affect or paralyse our natural ability to say that we can 'know' a piece of music. So does cataloguing help define identity? Are we assisted by an overview of the whole corpus towards appreciating and defining the individual work? After all, we pass wide-ranging opinions on Sophocles, despite only knowing seven of his 120 dramas. Is there a value in seeing the part in the whole? The Linnaean system of plant and animal classification (see Chapter 3) was the model adopted by Ludwig Ritter von Köchel, a botanist by training, as the basis of his approach to cataloguing Mozart (and the drawbacks to trying to list the works chronologically have haunted us ever since). The new edition of the Köchel catalogue promises to omit from the *Anhang* many of the details of spurious works and arrangements which were, until recently, thought to be *bona fide* Mozart. Although they are now disproved, they nevertheless constitute the reception history of Mozart's music and explain the image of him that we have inherited from the past two centuries. It is still important to establish what people *once* thought they knew, rather than exclusively admitting only what we think we know now; what was *once* understood as Mozart has contributed to the picture we have inherited of Mozart (via Eberl, Müller and a host of fine artists held in suspension in the *Anhang* of the Köchel catalogue).

We have disposed of the classicists' way of looking at music (mountain tops only), the purists' attitudes to both performing and cataloguing and outlined some of the processes in which we all connive when 'enjoying' music. We are more aware of the context that creates the halo and colours identity, whether or not we are conscious of it in practice. But for a more rigorous scrutiny we should momentarily relinquish the position of the conventional music-lover and adopt some other points of view.

The scientific viewpoint

Scientists seek to find universal laws or universally applicable methodology that will produce repeatable results. Many music analysts hanker after similarly basic laws, applicable to all music, that will pin down a work's identity once and for all.

Early systems of teaching composition propounded the use of *modelli*:[16] observing existing pieces and varying units from them by means of pre-defined formulae (the type of subversion later used by Satie in his *Sonatine bureaucratique*, a spoof of the popular beginner's Sonatina Op. 36 no. 1 by Muzio Clementi) – in fact an early manual application of the principles used by computer-generated music systems.

More reductive forms of musical analysis are practised nowadays (the system of Heinrich Schenker is particularly capacious) searching for a hierarchy of notes, gradually relegating more and more of them to being 'ornamental' until only a short pitch-structure remains; this may claim to be the DNA of the piece, but even if it identifies a piece to fellow analysts, it is no help at all to performers or listeners. It is like presenting you with a printout of a friend's DNA sequence, from which you don't recognize him at all, whereas the expression of that sequence as dark hair, brown eyes and a crooked nose produces instant recognition. You need only resort to DNA analysis when you don't have the whole person.

---

[16] Exemplified in A. F. C. Kollmann's *An essay on practical musical composition, according to the nature of that science and the principles of the greatest musical authors* (London: printed for the author, 1799).

Such analytical systems appear to have two ambitions, one open and one more covert. The first is the straightforward search for a code in the construction of the music (similar to the numerology and use of harmonic proportion found in Bach, Bartók, Liszt, Debussy, Haydn); very useful if, for instance, you are completing an unfinished piece – Süssmayr would have done better had he been aware that Mozart was employing a 'leitmotiv' in the unfinished Requiem.

Practitioners of computer-generated music have a more worrying agenda: intrusion into the subconscious of the author, and even into the very nature of 'inspiration' itself. The idea of composing by a mechanical device isn't new. Mozart's Musical Dice Game (or the game traditionally ascribed to him, or Haydn, or Dittersdorf, or . . .) used the roll of dice to select individual bars of prepared music which could stand together in many combinations, in fact employing the same algorithms as computers do now. But a computer cannot be 'inspired', it can merely 'manipulate' material it has been fed. Like us, the computer has been given only the very best musical diet; like us, it has remembered some very typical germ themes and been programmed to digest, separate, recombine and excrete them. Such manipulation, of course, is what computers and 'composing programmes' can readily undertake and there are now computer-generated scores (for performance by humans) in the style of Mozart, Bach, even Schoenberg (it is not necessarily easier to imitate Schoenberg than Palestrina by computer). We can be offered Mozart's 42nd symphony or a new Brandenburg Concerto or even enterprising genetic modifications, such as Bach crossed with the Spice Girls.[17]

[There followed three examples drawn from the work of David Cope, 'in the style of' Bach, Mozart and Mendelssohn.][18]

One must distinguish between computer-music and computer-performance; the human element makes a big difference, and normalizes many gaucheries; but what is often missing in the composition is both a 'sense of etiquette' and also the sudden breach of etiquette, an

[17] See the work of Charles Fox: charles.fox@cantab.net and www.robots.ox.ac.uk/~charles, especially his <crossbreed mp3> as an example of genetic hierarchical music structures.
[18] *Virtual music: Computer synthesis of musical style* (Cambridge, MA, and London: MIT Press, 2001).

unexpected cross-fertilization which only the living composer is able to initiate. If the available information is taken exclusively from within the designated category (the new 'Brandenburg Concerto' derives its formulae purely from the six Brandenburg Concertos), then you will never have the opening up of foreign possibilities, as when Mozart injects a moment of operatic inspiration into a keyboard sonata, or a patch of church counterpoint into a string quartet.

Two earlier systems employed before the advent of artificial intelligence to mine for musical identity need a mention here, since both are allied to the science of linguistics. Deryck Cooke in *The language of music*[19] posited the most convincing argument on paper for particular melodic and harmonic turns having a timeless validity in Western music: certain combinations of notes, he claimed, are supra-inspirational and used (consciously or unconsciously) by composers of different periods to represent the same emotive message. The best system of analysis accomplished solely by ear, without the aid of paper, was presented for the BBC between 1959 and 1979 by Hans Keller under the title of 'Functional Analysis'. It consists of a self-explanatory sequence of musical variants without verbal commentary to show the development of a composer's thought – the equivalent of the 'direct method' of learning a language, and remarkably useful to the performer, since the argument is entirely presented *by means of* performance.[20]

The legal viewpoint

The questions already raised about plagiarism and originality in musical identity can perhaps best be surveyed from our second standpoint. Here a strong test case is that of Handel. Sir Uvedale Price, a staunch eighteenth-century Handelian (but best remembered for his theories on landscaping and the sublime) described the problem:

> If ever there was a truly great and original genius in any art, Handel was that genius in music; and yet, what may seem no slight paradox, there never was

[19] Deryck Cooke, *The language of music* (London: Oxford University Press, 1959).
[20] See Hans Keller, *Music and psychology: from Vienna to London (1939–1952)*, ed. Christopher Wintle (London: Plumbago Books, 2003), and Hans Keller, *Functional analysis: the unity of contrasting themes: complete edition of the analytical scores*, ed. Gerold W. Gruber (Frankfurt am Main and New York: Lang, 2001).

a greater plagiary. He seized, without scruple or concealment, whatever suited his purpose. But as those sweets which the bee steals from a thousand flowers, by passing through its little laboratory, are converted into a substance peculiar to itself, and which no other art can effect, – so, whatever Handel stole, by passing through the powerful laboratory of his mind, and mixing with his ideas, became as much his own as if he had been the inventor. Like the bee, too, by his manner of working, he often gave to what was unnoticed in its original situation, something of high and exquisite flavour.[21]

Many unsuspecting listeners today are disturbed to find that much of their favourite Handel repertoire – music ranging from the so-called 'Largo', to 'I know that my Redeemer liveth', through *The arrival of the Queen of Sheba* and even the opening of the *Hallelujah Chorus* – is, to some degree, indebted to other composers for its germ material. The commonly held English view in Handel's own century was expressed by Charles Burney at the time of the 1784 Handel Commemoration:

All that the greatest and boldest musical inventor *can* do, is to avail himself of the best effusions, combinations, and effects, of his predecessors: to arrange and apply them in a new manner; and to add his own source, whatever he can draw, that is grand, graceful, gay, pathetic, or, in any other way, pleasing.

The analogy of the bee was widely adopted, together with William Boyce's charming proof of greatness: 'He takes other people's pebbles and polishes them into diamonds.' But in the nineteenth-century critics became more censorious – a reflection of the prevailing moral code rather than any greater insight into Handel – and 'borrowing' was assumed to be freighted with guilt.

From the start, 'borrowing' (*Entlehnung*) was probably the wrong word, being strongly loaded with moral and legal resonance. We must distinguish between a full, recognizable 'theme' and a commonplace 'motive' or trivial 'motto'; then there is the distinction between outside borrowings and self-borrowings; we must allow for subconscious memory, after long experience playing other people's music that shared a common language; there could be open borrowing in the spirit of competition; and finally there is the

[21] Uvedale Price, 'Essay on decorations', in *An essay on the picturesque, as compared with the sublime and the beautiful, . . .* (Hereford: printed by D. Walker for J. Robson London, 1796), vol. II.

obligation that the eighteenth century laid on the greater artist to improve on the lesser, well expressed by Handel's contemporary, John Byrom:

> Crime in a Poet, Sirs, to steal a Thought?
> No, that 'tis not; if it be good for aught:
> 'tis lawful Theft; 'tis laudable to boot;
> 'tis want of Genius if he does not do't:
> The fool admires – the Man of Sense alone
> Lights on a Happy Thought – and Makes it all his own.[22]

The identification of a musical theme is nowadays done primarily by its melody; judges recognize only tunes, catalogues are thematically searchable by a sequence of pitches, rather than harmonies or rhythms. But even here it is impossible legally to protect the very small (a single interval) or the very large (a complete tonal scheme). Definitions of illicit copying vary (it used to be conventionally defined as 'more than six consecutive notes borrowed') although, as we shall see, this has had to be relaxed in times of 'sampling'; a leading music litigation lawyer provided ample reasoning for why melody wins,[23] but then undermined the whole theory by himself composing a variant on the melodic notes of Scott Joplin's 'The entertainer', which he nicely titled 'The plagiarist'. Few analysts would be able to spot the similarity:

'The plagiarist'

'The entertainer'

---

[22] John Byrom, *Miscellaneous poems* (Manchester: J. Harrop, 1773), I, 133.
[23] Keyt, 'An improved framework', 421–64.

With such evidence devised by a lawyer, one has to question (as Uvedale Price did) whether the melodic raw material represents the sacred inspiration, the 'true identity', or whether it is the manner of working out. Currently the law is inclining towards a 'licence to borrow'; borrowing per se is held not to be theft since, although the material is duplicated elsewhere, the original remains complete, if not untouched. But, as the defence is quick to point out, the potential to exploit your original has been harmed. Previous attempts to legislate for such deterioration were graded according to the size of the portion stolen measured against the original whole: that is to say, to take an extract from a four-hour opera and make a four-minute pop song is allowable, but to take a four-minute song and weld it into your four-hour opera is not.[24]

This has led to a distinguishing between 'idea' and 'expression' (a not very satisfactory term for the working-out process) – what the eighteenth century would better have called the 'mood' and the 'plan' – and now the preferred policy, largely provoked by strategies in film and theatre music and the more recent rise of 'sampling', is one of 'apportionment of profits'. In future the charge would be in inverse proportion to new input: a commendable shift, since it automatically discourages uncreative borrowing.

The fine art viewpoint

This I currently find the most exciting new standpoint, offering several considerations which have not frequently been applied to the world of music. There is, for a start, a less strict application of 'uniqueness' in fine art; much borrowing and flattery by imitation is accepted comfortably (groupings, treatments, poses, detailing 'after Raphael' or 'in the manner of Turner').

One might compare the treatment of music, say, the B minor Mass, with that of a painting, maybe Vermeer, since both these examples, in fact, were rediscovered in the first half of the nineteenth century: Bach with the revival of the *St Matthew Passion* by Felix Mendelssohn in 1829, Vermeer with the work of Théophile Thoré starting in 1842. Both works

[24] Ibid., 439.

were reprinted, catalogued, analysed, performed and exhibited and made available to the masses. In both cases the means of transmission had changed into the forms of reproduction – at first with Vermeer (engravings), later with Bach (recordings). Both influenced later artists, who borrowed and copied from the style in a changed aesthetic and for a very different public than the original creations. Music has only recently developed an interest in 'reception history', but fine art, with its financial emphasis on 'provenance', has always been aware of the transit of artefacts.

A recent study of a single Vermeer painting deals not only with the content and creation (as you would expect with a musical work), but also the use of photography, the engravings and reproductions, the connoisseurship, the manner of hanging in galleries, the influence of donors, the pressures of patronage, and even the therapeutic effects of art, all this in respect of one work, the *Lady playing the virginals* in the National Gallery.[25]

Although painting is not a recreative art, from what we see of the connoisseurship required to authenticate or identify a painting, it is not hard to imagine the precision that would be required of recreation. Imagine the picture dissolving into several tubs of paint plus a recipe every evening as the gallery doors closed; there would be extreme concern that, when the paint had to be reapplied before opening the next day, it should be done *exactly* in accordance with the recipe.[26] One might say that the identity of the painting *is* the painting, whereas the identity of the music is a conglomerate of remembered performances, except that this distinction totters slightly when faced with paintings in multiple identities. Which of the several versions of *The scream* actually *is The scream*, or which of Van Gogh's eleven paintings of sunflowers is meant to spring to mind when the title is quoted?[27]

---

[25] Ivan Gaskell, *Vermeer's wager: Speculations on art history, theory and art museums* (London: Reaktion, 2000).

[26] One should not assume the permanence of paintings; all galleries require the helping touch of the restorer's brush, and many works of art, from prehistoric cave paintings to Van Gogh's *White Roses* (once pink) have suffered from fugitive colours; very often the paint-surface you see today was not laid down by the named painter.

[27] You can chose between 2, 3, 4, 5, 12 or 15 blooms, and even the art world remains confused; see Louis van Tilborgh and Ella Hendriks, 'The Tokyo Sunflowers:

From the graphic artist's viewpoint, all musical performances are, as it were, cover versions, since only Mozart playing Mozart could be the real thing. I well remember Sting, at a Brit Awards ceremony many years ago, being surprised, and possibly a little outraged, that the Academy of Ancient Music had won a prize for simply playing Vivaldi 'as he would have played it' ('You didn't do *anything* to it?' he asked, incredulously); now, I am intrigued to see, he records Dowland.

As well as a more relaxed attitude to 'uniqueness', connoisseurship in the fine arts has stronger economic teeth, and the results can be financially negative as well as positive: true, a validated Vermeer increases in value, but uninhibited research could be financially perilous to a gallery. This is a very real danger in those art establishments that are allowed deacquisition, and might well be tempted to inhibit pure research, since debunking their Vermeer will devalue their collection. By comparison, musicians are free to choose their own scale of values; we can happily ignore Beethoven's *Battle symphony* as though he had no hand in it, or accept parts of the Mozart *Requiem* as if they were true Mozart without incurring artistic derision or financial loss. By the same licence, of course, scholars can, without financial qualms, busy themselves with proving that Bach did *not* write the *Toccata and fugue in D minor*.

In the second place, the physical context of the fine arts is felt to be of more consequence than that of music; the manner and place of display is often more permanent (as far as an individual work is concerned) than the setting of a musical performance (although, conversely, the artistic verisimilitude of a CD recording is ranked higher than its graphic equivalent, the coffee-table book of reproductions). The Gaskell study, centring on the single Vermeer painting, devotes several chapters to the placement, photography and physical context of pictorial art; the comparison of two states of hanging in the National Gallery, one from 1979 and the other post-1995, demonstrates clearly how the physical surroundings change our appreciation and perception of an individual painting.[28]

a genuine repetition by Van Gogh or a Schuffenecker forgery?', *Van Gogh Museum Journal* (2001).

[28] Most recently we have been aware of the telling series of photographs by Thomas Struth, the result of twenty years documenting the display of art and its interaction with museum visitors in major 'concert-halls for paintings' such as

It is true that art historians may use a painting to attempt to penetrate the mind of the creator (writing more about Vermeer's intentions, less about Vermeer's figures), rather like the use of the original musical manuscripts to fathom the composer's processes; each study is aided by the latest technology (X-rays, computer analysis). But in this case the painting is the score, the work and the performance.

A third area of departure from traditional musical thinking is the study of transmission, the use of photography versus engraving, and especially the widespread circulation of an *image* in place of an *object*. Photography of fine art in the nineteenth century was thought to be less revealing than a fine engraving (the personal was preferred to the impersonal, which could merely 'copy'); similarly early acoustic recordings were thought less musically useful than a well-performed arrangement. To our great-grandparents the 'identity' of a Beethoven symphony would be better revealed in a piano duet performance than in a tinny recording; we would now assume the opposite, having taken against arrangements as the epitome of misrepresentation. The monochrome photo which shows up details which the naked eye does not see is balanced by the CD which reveals details not audible in a live concert, just as the engraving 'after Rembrandt' could emphasize or reduce ingredients in the same way that an arrangement of the Mozart *Requiem* for string quartet can lead the ear to aspects on which it had never focused before. More provocative to a musician is the question of an *image* (a photo in an art book, of uncertain scale and without its frame and surroundings) replacing the actual *object*. Does not this separation occur with all recorded performances – disembodied sounds delivered to your sitting room or directly to your ear, minus all evidence of performance: the musicians, the instruments, the sheets of music – scale-less images stripped of their proper surroundings?

Still further, the modern habit of over-restoring and over-lighting pictures in galleries in order to compete with the glamour of a projected colour transparency has been anticipated by the recording industry's

the Prado, the Munich Alte Pinakothek, the Art Institute in Chicago, the Louvre, and the Museum of Oriental Art in Tokyo. See Hars Belting, *Thomas Struth: Museum photographs* (Munich: Schirmer/Mosel 1993, rev. 2005).

well-established 'rebalancing' of the sounds of a musical score – in opera, the forward voices, the background orchestra; in symphonic music the specially 'assisted' solos, the extra microphones for the brass section (or even the violas) producing effects which have now fed back to live performance. The result is the ludicrous scene of musicians on stage wearing legally enforced ear-plugs or with perspex sound-baffles for protection from the ever louder brass sections of orchestras who are simply trying to live up to the enhanced and spotlit sound of their own recordings. Comic – were it not for the sad fact that, if they don't go down this path, their live audiences will drift away, complaining that 'they don't sound as good as they did on the recording'.

Two more substantial chapters in the Vermeer study deal with the therapeutic effect of art – the museum as a site of 'beneficent security' – and the influence (sometimes control) of sponsors on collections and displays. It would still be thought unusual to find these factors considered together in a musical context, although such curatorial principles apply equally to those who are guardians or purveyors of recreative art.

Mythos

I should, at this point, divulge my own viewpoint, but since (as I admitted at the outset) we are demonstrably on very subjective ground, it should come last. Not only because it is individual, but because in my case it has changed over time, moving through several of the attitudes and viewpoints which we have just explored.

At first I tended to the scientific, *Musikwissenschaft* – analysis will answer everything, an 'echt' or 'Ur-' version is possible and theoretically the Platonic ideal would have to be the first performance by the creator. Then, especially after working on Handel, I discovered the power, and dichotomies, of borrowing; contrary to what I had been taught, original melodic inspiration was not the most necessary ingredient of musical creation and I began to lean towards the more tolerant attitude of licensed borrowing.

Now I am more at home with the fine arts theorists, and discover that the context and the adaptations and effects of a work in its 'after-life' (what musical historians grace with the ugly term 'Reception History') appeal more; I have an increased affection for arrangements and adaptations (of the period or by an artist comparable to the composer). Even the therapeutic angle now strikes a chord: if thousands of people annually feel better, healthier and happier after singing *Messiah* in choirs of several hundred voices, what is the value of my carping that this is 'historically uninformed' other than as a private reminder that I myself would feel better, healthier and happier doing it differently?

Gilbert Murray pointed out, in his preface to a fine translation of Aristotle's *Poetics*,[29] that to the ancient Greeks *mythos* could mean either historical fable (that which really happened) or plot (material invented by the poet). Poetry itself was either the art of 'making' (from hard facts or materials) or 'inventing' (from thin air) and the construct is not affected when a 'fact' is shown to be fiction (or vice versa).[30] I left Classics because of insufficient faith in the bottom line (did it really happen?), just as many people abandon religion; I have now come around to a sympathy for the Myth in Music: does it matter whether there is reality at bottom or not? Or correct attribution? Or authenticity? After a period of enthusiasm for 'cleaning the picture', I find I have now come to love the presence – or at least the implications – of the patina, the evidence of age, usage and transmission almost as much as the original piece; a fuzzy logic is fine, and the music will continue to present its identity, even to those of us still wondering 'What *are* Brahms?'

---

[29] Gilbert Muray, Preface, *Aristotle on the art of poetry*, tr. Ingram Bywater (Oxford: Clarendon Press, 1920).

[30] The recent publication by Robert Bittlestone, with James Diggle and John Underhill, identifying the true island of Ithaca, *Odysseus unbound: The search for Homer's Ithaca* (Cambridge University Press 2005), although fascinating as an archaeological hypothesis, does nothing to change the status of the *Odyssey* as art.

8 Identity and the mind

RAYMOND TALLIS

Like other contributors to this series I ought perhaps to define my topic more precisely.

I am concerned mainly with *personal* identity – the continuing sense of who or what one is – rather than identity in general. This is not such a restriction as it may at first sight seem – and is certainly an insufficient ground for invoking the Trade Descriptions Act – for it will be central to my argument that the notion of identity, except in a strictly logical sense, is properly located in first-person being; and even that strictly logical sense is ultimately rooted in intuitions whose primary provenance is identity as it applies to persons.

I shall not have much to say about identity as it plays out in identity politics; for, notwithstanding the passions it invokes, and the blood that has been spilt, this is a secondary or derivative aspect of identity. My interest in personal identity has little to do with the frankly tedious question of, say, how English I feel; or with identity as something that is asserted, affirmed, protested or sought when people feel marginalized, misrepresented or threatened. My present concern is with identity at the most fundamental level.

As if by way of compensation for narrowing the notion of identity, I want to look beyond the mind – the other abstract noun in my title – for the basis of personal identity. I shall argue that, although the mind – self-consciousness, memory – is central to personal identity, a stand-alone mind is insufficient to establish or sustain it. Nor indeed can the body either as a material object or a living organism alone deliver

Identity, edited by Giselle Walker and Elisabeth Leedham-Green. Published by Cambridge University Press. © Darwin College 2010.

what is required. Both body and mind are necessary to underpin personal identity, both as it is subjectively experienced and as it is objectively acknowledged. In addition, the community of bodies and minds that we call the world is necessary to elaborate and sustain it. This may come as a surprise only to philosophers.

In what follows, I may be seen to slither between terms such as 'personal identity', the person, the self, the I, first-person being and so on. The impression of sloppiness this may give is not entirely unconscious; for the terms capture different aspects of the beast in question and trying to call them to conceptual order is a forlorn exercise. More importantly, I believe that these notions are all derived from a single ancestor, which I have called the 'Existential Intuition'. The Existential Intuition is the key concept in this essay and it corresponds to the sense that 'I am this' where 'this' in the first instance is my self-aware body, though it subsequently unfolds into a massively elaborated self, a correlative of an individual world.

Readers who are familiar with the philosophical literature may be disappointed, even outraged, that I shall have little to say about the famous thought-experiments which have dominated discussions of personal identity in recent decades and have been endlessly picked over by philosophers. I am thinking, for example, of imaginary scenarios in which whole brains, or cerebral hemispheres, are transplanted from one body to another and we are invited to consider whether the new body or bodies containing the brain or bits of brain do or do not take on the identity of the owner of the brain. I think such thought-experiments unhelpful and confusing and shall later explain why.

Let me widen the discussion for the moment and consider identity per se. This is a *relation* – the relation something has to itself – and at first sight nothing could seem simpler. While we may use the term 'identical' in a loose sense – asserting that you and I have identical motives for doing something or that twins are identical – in the strict sense identity is, as the American philosopher Quine said, 'as tight as a term can be'.[1] A thing is strictly is identical with itself: A is A. Not only

---

[1] W. V. O. Quine, *Quiddities: An intermittently philosophical dictionary* (London: Penguin, 1990), 89–90.

simple then, but boring. To quote Quine again, 'to say of anything that it is identical with itself is trivial, and to say that it is identical with anything else is absurd'.

Let us not be deceived: the notion of identity is neither simple nor trivial even in its strict, logical sense. Firstly, while 'A is A' is both simple and trivial, the prior conditions of this assertion, and the contexts that make it worth asserting, are not. The tautology 'A is A' – the sort of thing that gives logic, and philosophy by association, a bad name – has extraordinarily deep foundations. These are largely off-stage – or off-page. Logicians prefer it that way, liking their logic uncontaminated with the muddle and malodour of the human. But we cannot ignore what is off-stage. It is actually central to our theme today and to my claim that the primary mode of identity is *personal identity* and that other expressions of the identity relation are parasitic; that first-person identity, 'I am this', is primary and third-person identity, 'A is A', is secondary.

To understand this, it helps to appreciate that, while an entity is necessarily identical with itself, *the identity relation exists only insofar as it is made explicit and/or asserted*, and this requires at least two things. The first is the dissecting out of A as *an* entity. I may look at you, my audience, and see one audience or several hundred people; several hundred people or twice several hundred arms; an audience plus a lecture theatre or a packed lecture theatre. The way the world is divided is relative, amongst other things, to the way we perceive it and the language we use to describe it, which is in turn relative to our purposes. There are constraints, of course. I cannot see my audience as being composed of 25,000 human beings or, you may be relieved to know, of 600 chimpanzees.

The second requirement to make the identity relation explicit – and hence exist – is encompassed by expressed doubts as to whether A really is A. There are many circumstances under which such doubts may arise. First, I might encounter 'A' at two different times and wonder whether I have encountered the same thing or two similar things. Secondly, I might bump into A in 1965 and then again in 2007 and, seeing that it has changed, wonder whether it is right to say it is the same thing. Has it changed sufficiently for me to say, 'It is no longer the same thing – it has become something else'? Thirdly, I might hear of an item that it is 'the boat belonging to Jo' and wonder whether this is identical with the boat that I can see over there, or the boat that someone said is next to mine. Whether, in short, two experiences or two descriptions are accessing the same entity or accessing different entities.

Once we bring in from the cold and on to the page the context necessary to make identity assertions happen, we move from the banality and triviality of 'A is A' to the real meat of identity. Perceptions, the passage of time, language – all clothe naked tautology in matters of substance. The appearance of triviality proves to have been deceptive. Most importantly, we can now see how the concept of identity cannot get a foothold in the absence of self-conscious beings. Yes, it will be agreed, Chair A is Chair A but it does not have an intrinsic identity, unlike self-conscious beings. It does not carve itself out – out of a row of chairs or an auditorium – nor does it have the intuition that it *is* itself, the self-iteration, the italicization that marks the identity-relation. That ability is something unique to self-conscious beings.

This is scarcely original. The eighteenth-century philosopher Thomas Reid also argued that persons alone can be considered as having identity and that the identity of material bodies, or material events, is not intrinsic to them but stipulated from without. One of the favourite examples for those who inquire into identity is that of a club. If a club changes its members, its premises, its rules and has only an audit trail linking each phase with the next, is it the same club or not? If it has the same name, we might think so. But that is an arbitrary criterion. In fact, there is, to use Derek Parfit's phrase, 'no fact of the matter'. This is Thomas Reid's position:

> The identity, therefore, which we ascribe to bodies . . . is not perfect identity; it is rather something which, for the convenience of speech, we call identity. It admits of great change of the subject, providing the change be gradual; sometimes even of a total change . . . [Identity] has no fixed nature when applied to bodies; and questions about the identity of a body are very often questions about words. But identity, when applied to persons, has no ambiguity, and admits not of degrees, or more and less.[2]

---

[2] Thomas Reid, *Essays on the intellectual powers of man*, Essay 3: 'Of memory', Chapter 4, 'Of identity', ed. A. D Woolzley (Charlottesville, VA: Lincoln-Rembrandt, 1986).

In the case of persons, or selves, identity is not conferred from without. It is at least in part – and the most important part, the ground floor as it were – stipulated, or imposed from within. Identity is something that, first and foremost, is *felt*. Hence its restriction to persons: identity is 'I-entity'; an assumption, as we shall see, that straddles flesh and logic.

Even as applied to persons, identity is by no means a concept that is easy to grasp. Many of the difficulties in pinning down personal identity result from conflating different aspects of this rather complex notion. We need to tease out these different aspects so that we shall see it in the round, and grasp what is fundamental, what underpins all the various aspects of identity that are highlighted in different circumstances.

First, there is my sense of who and what I am at any given time; and, secondly, there is my sense of being the *same* who or the *same* what over time. These subjective dimensions in turn have many elements, and I will examine some of these presently. For the moment, I would like to note that it is this second aspect of the subjective dimension of personal identity that has attracted the lion's share of philosophical attention. I shall argue that this question about the endurance of personal identity over time, while important, and a main theme of this talk, is not the fundamental question. Fully to address it, to grasp the essence of personal identity, we need to understand the sense of self, *at any particular time*.

There are also what we might call 'external' aspects of identity: those characteristics by which I am identified and classified by others, or by myself, taking an objective view of myself. It is these that supply object-ive criteria for my being counted, recognized, acknowledged as such and such a kind of person and as the same person on different occasions. These aspects are closer to those utilized in identification. They under-pin my claim to be identical with Raymond Tallis, a person others have met before, of whom certain things can be expected, a person who has rights, duties, possessions and so on. Identity cards underline the link between identity and entitlements, the aspect of the problem that par-ticularly exercises the *Daily Mail*. These external aspects also fall short of being fundamental: they would not have any meaning without the subjective aspect of identity.

The (in my view erroneous) primary focus on identity over time and (the equally erroneous) focus on external criteria for identity both distract from the core of the matter – the experience 'that I am'. It explains, what is more, the tendency among some contemporary philosophers to reduce personal identity to impersonal facts; to imagine that a third-person account will reveal the true nature of first-person being.

I have distinguished objective from subjective aspects of identity, but they are, of course, profoundly interrelated. My subjective 'who' will be shaped, coloured, in the most intimate and complete sense informed by the objective 'what'. Much of my sense of who I am will be an internalization of the objective facts about me and the behaviours these facts require, the expectations they will raise regarding others' behaviour towards me. My belief in the objective fact that I am my wife's husband will influence my expectation of how she will behave towards me. So when I enter our house, she acknowledges my identity, rooted in part in our shared life, by asking me if I have posted a particular letter rather than by calling for the police to expel an intruder.

This illustrates how the world in which we live provides a scaffolding supporting an elaborate sense of self, which would otherwise be highly volatile. I emphasize this because, while I am going to talk mainly about the psyche and the body in the creation and sustaining of personal identity, once we move beyond the bare sense that I am – or as that sense that I am grows in complexity and evolves towards a socialized or narrated self – the collective of minds and the culture they create and uphold is of huge importance in establishing what I am.

So much for the subjective and objective aspects of personal identity. Before we examine them further, it is appropriate to ask why personal identity is so important and under what circumstances it may become a pressing problem or even cause of anguish. Here are some. In adolescence, when we awaken to the possibility of an independent life, in which we to some degree define what we are or shall become, we search for an image and idea of ourselves that will flatter us or satisfy our desperate need for self-esteem. And then there are times when we have to make decisions that are of such fundamental importance that we have to know what we truly are, so that we shall know what to stand for. At other times, we may look back over our lives and, seeing that we – our values, our priorities, our entire way of life – have changed, wonder whether we are the same person. In illness – head injury, dementia – others may question whether we have ceased to be the person we once were or, indeed, any person.[3]

These occasions when identity becomes an issue to some extent justify the emphasis in the philosophical literature on the endurance or continuity of the self over time, as opposed to the more fundamental question as to the nature of selfhood at a particular time; on what makes one the same person, as opposed to what constitutes personhood itself. Pretty well everything that matters in identity is gathered up in the idea of the self as something definite, enduring, singular, unified – as tightly interconnected. For this notion of being internally stitched, biographically coherent beyond mere succession of events, seems to lie at the heart of any claim we have to dignity as moral agents. It is, as Thomas Reid said, 'the foundation of all rights and obligations, and of all accountableness'. A key notion is that of 'integrity' – the sense that I am one, enduring thing; that there is a unity across the different aspects of my life and behaviour. This justifies our expectation that we shall be respected: other people feel that they know what to expect of us. In return, we shall feel entitled to expect that others, too, will be consistent; that they will have stable dispositions. And it is not enough that people should be programmed to replicate the same patterns of behaviour; that same pattern has to have a coherent inside.

This idea of a coherent, enduring self has faced many challenges. The most famous was lodged by David Hume in what must be one of the most quoted passages in philosophy. He sought his self through introspection and this is what he found:

> For my part, when I enter most intimately into what I call *myself*, I always stumble on some particular perception or other, of heat, cold, light or shade, love or hatred, pain or pleasure. I can never catch *myself* at any time without a perception, and can never observe anything but the perception.[4]

---

[3] There is a very large literature on the question of whether, or when, people with dementia lose personhood. One of the most interesting short treatments is A. Buchanan, 'Advance directives and personal identity', *Philosophy and public affairs* 17(4) (1988), 277–302.

[4] David Hume, *A treatise of human nature*, Book 1, Part 4, Section 6: 'Of personal identity' (New York: Doubleday, 1936), 228.

He concluded that humans 'are nothing but a bundle of different perceptions, which succeed each other with an inconceivable rapidity, and are in a perpetual flux and movement'. 'The identity we ascribe to the mind of man is only a fictional one,' he finally says.

Hume's search for the self was informed by an assumption that predetermined its negative conclusion. He assumed that the self should be a percept among percepts, and that it could be grasped through turning his attention inwards. At the same time, unlike the fugitive impressions that cross our minds, it should endure over time – the entirety of our life – and hence be unlike any ordinary percept or indeed perception. Two irreconcilable demands. As Kant recognized, it is a mistake to think of the self as a percept, or even as a super-percept; not the least because the self is *presupposed* in perceptions, in the implicit sense that they are mine, that it is I who am perceiving them, that I am their subject.

Kant suggested, in response to Hume, that 'It must be possible for the "I think" to accompany all my representations.'[5] Not a very satisfactory solution and much puzzled over. A constant iteration of 'I think' seems implausibly donnish. What is more, the 'I' of the 'I' think, which he specifically denied had a place in the empirical world of experiences, seemed to have no home at all. It was not easy to see how it engaged with, attached itself to, the actual experiences of actual beings. One consequence was that it was always at risk of being crash-dieted to a skinny, a size zero, purely logical, subject. But at least Kant's intuitions were sound.

Some thinkers have rejected the challenge to find an enduring basis of personal identity that surmounts all the changes suffered by the experiencing self. Indeed, some have embraced the Humean vision, out of suspicion that any notion of personal identity which denies Hume's findings will inevitably appeal to a Cartesian, Kantian, or quasi-theological transcendental *ego*.

This seems to have motivated many twentieth-century interpretations of the self, notably those of existentialist philosophers who, emphasizing

---

[5] Immanuel Kant, *Critique of pure reason*, trans. Norman Kemp Smith, 2nd edn ('The original synthetic unity of apperception') (London: Macmillan, 1933), 152.

its non-material nature and its role as the source of freedom, wanted to liberate it not only from thing-hood but from being any kind of substantive entity. The self, for Sartre, is nothingness, an imaginary construct.[6] Analytical philosophers such as Gilbert Ryle argued that the 'I' was not only elusive but systematically so: it could never become its own object, any more than I could stand on my own shadow.[7] In the second half of the last century, structuralist, poststructuralist and postmodernist thinkers mainly located in Paris – paradoxically the very capital of the ego – dissolved the self: it is a mere node in a system of signs; it is in the grip of various modes of the unconsciousness – political, socio-political, historical, psychoanalytical, linguistic, and so on – through which it misrecognizes and is alienated from itself; or it is a bourgeois or tropological construct or (in Jacques Lacan's echo of Hume) a 'fiction'.[8] Some neuroscientists, apart from those who locate personal identity in bits of the brain, irritated that they cannot find selves in neural activity, declare the 'I' to be an illusion.[9] Finally, there have been many philosophers influenced by the eminent contemporary neo-Humean Derek Parfit, whose position we shall discuss presently.

These views might have serious implications if we were to take them seriously: notions of the self as an independent point of departure, the font of genuine action, the place where the buck starts, might be undermined. Luckily we don't have to take them seriously. Indeed, we could have a lot of fun with them. We could ask Hume whether he thinks his repeated use of 'I' in the passage we have quoted is problematic. And we might ask the mighty egos that stalked the Parisian intellectual scene and attached so many publications and so much fame to their names whether this was all attached to nothing. But this is not today's business

[6] See Christina Howells, 'Sartre and the deconstruction of the subject', in *The Cambridge companion to Sartre*, ed. Christina Howells (Cambridge University Press, 1992).

[7] Gilbert Ryle, 'The systematic elusiveness of "I"', in *The concept of mind* (London: Penguin, 1963), 189.

[8] These attacks on the self are discussed in 'Realism and the subject', in Raymond Tallis, *In defence of realism*, 2nd edn (Lincoln: University of Nebraska Press, 1996), and 'Marginalising consciousness', in Raymond Tallis, *Enemies of hope: A critique of contemporary pessimism*, 2nd edn (London: Macmillan, 1999).

[9] An accessible account of the apparent case from neuroscience for denying the reality of the self is Rita Carter, *Mapping the mind* (Berkeley: University of California Press, 1999).

and I shall take it that my readers accept that there is something corresponding to the notion of the enduring self; that it is possible for the notion of personal identity to have a meaning irreducible to a Humean flow without it having to be some kind of thing-in-itself or quasi-material object, or life-long super-percept. So what is the basis of personal identity?

Though the endurance of identity *over time* makes sense, as we said, only on the basis of identity *at a given time*, the former provides a helpful entrée into the primary question of what personal identity is and why it matters. The philosophical question of endurance over time is expressed by Richard Swinburne as follows: 'What are the logically necessary and sufficient conditions for a person P_2 at a time t_2 being the same person as a person P_1, at an earlier time t_1 or, loosely, what does it mean to say that P_2 is the same person as P_1?'[10]

There is another question linked with this: what evidence of observation and experience can we have that P_2 is the same as P_1?

The search, therefore, is on for some basis of continuity over time in the face of change; something that is continuously and unchangeably present. Premodern philosophers would have invoked an enduring immaterial substance: the soul. Descartes partly modernized this as thinking substance. The truly modern engagement with the notion of personal identity over time, however, began with John Locke, who also chose an immaterial basis – though not a substance but the connectedness of the psyche.[11]

For Locke, identity lay in our consciousness. What was continuously present was not some individual mental item, such as a super-percept, but continuity over time located in the internal connectedness of consciousness. This connectedness was secured most obviously through memory – the memory of our experiences.

Locke's account has powerful intuitive attractions. It is still influential; for example, it is echoed in Thomas Nagel's assertion in his 1986 philosophical masterpiece, *The view from nowhere*, that 'I survive as long

[10] Richard Swinburne and Sydney Shoemaker, *Personal identity* (Oxford: Basil Blackwell, 1984), 3.
[11] John Locke, 'Of identity and diversity' in *An essay concerning human understanding*, Book 2, abridged and ed. A. S. Pringle-Patterson (Sussex: Harvester Press, 1978).

as I retain the capacity for conscious experience and my ability to re-identify myself by memory'[12] – though his views are not precisely neo-Lockean. Continuity of memory seems to underpin so many other continuities: my enduring sense of what, where, who; the familiarity that makes the world *my* world and guides me through my life; my commitment to my commitments; my responsibility for delivering on my promises; and, most directly, my sense of having temporal depth. Psychological continuity seems like the inner truth within the external facts of my constancy, reliability, predictability; the private, essential 'take' on the framework that gives stable sense to my life, and enables me to make sense of myself and others to make sense of, and to recognize, me.

But there are problems with Locke's theory. First, the temporal extent of ourself would be measured by the reach of memory, but memory doesn't seem to go back far enough. My memory gets patchier and patchier, and more and more reprocessed and hence unreliable, the further I go back. To describe my childhood, as Philip Larkin does, as 'a forgotten boredom' would be a little harsh on my parents, but I remember little of the 131,400 hours of the experiences of my first fifteen years of life. And yet that child Raymond Tallis and I are the same person.

We can mitigate the implications of this blankness a little by imagining a kind of relay, as Thomas Reid (who was opposed to Locke's theory) did.[13] He gives an example of an aged general who does not remember the boy who, so he has been told, he once was who got whipped for stealing apples. However, he can remember being a brave young subaltern and the subaltern recalls the lad who was whipped for stealing apples. This, however, does not really solve the problem; for we do not regain possession of our past through our memories, only infer that there is a chain of rememberers, going right back to the two-day-old infant who presumably has some kind of recall of the previous day's nappy changes. This, however, contributes nothing to our *sense* of personal identity. We have a merely theoretical rather than living connection to our remote past, not in our own keeping.

[12] Thomas Nagel, *The view from nowhere* (Oxford University Press, 1986), 41.
[13] See note 2.

Derek Parfit, for whom personal identity dissolves without remainder into psychological continuity,[14] tries to strengthen Locke, though Parfit is best thought of as a neo-Humean. He advances the notion of overlapping chains of 'strong connectedness' tying together successive phases of our psyche; these would include not only memories but other psychological components. Memory, however, it seems to me, remains central to the intuitive attraction of the theory: it is psychological connectedness made explicit.

If memory is so important to enduring personal identity, it is reasonable to ask whether memories have to be in a state of being remembered to bind the person together. It is obvious that we are not at any given time engaged in remembering more than a minute fraction of even those memories we have. If we had to keep a large number of our memories in play in order to count as being adequately connected with our past, so that ourselves at t_1 could count as the same person as ourselves at t_2, the price of having an enduring personal identity would be to live like Borges' mnestic monster Funes the Memorious, who could forget nothing.[15] We live by leaving things behind and we need amnesia if an overreplete present consciousness is not going to become a kind of delirium of reminiscence.

Most importantly, the Lockean account, which has a rather vague view on what counts as sufficient psychological connectedness to constitute continuity of self, seems to be at odds with our intuition that personal identity – to use Reid's phrase – 'has no ambiguity, and admits of no degrees, of more or less'. To translate this: 'I' does not pass through a penumbra of 'I-ish' as it fades to 'Not-I'. As the line of connectedness becomes less dense, the sense of 'I' does not attenuate. For Parfit, who does not believe that personal identity is determinate, yes–no, and that what matters is not the continuation of something called personal identity, but the future of the Humean series of experiences we have, this is not a problem. For me, who do not believe that Raymond Tallis dissolves into a succession of experiences, it *is* a problem. Either Raymond Tallis is

---

[14] Derek Parfit, *Reasons and persons* (Oxford: Clarendon Press, 1987).
[15] Jorge Luis Borges, 'Funes the Memorious', in *A personal anthology*, ed. Anthony Kerrigan (London: Picador, 1972).

or Raymond Tallis is not; at least that is what Raymond Tallis thinks. He doesn't think he can be a teeny-weeny bit Raymond Tallis any more than anyone can be a teeny-weeny bit pregnant.

There is a further problem with seeking continuing personal identity in psychological connectedness through memory. How can I be sure that a memory I am having now is a true memory of an actual experience – of an experience that I had? Vividness of recall is no sure guide to authenticity of apparent memories. The great psychologist Jean Piaget reported that his earliest memory was a very precise and terrifying image. He had a clear memory of being in the Jardin de Luxembourg with his nurse, when she was attacked by a man wanting to steal him from his pram. It was only many years later that his nurse confessed that she had fabricated the entire incident to earn herself praise.

This question of validation – what makes these memories authentic memories of experiences *I* have had – connects with the profound insight expressed by Bishop Butler when he challenged Locke's rooting of personal identity in 'sameness of consciousness'.[16] This, he said, was 'a wonderful mistake'; for it is 'self-evident that consciousness of personal identity *presupposes*, and therefore cannot constitute, personal identity' (my italics). In other words, personal identity is not an objective given, which we then discover, say on the basis of memories that we feel confident are ours. And this seems sound: to found one's sense of identity on anything else, even memories that are felt to be valid because one had the experiences corresponding to them, and one has evidence that there is the right kind of causal relationship between the memories and the experiences remembered, is to put the cart before the horse. Just as quizzing me on little known facts about the life of Raymond Tallis seems a good way for others to check my claim to be Raymond Tallis, a high score on such a quiz could not underpin, or even strengthen, my sense of being myself. Imagining that it could is connected with a failure to recognize that personal identity goes deeper, or is presupposed in, identification and reidentification. The feeling that these memories are mine, and are authentic because they are of experiences that are mine,

---

[16] Joseph Butler, 'Of personal identity', Appendix to *The analogy of religion, natural and revealed, to the constitution and the course of nature* (1736).

that I have had, must be itself rooted in a pre-existing sense of personal identity: that 'I am this', a 'this' that is currently having these memories and previously had the experiences preserved in the memories.

It certainly seems odd to think of personal identity as something you arrive at as a kind of conclusion. We are led down this peculiar path, as Bishop Butler pointed out, because we are using the term 'identity' loosely, as we do when we (illegitimately) apply it to objects such as trees, ships and gentlemen's clubs, when we do indeed have to invoke external criteria for justifying the use of the term and for arriving at what is an *identification*. The iteration – *that* I am – is a presupposition that precedes any determination of *what* I am. Psychological connectedness does not, therefore, deliver the sense of personal identity: it is presupposed in it.

Let me now examine something else that has been proposed for sameness of identity over time, and which has also been offered as the basis for my identity at any given time; namely my body. I *am* my body, it is argued, and my enduring self is rooted in my relatively stable body. Certainly, the body that I, and only I, have had all my life seems a plausible repository for my personal identity – at least when we focus on its continuity over time. This needs clarification, however: I am not just the physical material of my body, which outlasts me, even though it does not out*live* me; otherwise I might have to allow that my corpse which, for a while at any rate, is not materially much different from my body at the time of death, and certainly less different from my body immediately prior to my death than it is from my body as a child, would seem a continuation of my personal identity.

Eric Olson has recently argued in *The human animal* that identity resides not in the material of the body but in the biological processes in the *living organism* that is *H. sapiens*.[17] He is led to the conclusion that even people in a permanent coma or a persistent vegetative state still retain their identity. He enthusiastically welcomes these, to me unwelcome, consequences of his position, because he wants to separate personal identity from consciousness: the subtitle of his book is 'personal

[17] Eric T. Olson, *The human animal: Personal identity without psychology* (Oxford University Press, 1997).

identity without psychology'. Persons are human animals and 'no sort of psychological continuity is either necessary or sufficient for a human animal to persist through time'.

Admittedly Olson's identification of personal identity with the living animal body does dispose of some difficulties. It deals with our undeniable but seemingly puzzling connection with an object in the remote past that does not have personal identity: for example the foetus we once were. How can 'I' be linked to an 'I-less' foetus or neonate? The answer is straightforward if I believe that my identity resides in my animal body. I am this animal body which happens to have an ego-less phase preceding a phase with an ego.

Locating personal identity in the body is helpful in another regard. The body stands outside of the circularity we noted when we examined the attempt to locate continuing personal identity in psychological connectedness through memory. The body, unlike our experiences, endures through space and time, and has a public observable as well as a privately experienceable face. It can therefore act as a check on the relationship between past experiences and the present moment. For example, there is, as it were, an audit trail connecting the successive moments of the body. For the body has the handy property of being in a definite location at a particular time and of having to occupy all intermediate locations in between times. If I authentically remember being in Paris at a particular time, I know that I cannot also authentically remember being in Cambridge at that time. Nor could I have been in London ten seconds later. Nor even one day later, without a remembered form of transport. My publicly observable body also provides a means by which others may vouch for or contest my memories. By means of the body, our memories and other psychological states are located in a nexus of objective fact and checkable reality. Experiences, and the memories that make them part of my enduring identity over time, are tethered to real places and real times. (It is particularly unfortunate, then, that Olson is happy to do without these psychological items!)

My body, the public face of my identity, also connects identity with *identification*; that reinforcement of my sense of self that comes from others whose lives intersect or intertwine with mine; it links the private space of recollection with the public realm, with micro- and macro-society; the subjective sense of being me with the objective data recorded in ID cards.

While, by locating personal identity in the human organism, Olson gets round a few difficulties, he seems to by-pass the very essence of what lies at the heart of personal identity: the sense, the intuition, the feeling, the assertion that I am what I am. It gives a plausible *marker* of continuity of the self over time, but it doesn't seem to offer continuity of the *self* as such. As Locke says, '*Person* stands for . . . a thinking intelligent Being . . . that . . . can consider it self as it self'.[18] Most damningly, without this subjective dimension it is difficult to see how identity could arise in the body, for reasons I gave at the outset of this paper: identity is inseparable from conscious human beings because it has to be stipulated. A person-less body does not have the status of being a single, coherent thing. It can be taken as one body, many organs, millions of cells, trillions of atoms and so on. Unity does not come free.

We may therefore draw two conclusions. Firstly, personal identity is not a matter of the psyche solely: stand-alone memories cannot provide the basis either for the moment-to-moment sense of self nor for the confidence that we have in being the same person over time, that we are temporally extended. They are rootless or untethered. We need the body as well. But, second, a stand-alone body cannot provide personal identity, either. It is personless. We need both psyche and soma – with the psychological continuity providing the inner aspect of the enduring self and the corporeal continuity that outer aspect. But not one merely added to the other.

I want now to suggest a way of construing personal identity that combines both without the two merely being conjoined. Such an account of the self will takes its rise not from continuity of identity over time but from identity at any given time.

I envisage personal identity as something that begins with the awakening of the human body to itself; the intuition that it *is* and that it is *itself.* This is what I have called the Existential Intuition and this, it seems to me, is the *sine qua non*, the beating heart, of personal identity.[19]

---

18 Locke, 'Of identity and diversity', 188.
19 The origin of the Existential Intuition, and its uniqueness to human beings, is described in Raymond Tallis *The hand: A philosophical inquiry into human being* (Edinburgh University Press, 2003); its nature examined in Raymond Tallis *I am: A philosophical inquiry into first-person being* (Edinburgh University Press, 2004);

Raymond Tallis

The Existential Intuition cannot be readily described – it is immediately experienced – but it could be cast in the form '[That] I am [this . . .]' where 'this', in the first instance, is one's own body. This looks like an assertion or a proposition: that is how I have had to represent it. But to think of it as being in itself either an assertion or a proposition would be to replicate in part the error of Kant's notion of the 'I think that accompanies all my perceptions'. Even the word 'intuition' is too narrow, suggesting as it does an inchoate thought. We may think of the sense that one is this thing – in infancy this body – initially as a slowly spreading blush, engaging more and more of the body, with key land-marks such as the discovery of one's hands and, later, of one's toes. The human body, we might say, is itself by virtue of the fact that it *'ams'* itself.

At the point of origin of personal identity – in a newborn wakening towards itself – psyche and soma are one: the inchoate 'I' identifies with the sentient body. We may envisage a gradual awakening to the body as one's own, as one's self, and through the body to the world, so that bodily self-awareness becomes the elaborate correlative of a personal world. This is the context in which the 'I' emerges in the body and personal identity is established in and of a body that will precede and outlast it.

Without the Existential Intuition, which lies at the heart of first-person being, without this sense that I am this, *at any particular time*, there is no basis for the sense that I am the same thing *over time*. The intuition 'that I am this' must precede any question as to whether I am or am not the same 'this'. This really is the point of what Thomas Reid said: without, as it were, self-appropriation, self-stipulation, the question cannot arise as to whether or not something is the same thing over time. Or it can be resolved only by an external fiat that says that the acorn is or is not the same as the oak tree, the club is or is not the same club as the club that went under the same name but had different premises, rules and membership, as it did a hundred years ago.

In invoking the Existential Intuition, I have not provided a fully worked-out theory of personal identity – indeed, you may feel that, had

and its relationship to the origin of knowledge discussed in Raymond Tallis, *The knowing animal: A philosophical inquiry into knowledge and truth* (Edinburgh University Press, 2005).

200

you blinked, you would have missed my positive doctrine. (Most notably, I have not made enough of, even less attempted to give an account of, the sense of temporal depth that informs the moment-by-moment self, which draws on a past and reaches into a future.) Rather I have indicated a new point of departure for the philosophical investigation of this topic, which may redirect enquiry into what I believe may be more interesting areas. I devote the remainder of this paper to pointing to some of these.

The enquiry will not mobilize those endlessly recycled and picked-over and irritating thought-experiments – brain transplants, duplicates, transputers and so on – that have so bedevilled this field and so fascinated the film industry.[20] I find them unhelpful because it is difficult to judge their validity as one does not know whether it is logical or empirical possibilities which are being discussed. Contrary to what is usually assumed, such experiments are interesting only if they describe empirical possibilities. I happen not to believe that a stand-alone brain or part of brain could house personhood, identity or even memories. The Existential Intuition could not arise, and be sustained, in a stand-alone brain, as it would have no referent for 'this'. The brain is unaware of itself. Such thought-experiments therefore describe scenarios that cannot arise in fact, even if they are logically possible; and invoking logical possibility merely rules out 'Not (A and Not-A)' and 'Not (either A or Not-A)' variously dressed up.

One line of investigation might take its rise from the peculiar location of the Existential Intuition 'that I am this', on the borderland between a tautology 'I am I' and an empirical assertion such as 'I am Raymond Tallis'. This anomalous logical status of first-person being was first sensed by Descartes, for whom it became a subsequently much contested point of intersection between logic and existence, in the famous *cogito* argument whereby he proved his own existence – or rather reminded us that it could not be doubted: 'I think therefore I am'. This is not so much an argument – indeed there is less in the conclusion than in its premises – as a rather thin, brief rehearsal of the Existential Intuition, a paler

---

[20] Parfit, *Reasons and Persons*, and Olson, *The human animal*, rely very heavily on such thought-experiments. They are vigorously criticised by Kathy Wilkes, *Real people: Personal identity without thought experiments* (Oxford: Clarendon Press, 1988).

blush: 'I am'. At any rate, first-person being, awakening of parts of the material world to their own *existence*, a blush of self-realization, looks like a tautology that has empirical content. Of course, that content is available in the first instance only to the 'I' that has the intuition.

Does this mean that I am a supreme authority on what I am? There is an interesting problem of determining, in a principled way, the boundary between the sense of 'I', and of what I am, that is not open to challenge – a quasi-tautology – and that part of what I feel myself to be which is open to correction. I cannot be mistaken that I am I; I might be mistaken that I am Raymond Tallis, when 'Raymond Tallis' designates a set of biographical details; and I definitely could be mistaken in thinking that I was born in England or am 5 foot 10 inches tall; and I most certainly *am* mistaken in the belief that I am the tallest man in England. At first it seems that it should be easy to specify what characterizes those things about myself which I can be mistaken over and those over which I cannot be mistaken, but it is not. There has been a lively philosophical debate about the scope of self-knowledge; about whether we even know our own thoughts or whether, given that the meaning of the words in which they are expressed is externally determined, we cannot even know what it is that we are thinking.[21] Paul Valéry's delicious *aperçu* that 'we are made of many things that know nothing of us, which is why we do not know ourselves' captures an unease that we have about the cognitive transparency of this 'I' that is asserted quasi-tautologically in the Existential Intuition.

If incorrigible self-stipulation – 'That I am this . . .' which, as Reid said, admits of no degrees – is the core of personal identity, what is the scope of the 'this'? Descartes' systematic doubt placed even the body outside the charmed circle within which the Existential Intuition was an unchallengeable tautology. All I could be sure of was of myself as a currently thinking substance. P. F. Strawson[22] and many others subsequently, including Quassim Cassam,[23] have argued, I believe persuasively, that

---

[21] See, for example, Donald Davidson 'Knowing one's own mind', in *Self-Knowledge*, Oxford Readings in Philosophy, ed. Quassim Cassam (Oxford University Press, 1994). Cassam's introduction to this collection is also highly recommended.

[22] P. F. Strawson *The bounds of sense: An essay on Kant's* Critique of pure reason (London: Methuen, 1966).

[23] Quassim Cassam, *Self and world* (Oxford: Clarendon Press, 1997).

self-consciousness must refer itself to, have as its internal accusative, an object in the weighty sense, that is to say an item that 'is capable [not only] of being perceived but also of existing unperceived' – echoing Reid's observation that 'identity presupposes an uninterrupted continuity of existence' which perceptions and the like cannot boast. There seems to be only one candidate for this post of 'object in the weighty sense': my body. And this is central to the notion of personal identity as developed here. But what exactly do we mean by the body in this context?

This is not an empty question, for there is quite a lot of my body that has little to do with my self or my sense of self: my spleen, bone marrow, toe-nails, etc., seem clearly outside the scope of the Existential Intuition: for the least we should expect of any part of the body that is gathered up in the 'this' that I intuitively am, that I assume as myself, is that I should be aware of it without mediation. We incompletely colonize our own bodies.[24] And even in the case of the more accessible parts of the body, it is possible to make very large mistakes as to whether parts of one's body are one's own: as in the case of stroke patients with alien-hand-syndrome or so-called neglect, who disown parts of their body and even the actions in which they are engaged. What is more, 'the phenomenal body' as Merleau-Ponty calls it,[25] that part which is explicitly engaged in my actions and feels like me, will vary from moment to moment, depending upon what I am engaged in. When I am lost in deep thought, nearly all of my body drops off the radar screen – which is perhaps why many philosophers, for whom deep thought is an occupational hazard, and who define themselves in relation to it, have been inclined to identify the self with the mind and even, as in Descartes' case, the thinking mind.

Furthermore, we have different, and fluctuating, relations even to those parts of our body that touch on our self-awareness and seem eligible for inclusion in the scope of the Existential Intuition. We

---

[24] See Raymond Tallis, 'Reports from embodiment', in *I am: A philosophical inquiry into first-person being.*
[25] This concept is introduced in Maurice Merleau-Ponty, *The phenomenology of perception*, trans. Colin Smith (London: Routledge & Kegan Paul, 1962). See especially Part 1, 'The body', and, within this, Chapter 3, 'The spatiality of one's own body and motility'.

variously own, utilize, suffer, enjoy, take care of, and know portions of our body. None of these relations quite amount to gapless identity; indeed, as we introspect our experiences of our body, candidates for being what we are seem to retreat to the far end of our inner gaze – another manifest-ation of Ryle's systematic elusiveness of the 'I'. And this is to be expected because 'am' is an *assumption* not an inference – we assume and are assumed by the fleshly basis of our identity, rather than discover or identify it. As a relation, of course, true identity is so close as not to count as a relation at all; or to be a relation that holds up only so long as it does not differentiate into separate *relata*. Which is exactly what you would expect: in strict identity there is only one *relatum* because it is the relationship an entity has to itself. At any rate, it is difficult to specify the scope of the Existential Intuition and its immunity from challenge; to define its domain as a quasi-tautology.

We have drilled to the bedrock of personal identity. But how does it grow beyond its bedrock? Our sense of identity extends beyond the body and the question then arises as to how Existential Intuition anchored in the body unfolds into a self that is the complement of a world. How does this awakening *to* our bodies awaken *out of* our bodies to an objective shared reality that is sustained by the community of human minds? How does the 'I' crystallize out of the self-aware body and evolve to a social self? How does a robust, accountable ego arise out of the sensory delirium of infancy? And there are deeper questions. What is the relationship between the instantaneous, iterated Existen-tial Intuition, its continuous now, the inner time sense of the self that is rooted in an explicit past and reaches into an explicit future, and the objective temporal order of the common world which, among other things, upholds and validates our narrative sense of self and the story of our lives?

When we think about the interface between the subjective self and the objective world, we come upon an issue of great existential moment. As I cross the boundary between that of which I cannot possibly be mistaken to that over which I might be in error or deceived, we enter the realm of 'the facts of my case'. There is something disturbing about being attached to such facts: we find it difficult to be, or to coincide with, them, in order that the immediate apprehension of what I am should give personal colour to the objective facts about me. There is a drift towards the impersonal, from 'I am' to 'It is'. The assertion 'I am 5 foot 10' can be glossed as 'Raymond Tallis is 5 foot 10' or 'It is 5 foot 10'. Even the representation of the Existential Intuition as a proposition makes it a touch third-personal.

This is connected with the vexed question of the relationship between the singular 'who' and the general 'what' in personal identity. When as adolescents, we ask, 'What am I?', we long for an answer that makes us seem singular and thus irreplaceable. And yet at the same time, we want to identify with something larger than ourselves – a cult, a cause, a fashion, a nation. We come to our 'who' via a lattice of 'whats' that are not unique to ourselves. The Existential Intuition is reinforced by seeing itself in a mirror of generalities. The tendency for the search for a singular 'who' to drift into an inventory of general 'whats' is a consequence, ultimately, of the fact that, in making ourselves intelligible to ourselves, indeed, in making ourselves visible to ourselves, we need to place ourselves under the aspect of generality. The sense of being a substitutable anyone is mitigated by our somewhat vulnerable belief that the combination of generalities is unique, and the unquestionable truth that they are attached to a body that has a unique trajectory through space-time.

The very things that seem to nail us to a general identity – generality and intelligibility going together – seem also to elude us. This is not just a question of role–distance – as in the case of Sartre's waiter who is trying to be a waiter, as an inkwell is an inkwell, but ends up only playing at being a waiter[26] – but of the relationship between the bodily awareness in which the Existential Intuition arises, and in which it remains anchored, and the facts that we live by, and take account of, and accept when they are imputed to us. The pervasive sense that we fail fully to be the facts of our case, those facts in which we see an image of ourselves, those generalities through which we become intelligible to ourselves, is experienced as a kind of hollowness.

---

[26] See Jean-Paul Sartre 'Bad faith', in *Being and nothingness: An essay in phenomenological ontology,* trans. with an introduction by Hazel E. Barnes (London: Methuen, 1957).

This, perhaps, is the defining character – or, if one was inclined to take it tragically, the defining tragedy – of the human consciousness, of our being self-conscious knowing animals. Our 'who' constructs itself as a 'what' that it cannot entirely or stably be. Nevertheless, this failure of coincidence may be the basis of our freedom: we are liberated from our bodies by the generalities of cultural facts and from our culture by the unique trajectories of embodied selves. I offer this suggestion somewhat tentatively.

One master theme informing these observations is that of the relationship between subjective and objective aspects of identity, between the unassailable sense *that* I am (which must have some content) and *what* I am (which also has content but not the same). The latter grows out of the former, but there are tensions between them. This becomes especially noticeable in the slippage, or disconnection, between my subjective unchanging sense of 'I' and the objectively changing person others see me to be. 'I am I' whatever objectively I am; the iteration, the core sense of being myself, feels the same irrespective of whether that which is iterated in the Existential Intuition changes. Changes do not lead to the feeling of depersonalization: we feel we are this person, even if others think we are this person no longer. We are often the last to notice changes in ourselves; and, most poignantly, people with dementia seem to have a relatively strong Existential Intuition, and I-based wishes, to a very late stage, when the connected world of their fully mature adult self has been pretty well dismantled.

These then are potentially interesting fields of enquiry opened up by an approach to personal identity that insists on the priority of the subjective over the objective and of identity at a given time over enduring identity over time, secured by placing the Existential Intuition at the heart of personal identity. Let me now end by reminding you of the key claims I have put forward in this chapter.

Firstly, along with Bishop Butler and Thomas Reid, I have argued that there is no real identity outside of personal identity. Second, identity itself is not to be reduced to the objective basis of, or the criteria for, its own continuity over time, though the latter is important. Third, personal identity is not to be found either in the mind alone or the body alone: it is in the human body's awakening to itself *as* itself, in the Existential

Intuition 'That I am this'. Finally, while this account of personal identity avoids some problems associated with purely psychological or purely corporeal accounts of personhood, it leaves much unfinished business. Indeed, it highlights many new problems; or it casts the existing problems in a novel and, I would like to think more interesting, light.

Notes on contributors

Lionel Bently is Herchel Smith Professor of Intellectual Property Law and Director of the Centre of Intellectual Property and Information Law at the University of Cambridge. He is a Professorial Fellow at Emmanuel College, Cambridge. He is author of *The making of modern intellectual property law: The British experience, 1760–1911* (Cambridge University Press, 1999) (with Brad Sherman) and *Intellectual property law*.

Sir Peter Crane, FRS, is Carl W. Knobloch, Jr. Dean of the Yale School of Forestry and Environmental Studies at Yale University. He is a Fellow of the Royal Society and a Foreign Member of the German, Swedish and US academies of sciences. From 1992 to 1999 he was Director of the Field Museum in Chicago; from 1999 to 2006 he was Director of the Royal Botanic Gardens, Kew; from 2006 to 2009 he was John and Marion Sullivan University Professor at the University of Chicago in the Department of the Geophysical Sciences and on the Committee on Evolutionary Biology. He currently serves on the Boards of the Global Crop Diversity Trust, the Chicago Botanic Garden, the Lady Bird Johnson Wildflower Center at the University of Texas and the Gaylord and Dorothy Donnelley Foundation. His published research and other work focuses on the origin, fossil history, current status, conservation and use of plant diversity. He was knighted in the UK for services to horticulture and conservation in 2004.

Marcus du Sautoy is Charles Simonyi Professor for the Public Understanding of Science, Professor of Mathematics at the University of Oxford and a Fellow of New College, Oxford. He is Senior Media Fellow at the EPSRC. He has been named by the *Independent on Sunday* as one of the UK's leading scientists. In 2001 he won the prestigious Berwick Prize of the London Mathematical Society, awarded every two years to reward the best mathematical research made by a mathematician under forty. In 2004 *Esquire* magazine chose him as one of the hundred most influential people under forty in Britain. He is author of numerous academic articles and books on mathematics. He has been a visiting Professor at the Ecole Normale Supérieure in Paris, the Max Planck Institute in Bonn, the Hebrew University in Jerusalem and the Australian National University in Canberra. He is author of the best-selling popular mathematics book *The music of the primes*, which has been translated into ten languages. It has won two major prizes in Italy and Germany for the best popular science book of the year. He writes for *The Times*, the *Daily Telegraph*, the *Independent* and the *Guardian* and is frequently asked for comment on BBC radio and television. In September 2004 he presented his own series, *5 Shapes*, on Radio 4. He is also presenter of BBC 4's TV game show *Mind Games*, for which he has been nominated for the Royal Society of Television's Best Newcomer to a Network award. In 2005 he presented a one-hour documentary for BBC 4 based on his book *The music of the primes*. He gave the Royal Institution Christmas Lectures in 2006 entitled *THE NUM8ER MY5TERIES*, broadcast on Channel Five. His presentations on mathematics, which include 'Why Beckham chose the 23 shirt', have played to a wide range of audiences: from theatre directors to bankers, from diplomats to prison inmates.

Christopher Hogwood, CBE, conductor, keyboardist and musicologist, is one of the leading pioneers of the early music movement, as well as a renowned conductor of nineteenth- and twentieth-century works. In 1973 he founded the Academy of Ancient Music, and he has appeared regularly with many of the world's greatest orchestras (Berlin, Los Angeles, New York, San Francisco and London Philharmonics, Vienna Symphony and Leipzig Gewandhaus) and opera companies including the Royal Opera House (Covent Garden), La Scala (Milan), Sydney Opera House, Leipzig Oper and the Royal Operas of Stockholm and Madrid.

Hogwood began his career as a keyboard player on harpsichord and clavichord and has been a major force in the revolution that has forever changed the way music is performed, recorded and heard. Based on the principle of discovering and recreating the composer's intentions, his approach begins with musicology – going back to the original sources, correcting published errors and tracking subsequent changes. His repertoire ranges from medieval to contemporary music, but with a particular affinity for Haydn and Handel and, in twentieth-century music, for the neo-baroque and neo-classical schools. His current editorial work varies from the overtures and symphonies of Mendelssohn to the Fitzwilliam Virginal Book, and from Stravinsky, Elgar and Martinů to overlooked early versions of music by Haydn, Mozart and their contemporaries.

Hogwood's catalogue of more than 200 recordings with AAM includes much Vivaldi, Handel and Bach and the complete Mozart and Beethoven symphonies on period instruments, and is balanced by orchestral CDs of Martinů, Stravinsky, Tippett and Copland. His many scholarly publications include a survey of patronage through the ages (*Music at court*) and biographical studies of Haydn and Mozart. His handbook on Handel's *Water music* and *Music for the royal fireworks* was recently published by Cambridge University Press and a revised edition of his classic Handel biography appeared in 2007. From 2002 to 2008 Hogwood was Honorary Professor of Music at the University of Cambridge and received its Honorary Doctorate of Music in 2008.

Ludmilla Jordanova has been Professor of Modern History at King's College, London since January 2006 and previously worked at the Universities of Cambridge, East Anglia, York, Essex and Oxford. She was trained in the natural sciences, history and philosophy of science and art history. A Trustee of the National Portrait Gallery, London (2001–9), she also writes about the discipline of history (*History in practice*) and gender (*Nature displayed: Gender, science and medicine 1760–1820*) and other topics in cultural history and historiography. She is currently writing about the ways in which historians use visual and material evidence.

Philippa Marrack took her undergraduate and postgraduate degrees at New Hall, Cambridge. For her Ph.D. she worked with Dr Alan Munro in the Department of Biochemistry and at the MRC Laboratory for Molecular Biology on Hills Road. In 1971 she moved to the University of California at San Diego, where she did post-doctoral work with Dr Richard Dutton. Since then she has worked at the University of Rochester in New York and at the National Jewish Medical and Research Center in Denver, Colorado. She is currently an Investigator at the Howard Hughes Medical Institute and a Professor at the National Jewish and the University of Colorado Health Sciences Center. In 1967 she began to work on T cells. In collaboration with her husband, Dr John Kappler, Dr Marrack discovered how T cells act to help other cells reject infections and how they distinguish between invading organisms and their own host. These investigators also showed that some bacteria and viruses are particularly damaging because they produce powerful stimulants of the immune system which, paradoxically, kill rather than protect their hosts. Recently Dr Marrack has been studying adjuvants, crucial components of human and animal vaccines. She is a member of the Royal Society and the National Academy of Sciences, USA, and has received many awards including the Royal Society Wellcome Foundation Prize, the Paul Ehrlich and Ludwig Darmstaedter Prize, the Louisa Gross Horwitz Prize - Columbia University, the Rabbi Shai Shackner Prize - University of Jerusalem, the Lifetime Achievement Award of the American Association of Immunologists and the L'Oréal UNESCO Women in Science Award.

Adrian Poole is Professor of English Literature and a Fellow of Trinity College, Cambridge. He has written widely on tragedy, translation, and nineteenth-century literature; his publications include *Shakespeare and the Victorians, Tragedy: a very short introduction* and *The Oxford book of classical verse in translation* (1995), co-edited with Jeremy Maule.

Raymond Tallis, FRCP, F.Med.Sci., D.Litt., Litt.D., FRSA, is Emeritus Professor of Geriatric Medicine, University of Manchester. His research, for which he was elected Fellow of the Academy of Medical Sciences, was in stroke and epilepsy. He has published many non-medical books in the fields of literary theory, cultural criticism and the philosophy of mind, a novel, many short stories and three volumes of verse. His most recent books are: *The enduring significance of Parmenides: Unthinkable thought; The kingdom of infinite space: A fantastical journey round your head;* and *Hunger.*

Index

ABBA 35
Abbott, Lemuel Francis 138, 140, 143
Achilles 17, 20, 24
African Plants Initiative of ALUKA 86
Alcott, Louisa May 16
Alhambra, The 92, 97, 98
American Law Institute 32
Andrew W. Mellon Foundation 86
Andromache 17, 18, 19, 22
Antanarivo herbarium 72
antibody 117, 119, 120
   heavy chain 119, 120
   light chain 119, 120
Aristotle 183
arthritis (rheumatoid) 124
Astyanax 17, 23
Atiyah-Singer Index Theorem 107
Atropa belladonna 80
Augustine, St 9
Austin, Robert Sargent 153
Australian National Herbarium 76, 85
autoimmunity 121, 122, 124, 125

B cell (lymphocyte) 119, 120,
   124, 125
Baack, E. J. 73
Bach, Johann Sebastian 161, 162, 163,
   164, 165, 166, 168, 172, 174, 178,
   179, 180
Bach, Carl Philipp Emanuel 160, 162
bacteria 5, 69, 111, 113, 126
Balfour, Arthur James 132
Banks, Sir Joseph 63
barcoding 82, 83

Baricco, Alessandro 20
Barnes, Julian 167
Bartók, Béla 174
Bartolozzi, Francesco 142
Bauhin, Caspar 61, 63
Baxandall, Michael 152
Beck, Harry 99
Beethoven, Ludwig van 157, 162,
   163, 164, 180, 181
Beverley-Smith, H. 43, 44
biodiversity 59–71
Birch, Thomas 150
Birch Swinnerton-Dyer
   Conjecture 107
Blair, Anthony (Tony) 11
Blake, William 139, 142, 144
Bloustein, Edward 32
Borcherds, Richard 107
Borges, Jorge Luis 10, 195
Boyce, William 176
Brahmagupta 104, 105
Brahms, Johannes 7, 158, 171, 183
Branagh, Kenneth 22, 23, 25
Brandeis, Louis Dembitz 27, 28
Brendel, Alfred 164
British Ecological Society 70
Brown, Gordon 11
Brown, Lord 40
Buffon, George-Louis Leclerc,
   Compte de 84, 85, 87
Burke, Peter J. 53, 54
Burney, Charles 176
Butler, Joseph, Bishop 196, 197, 206
Byrom, John 177

Cambridge, University of 95, 146, 158
Cambridge University Botany
    Department 81
Cambridge University Library 131
Campbell, Naomi 33, 37, 38, 44
cancer 116, 121
Cannabis species 60, 61, 62, 63, 64,
    65, 67, 68, 77
Cantor, Georg 89, 91, 92
Caroline (von Hannover) of Monaco,
    Princess 41, 42, 43, 44, 45, 46, 47
Carson, Johnny 50, 51, 52
Cassam, Quassim 202
Cayley, Arthur 95, 96
Celsius, Anders 59
Cervantes Saavedra, Miguel de 10, 12
Chamaecyparis nootkatensis 76, 77
Charles, Ray 166
Chesterfield, Philip Dormer Stanhope,
    Earl of 167
Chopin, Frédéric François 162, 166, 169
Cibber, Colley 21
Clark, Sir James 35
Clementi, Muzio 173
Clifford, George 62, 63
clonal selection theory 117, 118, 119,
    120, 121, 122, 124
Concord Township, Massachusetts 73
Convention on International
    Trade in Endangered Species
    (CITES) 79
Cook, Captain James 132
Cooke, Deryck 175
Coombe, Rosemary 27, 57
Cope, David 8, 174
Corelli, Arcangelo 167, 169
cow (*Bos taurus*) 121, 122, 123
Cowper, William 138, 139, 140, 141,
    142, 143, 144, 145, 156
Crane, Stephen 19
Crohn's disease 113

Dahlhaus, Carl 159
Daily Mail 38, 188
Daily Mirror 33, 37

Darwin, Charles Robert 65, 66, 67,
    86, 109
    Origin of species 67, 86
Debussy, Claude Achille 174
Denning, Lord 53
Descartes, René 193, 201, 202, 203
diabetes (juvenile/Type I) 124
Dirichlet, Lejeune 107, 108
Disney, Walt 169
Dostoevsky, Fyodor Mikhailovich 11
Douglas, Michael 34, 39, 40
Dowland, John 180
Downing College, Cambridge 152, 154
Du Boulay (case) 58

Eberl, Anton 173
Eckard, Johann Gottfried 160
Eco, Umberto 9
Einstein, Alfred 160
Endangered Species Act 79
Escherichia coli 111
Euclid 98
    Elements 98
eukaryotes 69
Euler, Leonard 3, 100, 105
European Convention on Human Rights
    27, 36, 42, 43, 44, 46
European Court of Human Rights 36,
    41, 42, 43, 44
Evans, Sir Arthur 160

Farnaby, Giles 160
Fisher, Matthew (Procul Harum) 164
Franklin, Kenneth 147, 148
free-martin 121, 122
Functional Analysis (music) 175

Galois, Evariste 95, 97
Gaskell, Ivan 179, 180
Gauss, Carl Friedrich 3, 108
George Clifford Herbarium 62, 63
German Civil Code 42
German Federal Constitutional Court 42
German Federal Court of Justice 42
Gilbert, William Schwenk 165

Ginkgo biloba 75, 81
Godwin, Harry 81
Gounod, Charles François 163, 165
Granada 92
Greene, Richard 52
Greenham, Peter 152, 154
Grossman, Loyd 35
Gyrowetz, Adalbert 159

Hale, Baroness 33, 38, 40
Handel, Georg Frideric 160, 175, 176,
    177, 182
Hannover, von (case; see Caroline of
    Monaco) 41, 43, 44, 45, 46, 47
Harvard University Herbaria 76, 85
Harvey, William 146, 147, 148, 149,
    150, 151
Hasselquist, Frederic 63
Hawthorne, Nathaniel 144, 145, 146, 156
Haydn, Franz Joseph 7, 159, 171, 174
Hayley, William 139, 141, 142, 143, 156
Hector 17, 18, 19, 20, 22, 23
Heine, Heinrich 157
Hello! (magazine) 34, 39, 40, 41
herpes viruses 114, 116
Hesketh, Lady Harriot 138, 142, 143
Hilbert, David 3, 91
HIV (Human Immunodeficiency Virus) 114
HM Revenue and Customs 80, 82
Hoffmann, Lord 34, 37, 38, 40
Homer 12, 17, 19, 20, 23, 24, 25, 183
Honauer, Leontzi 160
Hooker, Joseph Dalton 86
House of Lords 33, 37, 39, 40, 44
Human Rights Act 1998 36
Hume, David 190, 191, 192, 193, 195
Hunter, John 129, 130, 134
Hunter, William 134, 150
Hynes, Samuel 19, 24

immune system 1, 5, 110–26
    acquired 110, 116–25
    innate 111–13, 126
International Association for Plant
    Taxonomy 64

*International Code of Botanical
    Nomenclature* 5, 65, 66, 77
International Plant Names Index 76, 85
International Treaty on Plant Genetic
    Resources in Food and Agriculture 79
invertebrate (animal) 83, 84, 85, 110, 111,
    125, 126
Iraq (war) 14, 23, 24
Irvine, Eddie 36, 46, 49

Jackson, S. T. 81
Janeway, Charles 112, 126
Janisch 60
Jerome, St 9
John, Elton 38, 45
Johnson, John 140, 143
Jones, James 24
Joplin, Scott 177

Kalm, Pehr 63
Kant, Immanuel 48, 63, 191, 200, 202
Keller, Hans 175
Kew *see* Royal Botanic Gardens, Kew
Keynes, Geoffrey 146, 148
Kirkby, Emma 160
Köchel, Ludwig Ritter von 172, 173
Koželuch, Leopold 159

Lacan, Jacques 192
Laddie (Judge) 36
Lagrange, Joseph Louis 105
Lamarck, Jean-Baptiste 60
Landau, David 51
Larkin, Philip 194
Lasdun, Denys 150
Lawrence, Thomas 139, 142
Leavis, Frank Raymond 152, 153, 154
Leyland Cypress (x *Cuprocyparis
    leylandii*) 76
Lichtenthal, Peter 169
Linnaeus, Carl 59, 60, 61, 62, 63, 64, 65,
    66, 69, 72, 76, 77, 78, 83, 84, 85, 87
Linnean Society of London 64, 77
lipopolysaccharide 5, 111, 113
Liszt, Ferencz/Franz 174

Locke, John 4, 193, 194, 195, 196, 199
London Underground 99, 100
Loussier, Jacques 168
Lucas-Schloetter, A. 43
lupus 124
Lutoslawski, Witold 159, 165, 166
lymphocyte 114, 116, 117, 118, 119, 120, 121, 122, 123, 124, 125

Madagascar 70, 71, 72
Madow, Michael 48, 57
Malthus, Thomas 66
Mann, Thomas; *The Magic Mountain* 93
Mayr, Ernst 67, 73, 84
McCulloch, Derek 35
Mead, Richard 149, 150, 156
Medical Control Agency of the UK Department of Health 79
Medical Toxicology Unit of Guy's and St Thomas' Hospital Trust 80
Mendelssohn, (Jacob Ludwig) Felix 174, 178
Merleau-Ponty, Maurice 203
MHC (Major Histocompatibility Complex) 114, 116
Midler, Bette 26, 50, 56
Millett, Lord 53
Missouri Botanical Garden 72, 86
Moreschi, Alessandro 163, 164
Moses, Anna Mary Robertson (Grandma) 169
Mozart, Wolfgang Amadeus 7, 159, 160, 164, 166, 168, 169, 171, 172, 174, 175, 180, 181
Müller-Molinari, Helga 173
multiple sclerosis 124
Munch, Edvard; *The Scream* 179
Murray, Gilbert 183
Musée national d'histoire naturelle 72
Mytens, Daniel 149

Nagel, Thomas 193, 194
National Gallery, London 179, 180
National Poisons Information Service (UK) 80

National Portrait Gallery, London 132, 134, 139, 140, 142, 143, 146, 148, 151, 153, 156
Natural History Museum, London 63, 77
Natural Killer (NK) cells 114, 115, 116, 125, 126
natural selection 65, 67, 68, 125
Newman, Paul 35
Newton, Isaac 2, 3, 152
Nicholls, Lord 37, 38, 40, 52, 53
NLR (NOD-like receptor) 112, 113
non-self (immunity) 111–13, 116–20
Noonan, Circuit Judge 50, 56

Ohly, A. 43, 44
OK! (magazine) 39, 40
Okeghem, Johannes 160
Olivier, Lord (Laurence) 21, 23, 24
Olson, Eric 197, 198, 199, 201
Onassis, Jackie 41, 55
Orwell, George 5, 9
Owen, Ray 121, 122, 126

Page, Christopher 160
Palestrina, Giovanni Pierluigi 169, 174
Parfit, Derek 187, 192, 195, 201
Parsons, Nicholas (*Just a Minute*) 166
Parton, Dolly 166
passing-off 34, 35, 36, 41, 49, 56, 57
Pathogen-associated molecular patterns (PAMPs) 112
Pavesich, Paolo (case) 28, 30, 31, 32
Perelman, Grigori 103
personal identity 44, 47, 184, 185, 186, 188, 189, 190, 191, 192, 193, 194, 195, 196, 197, 198, 199, 200, 201, 202, 203, 204, 205, 206, 207
Phillimore, Sir Robert 58
Phillips, Tom 129
Physostigma venenosum (calabar bean) 81
Piaget, Jean 196
Picea critchfieldii (spruce) 81
Picea glauca (spruce) 81
placenta 119, 121, 123
plants 60–71, 110

Plato 5, 13, 182
Pleyel, Ignaz Joseph 159
Poincaré, Henri 101, 102, 103
Pointon, Marcia 135
portraiture 3, 128, 129, 131, 132,
    133, 134, 135, 138, 144, 145, 146,
    153, 156
Price, Sir Uvedale 175, 176, 178
Privy Council 58
Procul Harum 164
property in identity 4, 27, 48
Prosser, Dean William L. 27, 28, 31,
    32, 33, 50

Quine, Willard Van Orman 185, 186

Rachmaninoff, Sergei Vassilievich 172
Ramanujan, Srinivasa 3, 105, 106
Ras (cell activation protein) 116
Raupach, Hermann 160
Redpath, Theodore 10, 11
Reid, Thomas 187, 190, 194, 195, 200,
    202, 203
Reiseberg, Loren H. 73
Restatement (Second) of Torts 32, 33
Restatement (Third) of Unfair
    Competition 32, 33
Reviewing Committee on the Export
    of Works of Art 148
Reynolds, Sir Joshua 129, 130, 135, 156
Richardson, Jonathan 150
Riemann, Bernhard 3, 108, 109
Rochlitz, Friedrich 159
Romney, George 138, 141, 142, 143, 156
Rosen, Charles 158
Rossini, Gioachino Antonio 164
Royal Botanic Gardens, Kew 71, 72, 76,
    79, 80, 81, 85, 86
Royal College of Physicians of London
    146, 147, 148, 150, 156
Royal College of Surgeons of London
    130, 134, 156
Royal Society, The 150, 152
Royal Swedish Academy of Sciences,
    The 59

Rubik's cube 104, 105
Ryle, Gilbert 192, 204

Saint-Foix, George de 160
Salmonella typhi 111
Saramago, José 11, 12
Sargent, John Singer 132
Sartre, Jean-Paul 192, 205
Satie, Erik (Eric Alfred Leslie) 173
Scheemakers, Peter 150
Schenker, Heinrich 173
Schobert, Johann 160
Schoenberg, Arnold 174
Schubert, Franz Peter 164
Schwencke, Christian Friedrich
    Gottlieb 162, 163
Scream, The (Munch) 179
self (immunity) 113–16, 121–5
Sen, Amartya 13, 14, 15
Septuagint 9, 11, 19
Shakespeare, William 11, 12, 13, 14,
    17, 19, 20, 21, 22, 23, 25, 157
    Comedy of Errors, The 13
    Hamlet 13, 20, 21
    Henry IV, Part I 22
    Henry V 20, 21, 22, 23, 24, 25
    Henry VI, Part I 20, 23, 24
    Julius Caesar 14, 25
    King Lear 20, 21
    Merchant of Venice, The 21
    Richard III 21
    Romeo and Juliet 11
    Troilus and Cressida 19
Sharp, William 129, 130
Simpson, Homer 101
Skalkottas, Nikos 160
Smith, James Edward 64
Solander, Daniel 63
Solanum dulcamara (woody nightshade) 80
Solanum nigrum (black nightshade) 80
Sophocles 14, 157, 172
species 59–71
Spencer, Herbert 13
Spice Girls 174
spruce (Picea species) 81

Star Trek 82
Stearn, W. T. 77
Sting (Gordon Sumner) 62
St Lucia, Royal Court of 58
Stone, Oliver 19
Stravinsky, Igor 169, 171
Strawson, Peter F. 202
Sullivan, Arthur Seymour 165
Sulston, Sir John 129
Supreme Court of Georgia 28, 29
Süssmayr, Franz Xavier 174
Swinburne, Richard 193
symmetry 92, 93, 94, 95, 96, 97, 98

T cell (lymphocyte) 114, 116, 119, 120,
    124, 125
Talksport 36, 46
Thoré, Théophile 178
Thoreau, Henry 73
Thunberg, Carl Peter 63
Thurston, Bill 103
TLR (Toll-like Receptor) 112, 113
tolerance (immunity) 121–4
Tolstoy, Count Leo 19
Tonegawa, Susumu 119, 126
topological identity 2, 88, 98, 100,
    101, 102, 103, 107, 109
Traditional Chinese Medicine
    (TCM) 79, 80
Trinity College, Cambridge 95
tumour 116, 121

Underground, London 99, 100
Uppsala University 59, 64, 66
US Court of Appeals for the Fifth Circuit 30
US Court of Appeals for the Second
    Circuit 30
US Court of Appeals for the Ninth
    Circuit 51

Valéry, Paul 51
Van Gogh, Vincent 179, 180
Vermeer, Johannes 178, 179, 180, 181, 182
vertebrate (animal) 67, 85, 110, 111, 116,
    119, 120
Vivaldi, Antonio 180
Voltaire, François Marie Arouet de 12
von Bemmel, Wilhelm 150
von Bingen, Hildegard 160
Vonnegut, Kurt 19

Wagner, Wilhelm Richard 11, 157, 172
Walker, Lord 34, 40, 41
war 14, 17, 19, 20, 23, 24, 66
Waring, Edward 105
Warren, Samuel D. 27, 28
Webber, John 132
Weng, C. 81
Westfall, David 51
White, Vanna 32, 50, 51
Wilde, Oscar 135, 136, 137, 155
    The Picture of Dorian Gray 135, 137
Wilson, Edward O. 86
Windward Islands, Court of Appeal
    for the 58
Wittgenstein, Ludwig 10, 11, 16
Wood, T. E. 73
Wyzewa, Téodor de 160

Xanthocyparis nootkatensis (Nootka
    Cypress) 76
Xanthocyparis vietnamensis 76
    x *Cupressocyparis leylandii* 76
    x *Cuprocyparis leylandii* 76

zeta function (Riemann's) 108
Zeta-Jones, Catherine 39